MW00780053

My Pilgrimage of Faith

The Memoir of a Baptist Minister whose path at crucial points has seemingly been shaped by divine guidance.

Buddy Clay McGohon

Parson's Porch Books

My Pilgrimage of Faith
ISBN: Hardcover 979-8-8690-0423-9
Copyright © 2023 by Buddy Clay McGohon

Parson's Porch Books is an imprint of Parson's Porch *&* Company (PP*&*C) in Cleveland, Tennessee. PP*&*C is a self-funded charity which earns money by publishing books of noted authors, representing all genres. Its face and voice is **David Russell Tullock** (dtullock@parsonsporch.com).

Parson's Porch *&* Company *turns books into bread & milk* by sharing its profits with the poor.

www.parsonsporch.com

My Pilgrimage of Faith

Dedication

Barbara, our three daughters,

Beth, Amy and Alisa and our six grandchildren,

Maegan, Sarah, Ann Marie, John Mark, Mitch, and Jackson.

Table of Contents

Prologue

At the midpoint of the ninth decade of a most fulfilling life I would like to share some of my reflections on that life with my children, grandchildren and others who may have an interest in reading them. These reflections make no pretense to objectivity or total accuracy for they have at least two major limitations. The first is a faulty memory. In this wander down memory lane I have discovered a host of blank pages. I've found to my distress many months and in a few cases years in which the memory bank was nearly empty. I now regret that journaling, even in its sketchiest form, was not one of my disciplines. Moments I was sure at the time would never be forgotten have slipped from my memory or are at best uncomfortably hazy.

A second limitation to total accuracy is an innate and often unconscious desire to cover or at least minimize unseemly warts and scars along with unflattering mistakes and sins. I am certainly no exception to this tendency. Before this little enterprise is completed those blank pages in the memory bank could prove to be a blessing in disguise for all of us.

A further limitation, or at least source of discomfort for me, is the glaring overuse of the personal pronoun. Unfortunately, it is the only way I know how to tell my story and take full responsibility for the living and telling of it.

Like the life of any person my life pathway has been filled with many twists and turns, along with its share of ups and downs. Thinking back especially on some of life's earlier events has been interesting, and in some ways quite revealing, at least to me. For instance, I have discovered to my amazement that often events that were seemingly insignificant at the time they occurred have proven to be life shaping.

I've renewed my appreciation for my parents. While the task of piecing together their influence on my life has been challenging and the results not totally satisfying, it has been a most helpful and enjoyable endeavor. I am now convinced I took much of their influence for granted. Unfortunately, I now find much of their lives shrouded in mystery. I know so little of the influences on their early life, of what they did and why they did it. Some of that I've tried to reconstruct, inadequately and perhaps in some cases even erroneously.

More than I ever knew at the time God's unseen hand, whether sought or unsought, has seemed to guide my path. In retrospect, events in one chapter seem to have been preparing me for the next. My last sermon at South Avondale based on Hebrews 11 and entitled "A Pilgrimage of Faith," was also my first sermon in Montgomery. While thousands before me have shared and given testimony to a similar experience, yet the contour of each experience, mine included, is unique.

If these ramblings should prove in some way interesting, informative or perhaps even helpful I will consider the time collecting and recording them (now stretched into 5 years) well spent.

I am deeply indebted to Dr. Norfleete Day, South Avondale Baptist Church parishioner, long-time friend, and current Vestavia Hills fellow church member, for the countless hours spent reading and providing editorial counsel for this manuscript. Finally, words cannot express adequately my gratitude for the joy my precious family has brought to my life and whose encouragement made this project happen.

A Seminal Year

From my present vantage point the year following my 17th birthday, December 19, 1954, was a seminal, yea even the pivotal, year in my life. It was certainly a year filled with events and decisions more monumental than I would have ever imagined at the time or for a number of years thereafter. For starters, it was the year I began taking full responsibility for my life. Steps were taken to further my education beyond high school by enrolling in the University of Kentucky's College of Engineering and preparing for a vocation quite different from the farming vocation of the generations before me. Knowing that paying for my education would be my responsibility I began making and for the first time saving some "real money" for that purpose.

In the summer of '55 I had my first "real date" with a girl. I had set next to girls on group outings, but this was the first time I had asked a girl to go with me on a "date." The girl's name was Barbara Heathman who two years later would become my wife. Finally, that fall I would hear and respond to a deep spiritual "Call of God" on my life to be a "preacher," a Minister of the Gospel. All three of these epic, life-shaping events occurred between May and November of 1955.

Graduating from Wilmore High School did not seem to be a big deal at the time, yet it provided unusual support for what would come later. Wilmore High School was a small school with an enrolment of 121 students in the 1954-55 school year. Twenty-eight of those students were my senior classmates. Thirteen of them (45%) went on to earn college degrees. (By comparison, less that 20% of the nation's high school students attended a college in 1955 and even fewer earned degrees). That abnormally large percentage of my peers attending college probability can be attributed to the fact that Wilmore, population less than 1500, was home of two Methodist institutions of higher learning, Asbury College and Asbury Theological Seminary.

The impact of these two institutions on the local public school was felt in a number of ways. They added an important moral dimension to the social and civic life of the community. A number of my classmates came from homes that placed a high value on personal spirituality and faithful church-life. One classmate grew up on a foreign mission field, and another became a missionary serving in Korea. Though the more zealous devotees were sometimes mocked and opportunities to "stray" were abundant the influence for good was unmistakable.

Two of my teachers, Jim Young and Joe Dawes were recent graduates of Asbury College. They were both very capable and highly motivated. Mr. Dawes taught math and a physics class in which I was one of 6 students. Mr.

3

Young taught English along with Drama and Speech. Mr. Young coached our debate team and encouraged us to participate in regional speech and drama contests. Before my senior year Young left the High School to teach and coach drama at Asbury College yet he continued to voluntary coach a few high school students on the college campus after normal school hours. I was fortunate enough to be one of those students. That coaching led to my receiving a Superior rating in both Dramatic Monologue and Extemporaneous Speaking contests. This would later lead to a much-needed speech scholarship when I transferred to Georgetown College.

Finally, both the college and the seminary communities considered supporting the local high school and elementary school an important part of their ministry. Our senior graduation activities included a Baccalaureate service, a worship service held on a Sunday night in the beautiful new Estes Chapel on the campus of Asbury Seminary. Though I am reasonably sure attendance was not mandatory, few if any students or their parents missed the service.

Upon graduating from High School, the next most important task at hand was earning money for college in the fall. Entering the work force was the normal "next step" for many of my friends and all of my family predecessors. To the best of my knowledge none of my father's or mother's siblings ever attended college. Of the 32 first cousins on dad's side of the family, to the best of my knowledge, only the oldest, Reb Jr., attended college.

I assume Reb Jr. graduated from college because of his career in the Secret Service. My parents thought he served for a time on President Eisenhower's presidential detail. He called mother several times in the waning years of her life, and I understood from her he had moved to Phoenix, AZ following his retirement. While preaching a revival and conducting a church consultation as part of a mission partnership between the Montgomery Baptist Association and the Apache Junction Baptist Association in the early 90's I met him for the one and only time I ever saw him. His phone number was not hard to find since there was only one McGohon in the Phoenix area phone directory. I called him and at his suggestion we met in Scottsdale at the San Francisco Giants spring training baseball facility where we watched an exhibition game between the Giants and the Cubs. True to his training and nature he revealed little of his past. I did learn he had worked for the Secret Service and for a time was a recruiter on college campuses.

Though attending college was not the norm for my family or many of my friends I do not remember a time I did not plan to go to college. I got good grades in school and when my future was discussed college was assumed. When Auntie or her sons Garnett and Pete mentioned my future the conversation went like, "When you go to college…" or "When Bud gets out of college…"

Well aware that my parents had few if any resources to devote to my college education, a job that paid real money was essential. Previous summers had been devoted to working on the farm with Daddy and helping neighbors. The latter often involved "swapping" work with neighbors who would repay us by working in our crops when needed. I only got paid if we worked for them more than they worked for us. Five to six dollars a day was the going wage for a farm hand and that had provided me with some spending money.

I got a steady "part time" job the summer of '55 at the Kroger store in Nicholasville, stocking shelves one or two nights during the week and sacking groceries at the checkout lane on Saturday. This allowed me time to still work on the farm when I was needed. Twenty hours a week was my normal workload at Kroger's unless one of the full-time workers was on vacation and then I got 38 hours. Had I worked 40 hours a week union rules would have required them to pay me $1.10 an hour instead of the 85 cents an hour I made as part-time help.

In my preparation to enter college there was never any discussion or question as to where I would go to school. The University of Kentucky was 13.5 miles away (1.5 miles to Nicholasville and 12 miles to the center of the UK campus). I could live at home, and easily hitchhike to school most days. Catching a ride to Nicholasville was easy and with so many people working or going to school in Lexington getting a ride with someone was seldom a problem. Coming back after class was even easier. After a couple of weeks, I discovered Lyman Cox, a fellow student from Wilmore, had a car and commuted regularly. His last class and my last class on Mondays and Fridays ended at the same time. I only had to get to the lot where he parked before he left. Another commuter from Nicholasville shared Chemistry for Engineers Lab with me on Wednesdays, so I rode with him the first semester.

Occasionally, I was able to drive the family car on the rare times I had a Tuesday or Thursday class, which was a big help. Unfortunately, this was not without its problems. For example, one Friday I rushed from my 2 o'clock class to the parking lot as usual to catch my ride to Nicholasville with Lyman. About a third of the way to Nicholasville, to the astonishment of our driver and two other passengers, I remembered I had driven the family car to school that morning. From that day forward the standard question before we left the parking lot was, "Buddy, did you drive to school today?"

On another occasion my sisters and brother missed the school bus one morning. Since I didn't have an 8:00 class and wanted to use the car that day I took them to their school in Wilmore. Less than a mile from the house I tried to catch a pestering fly as he flew by the rearview mirror. The car veered to the right off the road, down an embankment, through a wire fence and into a pasture. By God's grace no one was hurt though we had narrowly missed a telephone pole. Amazingly, the '52 Ford was still drivable having sustained only a few minor dents and scratches. The neighbor's fence was not as fortunate and since there were cows in the pasture the fence needed a few strands of barbed wire immediately.

A couple of days later as I was helping my dad make a more permanent repair to the fence he expressed his exasperation at both my inattentiveness and ineptness. "Aye God (more of a byword that an actual curse) Buddy, it looks like once would have been enough! When you got in the field why didn't you just stay there?" As the car had started over the 3 feet high, 45-degree embankment I steered hard to the left trying to get back on the road. Some 20 – 30 feet through the fence at the foot of the embankment the front wheels caught in the sod. Now the car turned abruptly, with its momentum carrying it back toward the road and into the fence again. It came to a stop at the foot of the embankment with the hood on the roadside of the fence and the remainder of the car in the pasture. It was now only a few feet beyond the gap made in the fence when the car entered the pasture, thus requiring two repairs instead of one.

In case you don't remember, a car going 35 mph travels 51 feet per second. Thus, it was less that a second from the time the car left the highway until it hit the fence the first time and little more than another second before it hit the fence a second time, even though I had my foot on the brake pedal part of that time. To get my driver's license I had to correctly answer a question about how many feet a car traveled per second at various speeds. Until that day, however, I never really understood how quickly an accident could occur, how little time you had to react, or how little control you had of a car once it left the road.

The course of study I would pursue in college received little more discussion than the college I would attend. Math had always been my favorite and easiest subject. So, studying to be an engineer appeared to be the most reasonable option. I had excelled in the math courses offered in my small high school (algebra I & II, geometry and physics). Though this was a limited math curriculum compared to that of larger schools I did not see this as a problem. Another big reason for settling on a course in Engineering was financial, pure and simple. Though I had no idea how much money engineers made I was sure it had to be more than tenant farmers. I have no doubts my parents shared the same idea

On Registration Day I signed up for the typical 18-hour course load for entering engineering students. All went well that first semester except for two courses. My innate lack of neatness and procrastination made Engineering Drawing a challenge and pure pride made Chemistry for Engineers tough. The latter class had 140 students and was taught by a professor who had worked on the Atomic Bomb at Oak Ridge, Tennessee. Two days each week the professor lectured to everyone. Wednesdays were devoted to lab work in small groups of 20 each and on Fridays the same 20 met in small classes to ask questions about the week's lectures and take a weekly test. A math test was given on the first day of class to determine the makeup of the lab groups and Friday classes. The top 20 scores made up the first group which the professor chose to guide, and the other 6 groups were determined accordingly and given graduate assistants as instructors.

My math score placed me in the first group with the professor as the instructor. At the beginning the professor took a few minutes of the lab period to discuss the experiment to be done that day and then left, assuming everybody understood what was to be done. As it turned out, 19 of the 20 students in that group had taken at least one Chemistry course in high school. While I had watched some experiments in my high school Physics class, I had never conducted or written up an experiment on my own. Unwilling to admit my limitation or ask to be transferred to another group that had a hands-on instructor for the full 2 hours of the lab period, I muddled on turning in at the end of the semester the write-ups of the few experiments I had completed. As usually happens I found an "accomplice" to hang out with during those 2 hours, an old buddy from West Virginia who didn't want to be an engineer but was there because his father insisted. Fortunately, when my "F" for my lab work was coupled with my "A" for the Friday tests I got a "C+" for the course. **An important lesson learned.** Indeed, *"Pride goeth before destruction, and an haughty spirit before a fall"* (Prov. 16:18 KJV).

Overall I found the classes my first semester in college to be interesting and fun, except for the frustration of the Chemistry Lab. The fact that I had no real "campus life" made no impression on me at the time since I had neither knowledge nor expectation of what it could be. Actually, the lack of financial resources made commuting the only option open to me and my siblings who would follow me to college. Ann completed Fugazzi Business School in Lexington, Carol attended UK and earned a degree from Mississippi State after she was married, and Ronnie earned a degree in Electrical Engineering from UK.

A very important social event in my life also occurred in the summer of 1955. For the very first time I finally summoned the courage to ask a girl for a date. To say I was shy or self-conscious around members of the opposite sex would be an understatement. As an 8th grader, a cute little girl from Nicholasville, not the school I attended, was the object of a definite crush. I thought about trying to sit next to her in the movie theater sometime, but that thought never passed the daydream stage probably because there was no effort on my part to make it happen.

Then, there was that afternoon in the summer following my junior year in high school. I was walking home from Nicholasville along the Keene Pike when a car loaded with girls, at least 3, some of whom I knew from our church youth group, stopped and asked if I wanted a ride.

"Naw, I can walk."

"Come on, get in we'll take you home," the driver said.

What a stroke of luck, "older women" interested in little ole me, I thought. Wow! Needless to say, that "accidental" encounter left an indelible impression on a bashful boy's mind, which would prove to be the beginning of a growing self-confidence.

Over the next few months at church I found myself more frequently sitting next to the girl behind the wheel that day, a Miss Barbara Heathman.

By the next summer following graduation from high school I finally gained the courage to attempt a daring act of bravery, asking a girl I really liked out on a date. During the spring I had detected what I thought were an increasing number of signals that she liked me too and would not reject my request. The primary signal I decoded came from some Sunday evening outings. Often following Sunday night church 8 to 10 young people would pile into a couple of cars and head to the Starlight Drive-in restaurant in Lexington, some 10 miles up US highway 27. On an increasing number of those trips I found myself sitting beside Barbara both going and coming. I began to suspect this was not coincidental. She would eventually confess it was not.

Having determined the time had come to ask Barbara for a date the remaining hurdle was "Where would we go?" This had to be more than a simple burger at the drive-in and a movie. This needed to be a big event. Surely, the Lexington Junior League Horse Show would fill the bill. Now in those days in Central Kentucky county fairs were big events and every county fair had two featured attractions, a carnival and a gaited horse show. The horse shows featured multiple classes for 3 and 5 gaited horses and usually concluded with a "Roadster Race" featuring drivers in two-wheel carts.

Barbara's first cousin, Ann Russell Carney, had a gaited horse she rode on the county fair circuit for several years during her early teen years and my neighbor Ann Parks whose father owned the farm just west of the farm where we lived had a show horse, which she occasionally showed at a county fair. The horse show circuit ended each year in September at the Kentucky State Fair in Louisville where the "National Champion" in each class was crowned. The Lexington Junior League Horseshow held each year in early July was second only in both prestige and prize money to the World Championship at the State Fair in Louisville. Barbara's Aunt Nelda, the first woman in the state of Kentucky to hold the title of Certified Life Underwriter, was also a gaited horse enthusiast. She was a volunteer in both Lexington's Junior League and the Kentucky State Fair horseshows. For several years she was responsible for securing the ribbons and trophies for the State Fair event.

So, we have a big event in which both of us have an interest. What next? Without asking her point blank for a date, I began a discussion as to where she would like to go the following Friday night. When I mentioned the possibility of the Junior League Horse Show Barbara informed me she had had been given 2 complimentary tickets by her dear Aunt Nelda to that very event. What a deal, a Big Deal event that wouldn't break the bank. "Tickets to the Junior League Horseshow" was only the first of many gifts and blessings Nelda would bestow upon us in the ensuing years.

The horses that competed and the various class winners that evening have long since faded from my memory but not that first real date. Barbara would be both the first and only girl I would ever date. While I was not her first dating partner, she assures me I was her last. I could not say ours was "love at first sight," but we both found a joy in one another's company. That joy and an easily recognized compatibility would quickly blossom into a deep love and unshakable commitment to one another. While there would be adjustments to be made and challenges to overcome they have seemed relatively minor compared to the love and joy we shared. At this point in time, some 67 years after that first date, it is easy to believe that our relationship had not only been blessed by God but perhaps even destined by Him. Not that we couldn't have messed it up, but by His grace we didn't.

The climatic event of 1955 came on a Sunday morning in late October. I do not remember if I attended Sunday School that morning, but I have a clear mental picture of sitting in the Sanctuary alone, unaccompanied by close friends or family members during the worship service that day. Barbara must have spent the weekend in Richmond where she was attending her junior year at Eastern Kentucky State University. I took my seat on 4th pew from the back, center section next to the right aisle.

The Nicholasville Baptist Church, an old historic red brick church with white antebellum columns located on the southwest corner of Main and Chestnut, was a Nicholasville landmark. The church had served as a hospital during the civil war, though not this particular building. I suspect this particular building had been built near the end of the 19th century and sometime later its attractive, though not ornate, stained-glass windows were added.

A couple of minutes before 11:00 A.M., Sunday School Superintendent Edgar Heathman, Barbara's uncle "Sue," stood up from his front pew seat on the left side and made an announcement or two then gave the Sunday School attendance for the day. Mrs. Hervey began playing the organ prelude, the choir filed into the choir loft and before they were seated began singing, "The Lord is in His Holy Temple, let all the earth keep silence before Him, keep silence, keep silence before Him." I mainly know the service began that way that Sunday because that's the way it began almost every Sunday.

After the congregational singing, offering, and choir special Pastor Pete Evans read his text for the day's sermon, Isaiah 6. He came to verse 8, "Then I heard the voice of the Lord saying, 'Whom shall I send? And who will go for us?' And I said, 'Here am I send me.'" He probably read more than that

8th verse, but for sure those words were the focus of his sermon. As the moments passed it seemed as though I was the only person in the congregation that morning and the words of that verse repeated several times constituted nothing less than a word from God directed straight to me. "Whom shall I send and who will go for us?"

I stood with the congregation as they began singing the "Invitation Hymn." With eyes focused unflinchingly forward and the congregation singing my heartbeat quickened and the words pounded in my brain, "Here am I send me!" "Here am I send me!" "Here am I send me!"

I barely nodded to a few familiar faces on the way out of that worship service, got in the family car and drove straight home. I kept thinking, "What has just happened? Is this what a "Call of God" is like?" The thought had never crossed my mind, at least not seriously. I had heard preachers talk about "being called to preach," by God but I had no real idea as to what they were talking about.

After the initial shock and its accompanying fright wore off I began to try piecing together in my mind what this would mean at least for my immediate future. I would certainly have to change my course of study at UK from the College of Engineering with its heavy math curriculum, at which I was adept, to the College of Arts and Sciences with perhaps an English major. Freshman English was without a doubt my most difficult subject. And what about schools? Could I continue at UK, or would I need to change colleges, from UK to Georgetown, the Baptist College in Kentucky attended by most Baptists I knew who were preparing for a church vocation?

Major questions also revolved around finances? Where would I get all the additional money to go to a private college? Then what about after college? I didn't know how much engineers made, but I knew it was a lot more than any preacher I knew. Finally, what would my parents think? They (certainly my mother) had planned on their son getting a good paying job some day and hopefully helping them in their retirement years.

I needed help to sort through the chaos in my mind. Brother Evans, my pastor who had preached what had proven to be for me an earth-shattering sermon seemed to be the logical person to whom I could turn. There was a problem, however. Since that fateful October Sunday Brother Evans had announced his resignation as pastor of the Nicholasville Baptist Church to accept the pastorate of a church in Meridian, Mississippi and was preparing to move. Finally, following my normal path of procrastination, on the Monday morning after his last sermon at Nicholasville Baptist I called the church parsonage and asked if I could talk to him. He said, "Yes, but you will need to make it fairly soon. The movers are here putting our furniture on the truck."

Fifteen minutes later we were sitting on a couple of boxes in his living room. For the first time I tried to describe for another person what had happened that Sunday morning in October of 1955. I asked him if it meant what I thought it meant. He assured me that it sounded like I had experienced a genuine "Call of God" on my life. As I bombarded him with questions about college, the seminary and a host of other issues he assured me I need not worry about all the questions clamoring for answers. God would work everything out in due time. There amid the boxes he placed his hands on my shoulders and began to pray. While I do not remember all of the words of that prayer two phrases burned themselves into my memory. "Help him to know he now stands in the line of your prophets, Isaiah, Jeremiah, Ezekiel and Daniel" and "Make your Word a fire in his bones that he may study it and proclaim it." While I do not remember them specifically, there must have been other words of thanksgiving for Christ's love and assurance of the Holy Spirit's empowerment.

Tears were running down my cheeks when he finished. As I walked from the church parsonage that Monday most of the questions I had when I arrived were still unanswered, except for one. I now knew that on that October Sunday morning in that strange, even mystical, experience God had somehow called me to a life of serving Him in pastoral ministry and to preaching His Word. In the years that followed there would be periods of hardship, uncertainty, discouragement, doubt and disillusionment. There would be moments of weakness, frustration, and failure but the memory of that mystical moment has been a powerful beacon and sustaining anchor. Fortunately, there have been many other moments of gracious affirmation through the ensuing years, which have supported and enhanced that moment, but none that changed its directive.

In retrospect at least 3 spiritually focused incidents still lingering in my memory served as a prelude to that mystical moment. They might be considered "seeds sown in fertile soil," that would eventually bear fruit. The first occurred on a Sunday night some 3 years earlier after I had "given a part" in BTU (Baptist Training Union, a disciple training program meeting on Sunday evening). Mary Katherine Evans our leader and pastor's wife, had commented, "Buddy, you ought to think about being a preacher." I took it to mean she thought I "had done good" and nothing more. The fact that I remembered it years later indicates it had an impact unrecognized at the time.

The second occurred the following spring when the church had a Youth Sunday. It was a day when young people assumed all the leadership roles in the church for one Sunday. I was asked to be the Youth Pastor and "preach." Since I was on the High School debate team and had participated in several "Speech Festivals," I felt confident enough to give it a try. My sermon was basically a personal testimony, which I entitled "The Christ I Know." There were some nice comments from friends in the congregation, but my motivation was simply to "help out" and nothing more.

Perhaps a year later, just prior to a Sunday Evening Service, the pastor asked if I would have one of the prayers that night. My response was a firm, "No, thank you." Jean Moss a, young college graduate, some 5 or 6 years my senior, had overheard the conversation and asked me why I turned down Brother Evans' request.

"I don't feel like praying before a bunch of mostly adults," I answer. "You've got to crawl before you walk."

"Just remember, you're not talking to those people, you are talking to God. He's the only one you need to worry about pleasing," she responded. "The next time he asks you, you might want to say 'yes.'"

Two Sunday nights later Brother Evans asked me again, I'm sure at Jean's prompting, and this time I agreed to try. (I now know that leading a congregation in prayer and praying personally to God are two very different kinds of prayer, but Jean's reasoning made sense at the time. God can use a good heart and spirit even if our knowledge is limited or even faulty).

These 3 occurrences, spanning 3 years and all seemingly trivial at the time, now appear connected if for no other reason than that they are still clearly embedded in my memory over 60 years later. Were these "acts of God" preparing me for that October Sunday morning? It now seems that way.

Imagine three signal events occurring between May and November of 1955 setting the life course of a very young 17-year-old man! Of course, the events of those 7 months had antecedents and they would set in motion other events, feelings, and activities that constitute a life which now seems divinely directed. It is to these that we now turn.

Where to Begin

Where to begin is always a difficult decision in the telling of any story, especially the story of a family. The long winding DNA roots providing the foundation and nurture of a family are always more intricate and complex than we can imagine. For this family story I shall begin with the birth of four children to four separate couples in the four consecutive years of 1911, 1912, 1913 and 1914. Three of the couples lived in the central region of Kentucky and the forth just across Kentucky's southern border in Tennessee.

The summer of 1911 had been typically hot and humid along the Kentucky River in Woodford County's Clover Bottom community. Merritt and Sue Ella (Stopher) McGohon were expecting the arrival of their 8th child, Hugh McLean, in what would ultimately be a family of 9 children, 6 boys and 3 girls.

Sue Ella born on New Year's Day of 1873 and Merritt born 5 months later on June 1 grew up in Mercer County. They married there in 1898 at the "ripe old age," of 25. In the next 13 years they had 8 children. In 1909 Merritt and Sue Ella along with their seven children moved to the Clover Bottom community in adjoining Woodford County. By 1911 they were well-established respected members of the Clover Bottom community near Nonesuch living in a rather large "L" shaped two-story red brick house on a farm located at the SW corner of the Fords Mill and Mundy's Landing Roads. Hugh arrived on August 13, 1911, and was delivered by Dr. McLean from nearby Wilmore, a small town 4.5 miles away.

I can only imagine the conversation that must have taken place when it came time to give the new baby boy a name. Dr. McLean must have said something like, "The new baby is here safe and sound. I've got one more thing to do, fill out the birth certificate. What name have you picked out for your new baby?"

Merritt, "I don't know Sue Ella usually takes care of that. Sue Ella, what are we going to name him?"

"I don't know, I only had a girl's name picked out. We've already used up all the family names for boys. What do you think?"

Merritt, "Beats me, whatever you think?"

Dr. McLean, "Well hurry up, I don't have all day. I've got to put down something."

"Well just put your name down there, you're a good man, maybe he'll turn out good like you. What's your first name?"

Dr. McLean, "Hugh!"

Merritt, "Well, Hugh it is!"

Dr. McLean, "What about his middle name?"

Merritt, "Do we have to have a middle name?"

Dr. "It would be helpful."

Merritt, "All right, Hugh McLean McGohon. How's that?"

Dr. McLean, "You want to give him both my first and last names?"

Merritt, "You're the one who said he needed two names."

So, Merritt and Sue Ella's eighth child and fifth son was named for the delivering doctor, Dr. Hugh McLean. I attribute the naming to Merritt and wonder why Sue Ella would have allowed it to happen. She was "Mammy" to everyone by the time I came along and as I remember her; she was not at all shy about expressing her opinion. Consequently, she must have been only semi-conscious during the naming process. On the other hand, they just may have had a lot of respect for their new young doctor.

Twenty-eight years later on February 19, 1939, in that same house, Hugh's young wife Marie gave birth to their second child, Gloria Ann, and the attending physician was none other than the still loved and respected Dr. Hugh McLean.

When Hugh was 3 months old his family experienced one of the most unusual weather phenomena ever to strike the United States, the "Cold Front of Nov. 11-12, 1911". In Lexington, Ky. at midnight on Nov. 11th the recorded temperature was 70 degrees. 24 hours later the temperature stood at 14 degrees and there was snow on the ground. In Louisville in the hour between midnight on the 11th and 1 am on the 12th the temperature fell 24 degrees, from 74 to 50. By daybreak the temperature stood at 24 and continued to fall throughout the day.

For 3 ½ years Hugh was the baby of the family until Robert came along, completing Merritt and Ella's family. Hugh grew up on that farm on the road to Mundy's Landing with his Mom, Dad and 8 siblings, at least for a short time. I suspect he developed a closer relationship to Hannah his older sister by two years and Robert his baby brother than to the rest of his siblings. At least during my childhood-years it seems we visited their families more often that the others.

According to the 1940 census Hugh completed 8 years of formal education, all received in the small 2/3-room school at Nonesuch.[1] Assuming he began first grade at age 6 and continued without missing a year, he completed the 8th grade in 1925 just prior to his 14th birthday.

When his older brothers, Reb and Jack left home is unknown but when Hugh was 12 his oldest sister Etta married Arthur Drury. When he was 13, 16 months later Hannah married Arthur's first cousin George Drury on Feb. 28, 1925, 2 weeks before her 16th birthday. Sister Josie married the next year and brother George married New Year's Day in 1928, Hugh was 16. When brother Grant left home is unknown, but he did not marry until 1937.

I've often wondered why Hugh never went on to High School and what effect that had on the remainder of his life. He certainly was intellectually capable. He was good at math and could do simple math and algebra in his head. On one occasion someone asked him a riddle that went like this; "I have so many sheep and you have so many sheep. If you give me one of your sheep I will have twice as many as you have but if I give you one of my sheep, we will both have the same number. How many sheep did each of us have at the beginning?" In a matter of a few seconds he gave the correct answer, "I have 5 and you have 7." He also enjoyed reading, especially Zane Gray and other western novels, on rainy days or during the winter when he had a few rare moments of spare time. The newspaper, especially the sports pages, was also a favorite daily read.

I suspect that with the older boys moving on, Hugh's hands were needed on the farm, and he stayed home and helped, little realizing at the time what he was missing. It was on that farm with the red brick house that he began to learn the art of farming, his occupation for all his life. He worked horses, tended livestock and learned to repair whatever needed mending. His brother George operated a garage in Nonesuch near the schoolhouse and in all likelihood, it was in that garage he learned and honed his skills as a mechanic. Though he referred to himself as a "shade tree" mechanic he was able to repair with his own hands most of his automobile malfunctions as well as "break downs" of his farm machinery.

It must have also been in the nearby Kentucky River that he was introduced to fishing, the passionate recreational activity of his life. It was there too he must have learned the skill of rowing a boat. As a boy on our fishing excursions to Herrington Lake or the Kentucky River I was always amazed at how smoothly the oars slid into and out of the water with each powerful stoke propelling our boat to the desired fishing spot.

Another important feature of the Clover Bottom community that made an indelible mark on Hugh's life was the Clover Bottom Baptist Church. When Hugh began attending that church and with what frequency I do not know, but he made a profession of faith in Jesus as his personal Lord and Savior, was baptized and joined that church early in his life. He learned some of the great songs of the faith and sang them in the car or in the field, as we would ride and work together. My earliest memory of a church service was attending a revival service at the Clover Bottom Baptist Church. He had a love for that church, and though he attended the Nicholasville Baptist Church regularly in his later years I think he was a member of Clover Bottom Baptist Church until he died.

No doubt character traits of honesty, personal integrity, hard work and respect for others, foundation stones for his life, in some measure can be traced back to the Clover Bottom Baptist Church. All of this was part of my heritage and contributed beyond measure to my life and the person I would eventually became.

Sometime between 1930 and '32 in the depths of the depression Hugh's life crossed paths with a beautiful young lady who had recently moved to the nearby community of Troy. Marie Rankin, 16 or 17 at the time, had recently moved from Henry County, Kentucky and had come to live with her aunt and uncle, Lilly and Martin Carroll, on their farm near Troy. Though Troy, little more than a bend in the road, was located in Woodford County the Carroll farm was located just across the Jessamine County line and about 2.5 miles up the road from the red brick house on the road to Munday's Landing.

Marie's early years in Henry county seem to have been much more turbulent and far less secure than Hugh's days in his one and only Clover Bottom home. Born on October 11, 1914, Marie was the first-born child of Grover Cleveland Rankin and Ethel James who had married a little over a year earlier and lived near New Castle in Henry County, Kentucky. In July of that year a regional conflict in the Balkans of Europe provided the spark for a war that would soon engulf the major powers of the world in what became known as World War I. On April 6, 1917, 6 months after Marie's second birthday the United States congress declared war on Germany. Young men throughout the country were called into military service and sent to the front lines of combat in France. Grover Rankin, Marie's father, was one of those young American doughboys who having known nothing, but the simple life of a rural farmer left his young family to fight a war in far off France.

Ethel with her two children, Marie and one-year-old Kelly, went to live with her mom and dad, Susie and Linden James, life-long Henry County residents. During those two to three years Marie's aunts and uncles became more like sisters and brothers. This was especially true with Emma, only a year older than Marie. Uncles included Chester, Russell, Lewis, Howard, Urban, and Morris. The James aunts and uncles always occupied a special place in Marie's mind and in the waning years of her life attending the James reunion at Butler State Park in northern Kentucky was a must if she was physically able.

When Grover returned from France to Henry county, life in the Rankin household became strained. He seems to have changed, or at least the relationship with his wife had changed. Marie never discussed those days with her family except for one occasion when she spoke briefly of the memory of a conflict between her mom and dad that had something to do with another woman. Whatever the problems, Ethel and Grover got past them and when Marie was 8 another brother, Garnett, came along. When Marie was 11 a sister, Marjory, was born. Sisters Joyce Dean, Sue, and Louise followed; however Louise was born after Marie had married.

During the 20's and early 30's Marie seems to have lived with her grandfather and grandmother James, at least off and on, attending schools at Pleasureville and Eminence with her aunts and uncles. In April of 1930 when the census was taken she was living with her parents and siblings, Kelly,

Garnett, and Marjory on Barton Lane east of New Castle. (The 1940 census indicated that Grover had moved his family to a house on the New Castle to Bethlehem Road). During these years Marie attended and joined the Point Pleasant Christian Church between New Castle and Pleasureville. She never moved her membership from that church. That church was the site of her brother Kelly's funeral in 2005 and he was buried in the nearby cemetery.

Marie's relationship with her father Grover continued to be strained and perhaps in the summer of 1930 at the age of 15, she went to live with her father's sister, Lilly, and her husband Martin, near Troy. On her 16th birthday she was living in Troy and received a piece of jewelry (which daughter Ann now has) as a birthday present from someone in the Troy community.

Lilly and Martin Carroll had two sons, Garnett, age 12, and Henry (Pete), age 11, when Marie arrived. Martin was also a farmer who owned his farm and house, at least in 1930. In perhaps the summer of '32 their house caught fire and while no one was injured in the fire, the house and its contents were lost, including Marie's clothes. Without adequate clothes to begin her senior year in the fall Marie's formal education ended with the 11th grade. (Since the Carroll's lived in Jessamine County and since Garnett and Pete attended and graduated from Wilmore High School it stands to reason that Marie must have attended Wilmore High School for one or two years, but I have no memory of her ever mentioning that fact. (If this was the case it may explain why Marie's children were sent to school in Wilmore where Marie knew some of the teachers, rather than the closer schools of Keene or Nicholasville).

"Uncle Martin" and "Aunt Lillie" or "Auntie" became Marie's surrogate parents and came to occupy an endearing place in her heart. She would name her first son Buddy for her "Uncle Martin" whose nickname was "Buddie," and her third child Lillian Carol for "Auntie."

In September of 1935 Hugh and Marie decided their courtship had gone on long enough and it was time to take the next step. Upon arriving at the Jessamine County Clerk's office in the courthouse in Nicholasville to get their marriage license they received a shocking bit of news. Because Marie was two weeks short of her 21st birthday a license could not be issued without the signature of her parent or guardian. Marie was tempted to "fudge" a bit on the date of her birth, after all it's only 14 days and the clerk didn't seem to mind. Hugh, however, would not hear it. So, hopping into the car they returned to Troy and persuaded Marie's "Uncle Martin" to accompany them back to the courthouse where he provided the necessary guardian's signature.

On Saturday, September 27, 1935, with the correctly documented marriage license in hand they proclaimed their love for each other and vowed to be faithful to one another until death should part them. Though the years ahead held many unexpected challenges and hardships their enduring love and those unbroken vows of commitment to each other were foundational pillars of a strong healthy home for rearing their four children.

The first challenge faced was a place to live. Like most Americans the residents of rural Clover Bottom and Troy were still struggling through the throes of The Great Depression. Nearly every head of the household was a farmer, and many were renters. In the1930 census Hugh, 18 at the time, was listed as a "general farm laborer" and that was still the case five years later. He worked primarily for his tenant-farmer father and occasionally for neighbors, as work was available, earning between $.50 and $1 a day. Consequently, Hugh and Marie began their married life living with his father and mother in the red brick house on the road to Mundy's Landing. They had an upstairs bedroom in the large house and while Hugh worked on the farm Marie assisted her mother-in-law, "Mrs. McGohon," with household chores. This was not an unusual arrangement for Merritt and Sue Ella. In 1930 George, Hugh's older brother, and his new bride Mary Lillian lived with them as did another brother Reb who was now divorced. However, because the Carroll's lived only 2-3 miles up the road Marie found living with her in-laws at least more tolerable.

This living arrangement would last for at least four years. During that time their first two children were born. Buddy arrived 6 days before Christmas in 1937 and exactly 14 months later Ann was born. As previously noted, Ann was born at home, delivered by Dr. McLean. Buddy, on the other hand, was born at Good Samaritan Hospital in Lexington, probably because his was a more complicated breach birth delivery. After nearly a week's stay in the hospital, normal for that time, the happy couple brought their "bundle of joy" home to the "oohs and ahs" of all, especially the Carroll's.

Now another grandchild was nothing new for the McGohons, I was number 25 of a group that would eventually number 38 grandchildren for Merritt and Sue Ella. But for the Carroll's, I was something special. Though technically a great nephew, because they considered and treated Marie as their child since coming to live with them seven years earlier, they considered and treated me as their first grandchild. Martin and Lilly Carroll were certainly my surrogate grandparents. He was "Old Buddie"[2] and I was "Little Buddy." Lilly, Marie's aunt, was simply "Auntie."

My earliest of many precious memories of times with Auntie and Old Buddie are of spending a few days with them when they lived in "temporary housing" at Fort Knox. Old Buddie was working as a plumber on the Fort Knox Army Base just before or in the early days of WWII, I have a mental picture of standing with Auntie watching a long row of tanks lumbering down a road and finally out of sight over a hill. I also remember going to a little "diner/store" at the entrance to the lane on which they lived where a jukebox seemed to play constantly Earnest Tubb's "Walking the Floor Over You." That song, released in May of '41, is considered the first "honkytonk" song of country music. It became an instant hit. So maybe that little "diner/store" was actually a little "honkytonk." At this point "Who knows?" Whatever the case, they sold milk and bread. The date that memorable visit occurred was either in the summer of '41 when I was 3, or more probably in the summer of '42 when I was 4.

There are other precious memories from overnight visits with Auntie and Old Buddie. Sometime before the war was over they moved to a farm on the Frankfort-Versailles Road and Old Buddie began farming again. A "Mr. Crutcher," who lived in Frankfort, owned the farm. It was on this farm that I traced my name with a stick in a freshly poured cement spillway for a pond near the house where Auntie and Old Buddie lived. It was also there while "helping" Old Buddie stomp out the last embers of a burning stump from a fallen tree that I caught my britches leg on fire. My journey back to the house carrying my pants in hand "burned" that event into my memory.

Another vivid memory from the Crutcher place days was helping work a jigsaw puzzle that depicted an aerial dogfight between American and Japanese fighter planes. The Carroll's oldest son Garnett was at that time serving as a bombardier on a B25 in the Army Air Corps, flying in the European theater. Anxiously listening to the radio for news of the war was an every-night activity in those days. Thankfully, Garnett returned from the war unharmed physically but there were emotional wounds that plagued him the rest of his life. He seems to have had great difficulty sleeping, often wakening up with nightmares. He regularly slept with a pistol under his pillow, an act for which other family members could find no understandable reason.

Old Buddie got sick late one summer while living at the Crutcher place and was unable to harvest his tobacco crop. I have a vivid memory of my father along with other family members and some neighbors working one weekend to harvest his crop. It was one of the rare occasions Daddy worked on Sunday. The illness, perhaps a heart problem, may have led Old Buddie to retire from farming that year because they moved from the Crutcher place to a house on Frankfort Ave. in Versailles shortly after the end of the war. It was on the sidewalk in front of the Versailles house just below a Catholic boarding school for girls I first learned to ride a bicycle.

After coming home from the war, Garnett flew a crop-dusting plane for at least one summer before he bought a restaurant business on Lexington Street in Versailles. It had a bar in the front that served sandwiches and mainly beer and there was a poolroom in the back. It was referred to in our home as the "beer joint" or "pool room." Garnett turned the upstairs into a nice 3-room apartment (kitchen, living room, bedroom and bath) for his parents.

Shortly after they moved into the apartment over the pool hall Old Buddie died unexpectedly of a heart attack Nov. 17, 1948. Auntie would live there until her death almost 24 years later on April 7, 1972. I was almost 11 at the time of Ole Buddie's death and in the following years I enjoyed many overnight visits with Auntie in her little apartment. I enjoyed watching from the second-story windows facing Lexington Street both people and traffic passing by. During those visits to Versailles I sharpened my skills at various card games, 7-up, Rummy, Pinochle, Hearts, Spades and Rook, to mention a few. I've been told I once cried to take a deck of cards to bed with me which surely must have happened before age 10. I also learned to play pool downstairs during slack business hours or when the pool hall was closed. Occasionally, I would rack the balls and collect the money for the next game, but I mostly watched others play.

Auntie's and Ole Buddie's sons Garnett and Pete would later marry and have two children each, but without a doubt I was their first "grandchild", and they were my only "real grandparents." They loved me, petted me and spoiled me. They probably taught me and let me do some things they shouldn't have, but I enjoyed a relationship and had privileges denied my sibling's.

Early Years

Growing Up on the Farm

My father was a farmer and a very good one all his life. He was a tenant farmer, meaning he farmed land owned by someone else. During the first four years of his and mother's married life he farmed with his father at the farm in Clover Bottom. Based on vaguely remembered statements being made in my childhood and from a conversation with my cousin, Johnny Drury, I believe at one time granddaddy Merritt thought he was part owner of the farm on which he lived. The house was known throughout Clover Bottom as the McGohon house.[1] Sometime between February of 1939 and April of 1940 (when the census was taken) Merritt and Sue Ella moved to a farm in Marion County Kentucky owned by their son Jack. It seems that Jack bought the farm and Merritt took his livestock (horses, mules and cows) along with all his farm machinery to the farm, thus enabling Jack to begin working on his recently acquired farm.

Hugh and Marie apparently moved with them to Marion County where they also lived on that farm for at least a few months. I heard stories about my learning to talk and mispronouncing the name Betty Stoffer, one of Uncle Jack's daughters for whom I had an affinity. At any rate, by April of 1940 the census taker found Hugh, Marie and their 2 children living as renters on a farm on Jessamine Station Pike in Jessamine County. In 1941 or '42 they moved to a farm in the Handy's Bend community, southeast of Wilmore.

In 1943 they moved again, this time to the McCauley place on the Lawrenceburg Road in Woodford County. That house, the first of which I have some memory, was "large," in that the rooms were large with high ceilings. Two big events occurred that year. In September I started school in Versailles. I was 5 at the time and would not have my 6th birthday until December, making me the youngest in my class. This would be the case throughout my elementary and secondary school life. Though I took pride in its status it may have been a disadvantage at least in some athletic endeavors. In the early fall days of the school year my mother would walk with me out a gravel lane over a set of railroad tracks to the highway where I caught the school bus, a total distance of perhaps 200 – 300 yards. The second big event was the birth of my second sister on November 21st. She was named Lillian Carol for mother's Aunt "Lillie" Carol. However, I must confess I have no memory of the arrival of the new baby in our home. I was told several times "She almost died her first year in this world because she caught all the childhood diseases I brought home from school."

During those years Hugh's primary work consisted of raising a small crop of tobacco each year as a tenant farmer and working on other farms as a day laborer when time and opportunity permitted. I think he may have also worked for a short time at a Whiskey Distillery in Millville, just east of Frankfort. I remember on one occasion some years later going with him in a truck to that distillery to get a load of "slop" to feed our hogs.

In January of 1944 Hugh and Marie with their 3 small children (Buddy just having turned 6, Ann about to be 5, and 6-week-old Carol) moved to the Paul Simpson farm on the Keene Pike in Jessamine County. The Simpson farm was located in the northwest corner of the intersection of the Keene and Harrodsburg pikes. Mr. Paul Simpson, the farm's owner, lived in a beautiful big red brick house on the northeast corner of the farm facing the Harrodsburg Road, US 68.

The 3-room tenant house into which we moved faced the Keene Pike to the south and was about 500 yards west of the Harrodsburg road. Covered in yellowish brown asbestos brick siding on the outside the house consisted of a bedroom, a living room/bedroom, a kitchen and a little screened-in back porch. A small steep stairway with a door two steps from the bottom led to a small attic that served as a storage room and an occasional children's playroom on rainy days. Mother would often say, "This house isn't big enough to whip a cat in," and compared to the "large" McCauley house the new house was small indeed.

However, the new farm offered a much-improved farming opportunity for Hugh. There was the usual 50% interest in a larger tobacco crop, perhaps 5 or 6 acres, the privilege of owning two or three milk cows, and for the first time Hugh was given a 1/3 interest in a small herd of 30-40 sheep. While many neighboring farms had cows and hogs very few raised sheep. The sheep would add an important dimension to both Hugh's workload and the economic productive of the farm.

A 4-years tenure on the Simpson farm also gave Hugh and Marie their first opportunity to put down real roots. For the first three years or more of their married life they had lived with Hugh's parents in the "McGohon House" in Clover Bottom. The next 4 years they lived in five different houses in three different central Kentucky counties.

The "little" house was heated by two stoves, a cooking stove in the kitchen and a "Warm Morning" stove in the living room, both fueled by coal. The living room served as my parent's bedroom and the family/entertainment room since the radio was located in that room. The large floor model radio was powered by a car battery that sat on a partially enclosed shelf in the bottom. The battery was charged by a windmill power generator daddy had assembled and fastened to the roof of the house.

Out back, beyond a couple of trees was the necessary "outhouse." It was a two-hole model well stocked with out-of-date Sears Roebuck catalogues. Baths were taken in the kitchen at least every Saturday and more often if absolutely necessary. A large galvanized # 2 washtub was filled with water heated on the kitchen stove. Fortunately, the door between the children's bedroom and the kitchen could be closed, but not locked, affording some small measure of privacy to a growing family.

The house was set back about 15 yards from the road making the front yard only about 45 feet deep and maybe 100 feet wide. The yard, more like a pasture field than a lawn, featured several potholes. On one occasion while learning to ride a borrowed girl's bicycle as I struggled to maintain my balance the front wheel hit one of those potholes. My body was thrown forward into the front angular bar. The injury caused considerable pain for several days and led me to conclude, inaccurately, that girl's bicycles were certainly not made with boys in mind.

There was also a nice garden spot west of the gravel driveway which daddy planted each spring. There were the early spring plantings of onions, beets, radishes and English peas. Later came tomatoes, potatoes, green beans, lima beans and sweet corn. Often there were later plantings of beans and corn. In the early years I "got to" help with the planting but as I grew older I "had to" help with the planting, hoeing, and picking the vegetables which made for an inexpensive yet very healthy diet.

Behind the house, perhaps 30 to 40 yards, was the livestock barn with a crib for corn, a hayloft, and stalls for the milk cows, and two workhorses. Our horseback riding as children was on the backs of "Big Red," a large roan colored gelding, and "Maggie" an older black mare, to and from the field where they were working. West of the horse barn was a low roofed "sheep" barn where the sheep were housed in the winter months when they were delivering their lambs.

The tobacco barn where the tobacco was hung for curing was on the back of the farm. It was in the pasture near that tobacco barn I received my most memorable "whipping." I received very few such punishments in childhood, not because I was a "good" little boy whose behavior didn't merit punishment, but because my father was usually quite lenient, and mother left punishment for serious misbehavior in his hands. However, on this particular occasion my actions reached a level of endangerment that could not be overlooked, even by my usually tolerant father.

It was tobacco housing time and two or three of my older cousins who lived about 5 miles away had come to help daddy "sucker" tobacco, an activity that preceded the actual cutting of the tobacco stalk. They had arrived in a large old flatbed truck and parked it next to the tobacco barn. While all the men were working on the far side of the field, out of sight, but not sound, of the truck. I along with a neighboring boy devised a most enjoyable activity. "Let's drive the truck around the pasture." Since both of us were under 10 at the time we would have to work together to manage the feat. One would work the pedals, gas, clutch, brake and gear shift, while the other with his knees on the seat would look through the windshield and guide the vehicle. My sister Ann had the exciting privilege of being the passenger riding on the truck bed. We drove in a wide circle and each boy had a turn at each major task.

We had just parked the truck and were getting out of the vehicle when daddy rounded the corner of the barn and hollered, "Buddy." My partner in crime started running in the opposite direction for all he was worth. I had taken a couple of steps when I heard that commanding voice again, "Don't you run from me!"

In addition to endangering our lives and especially Ann's it seems that we had used up most of the truck's remaining gas, which had been barely enough to get the Drury boys back home before our escapade. Now there was not even enough gas left to get the truck to a gas station. My legs and bottom stung for more than a few minutes after daddy turned me loose. Beyond that I seethed with anger at my neighbor friend who had escaped totally unscathed.

"Have you seen Danny?" I asked mother when I finally got to the house.

"He came running through the yard several minutes ago, on the way to his house I guess."

At that moment my intent was to inflict on him as much pain as my bare hands were capable of dishing out, if only I could have found him. By the time I saw him again several days later my anger had subsided but our friendship, which had never been great, was over for good.

Though we lived in the country we certainly were not isolated. Keene, a small community 1.5 miles to the west had two nice size country stores, Reynolds and Wilsons. Wilsons also housed the post office and a small inn. Keene was within easy walking distance. One winter when snow had made the roads impassable we walked to Reynolds and bought some candy and fireworks, firecrackers, cherry bombs and Roman candles. It must have been near New Year's Day for I remember daddy lighting the Roman candles and letting Ann and me take turns holding them while they shot their balls of fire into the air.

Four miles to the east of the Simpson farm lay Nicholasville, the county seat. It had a "big" courthouse surrounded by a distinctive stonewall plus the ever-popular movie theater which we were able to attend occasionally on a Saturday afternoon or evening. The "picture show" ran mostly westerns featuring popular cowboys like Roy Rogers, Gene Autry, Tom Mix, and Lash Larue. Each feature was preceded by a cartoon and a popular serial such as Batman and Robin, which always ended with the hero in a precarious situation and the announcer saying, "to be continued next week."

Downtown Lexington, the shopping and entertainment center of Central Kentucky, was only 12 miles to the north. It was also the center of the Burley Tobacco market where we took our tobacco annually to be sold. It was also the home of two large stockyards where daddy regularly bought and sold livestock, primarily sheep, cattle and hogs, at an auction. Each stockyard had a rink into which livestock were herded, sometimes individually and sometimes in a small group. I enjoyed sitting with daddy in the 4 to 5 row stadium surrounding the rink and watching him and other spectators following the chant of the auctioneer as they bid with a raised hand, a nod of the head or maybe just a wink.

Lexington was also the home of the University of Kentucky and the Kentucky Wildcats. My dad liked sports. He had played sandlot baseball as a youngster and followed the Cincinnati Reds baseball team in the sports pages and on the radio. One of my early memories was my first out-of-state trip to Cincinnati to see the Reds play at Crossly Field. We went with his younger brother Robert who had a glass eye. His eye had been put out a couple of years earlier in an accident while working in a garage. I was shocked, to put it mildly, when he took the eye out and showed it to us. I'm not sure which was most memorable, seeing Red's first baseman, Ted Kluszewski's huge muscular arms hanging from his jersey with cutout sleeves or Uncle Robert's glass eye.

Dad also enjoyed Kentucky football. With the arrival of Paul Bear Bryant as UK's coach in 1947 their football fortunes grew quickly. Though limited financial resources prevented him from attending games dad listened to radio broadcasts and avidly read all that was printed in the sports pages of the Lexington Herald newspaper.

Though my father enjoyed baseball and football his favorite spectator sport by far was basketball. He loved the Kentucky Wildcats. He loved reading about them, listening to them and talking about them. The Kentucky basketball dynasty, founded by Coach Adolf Rupp, was in its prime and unrivaled in the 15 years following WWII. They were NCAA champions in 1947, 1948, 1951 and 1958. In 1953-54, Rupp's only team to go undefeated (25-0), finished the season ranked #1 nationally. However, when the NCAA ruled 4 senior starters would be ineligible to play in the tournament, UK refused to compete without them.

Needless to say, I was totally infected with the Kentucky basketball virus early in life. Three memories stand out. A spring ritual for tobacco farmers was the preparation of a 100' X 10' bed in which tiny tobacco seeds were sown to produce plants that would later be transplanted into the field. To kill any weed seeds in the bed a wire sled of burning logs would be pulled across the bed allowing it to rest for 20 to 30 minutes in each place. The process would often last well into the wee hours of the morning.

One night in the spring of '47 when daddy was burning his tobacco beds Kentucky was playing Utah in the finals of the National Invitational Tournament in New York's Madison Square Garden. Daddy took the big floor-model radio to the tobacco bed, hooked it to the battery of the car and listened to the basketball game. When the game ended tears were rolling down my 9-year-old cheeks. The year before UK had burst on the national scene by winning the NIT but not that year.

The second memorable event occurred in the summer of 1948. The Kentucky team, that year's NCAA champions, played the Phillip's Oilers, the AAU champions, in a series of exhibition games in preparation for the Olympics in London. A basketball floor was set up in the middle of UK's football stadium and Daddy and I were among thousands of Wildcat fans who saw their beloved Cats for the first time in person. The Olympic team composed of half Wildcats and half Oilers would return from London with Olympic Gold.

The third memorable UK basketball event of my childhood occurred during the 1952-53 season. Because of a "points shaving scandal" at Madison Square Garden that occurred in '49 and came to light in 1951 the Kentucky team was banned from competing during the 1952-53 season. During that "off" year the team played 3 exhibition inner-squad games with the two stars of the team, Cliff Hagan and Frank Ramsey, serving as captains of the respective teams. Both were All Americans who would have long successful professional carriers. My dad and I were among 12,000 fans that packed newly constructed Memorial Coliseum to see one of those scrimmages at a cost of $1 per ticket. Thanks to those and many other transfusions in my formative years I would bleed blue the rest of my life, even if I only attended UK my first year of college.

The Christmas I turned ten I got a new bicycle and the news we were moving from the Simpson Place to the Taylor Place, also on the Keene Pike but 2.5 miles closer to Nicholasville. On a pretty day while school was out for the Christmas holidays I hopped on my new bicycle and rode the full 2.5 miles down the road to see the house that would be our new home.

"Wow!" It looked like a mansion, and compared to our current house it was. It was a "big" six room wood frame house painted white. It sat on the crest of a hill at the end of a tree-lined lawn and driveway nearly 100 yards from the road. The inside woodwork of the house was stained hardwood. The three coal burning fireplaces were framed in colorful ceramics and stained wood with mirrors over the mantles. Two pocket doors usually left open separated the living room and dining room. There were also two bedrooms, a kitchen and a breakfast room that had once been a porch connecting the kitchen and the dining room. An 18-inch square opening with a door was located on the wall between the kitchen and dining room, originally designed to pass food from the kitchen to the dining room. More importantly, there was a small room off the breakfast room that was to become a bathroom with running water as soon as a septic tank and field lines were installed. While daddy would still be a tenant, this was no "tenant" house. This was a sure enough "nice" house built for the owner at least 50 years earlier and lived in by the owner for many years before it became a tenant house.

The prospect of moving to a better house and farm must have filled my parents with renewed optimism because a little over 8 months later I had a baby brother, Ronald Wayne. Naturally, the newborn got most of the attention, at least in the beginning. Actually, I'm not sure that ever changed. Occasionally his older siblings treated him more like a toy. One day when he was 3 or 4 I tossed him over my shoulder and ran out the front door into the yard. As I went through the doorway he slid down my shoulder and his head hit the door frame. Thankfully, his head finally stopped bleeding and his crying subsided, but my feelings of guilt dissipated more slowly.

Ronnie, almost 11 years my junior, was too small to be a real playmate as long as I was at home. He was nine when Barbara and I were married. With his bright mind he graduated from UK becoming the electrical engineer of the family. He must have forgiven me, at least partially, for that bump on his head because he asked me to officiate at his and Donna's wedding.

By moving to the 157-acre Taylor Farm my father was able to significantly expand and diversify his farming operation. His sheep herd grew to 80 ewes. Beef cattle (cows and calves or stockers) and hogs were added to the livestock inventory. In addition to the larger tobacco allotment both wheat and corn were grown for feed, with any surplus being sold for a little extra cash. How he did all the work that first year with just one team of horses I do not know. However, by the second year, with the help of a sizable loan from the bank, he was able to buy a new Ford tractor. Diversified though the crops were, they were not large enough to justify buying a combine, corn-picker or hay-bailer. Work we couldn't do manually was contracted out to men who had harvesting equipment.

I learned to drive the tractor at an early age and helped with chores I was old enough to do. Milking cows (always 2 or 3, sometimes more) by hand twice a day was a year-around necessity. In summer, I helped with the many tasks required to raise tobacco. Hay was mowed, racked, bailed and stored in a barn loft. In my mid-teens I competed with other laborers to be the most productive.

In winter, livestock had to be fed daily and when ponds were frozen ice had to be broken so the animals could get water. In late winter and early spring when lambs were being born sheep required extra attention. Though on the farm there was always work to be done, dad never let farm work interfere with my schoolwork or activities.

Going to School in Wilmore

There was also a small elementary school for grades 1-8 in Keene. The building sat on the crest of a hill 150 yards or more from the road and had 3 rooms, one for grades 1-3 another for grades 4-6 and one for grades 7 and 8. Northwest of the school on adjoining property was the Mt. Pleasant Baptist Church building. The road to the church used the same entrance as the school but branched off to the church halfway up the hill. Though the Keene school was less than two miles from our house my parents enrolled me in the first grade at Wilmore some 6 miles to the south of the Simpson place. Though I do not recall the reason for that decision ever being discussed in my presence, I suspect they thought a school with one grade per classroom was worth the extra bus riding time. In addition, mother was friends with the second-grade teacher at Wilmore, Mrs. Braden. The school bus housed at a bus garage in Nicholasville picked me up on its way to Keene where it ran the Keene route. It then ran a route to Wilmore. In the afternoon the same route was run in reverse. While the "Keene kids" were being picked up I had the choice of staying on the bus and riding the Keene route or getting off at the schoolhouse and waiting for the bus to return.

The decision on whether to ride or stay at the school depended on the weather and who was around to play with. When the weather was nice one of our favorite games was anti-anti-over. We would choose up sides, one side on either side of the school building. One side would holler "anti-anti-over, here it comes over" and throw a rubber ball over the roof of the school. If someone on the other side caught it before it hit the ground they could run around the house and try to hit a member of the other team with the ball. The object of course was to get as many as possible on your side. No one ever really won, but it was a fun way to pass the time.

One winter following a "big" snow the roads became passable and school started back long before the snow was gone. In the morning on the school's long front yard we rolled up several large snowballs and stacked them on top of one another making 2 "forts" facing each other. In the afternoon we chose sides, made a lot of snowballs and had a prolonged fight, throwing at one another from behind our forts.

The Wilmore school I attended for 11 ½ years had a campus of 4 buildings. In the center was an impressive two-story stone building that housed the 3rd – 6th graders and a lunchroom in the basement. To the right was a newer one-story brick building that contained classrooms for 1st and 2nd graders and an auditorium with a stage and a seating capacity of perhaps 150. To the left was a longer stone building, two stories on the lower end, which housed the high school plus the 7th and 8th grade students. Behind the center building was a wood frame gymnasium with a basketball court and bleacher seating on each side of the court about 6 rows high.

Compared to some schools, the physical plant was modest, but faculty members and students associated with the college and seminary supported a quest for excellence in learning that exceeded that of the typical small-town school. I was the benefactor of that excellence though I would not recognize or appreciate it until several years later.

Early Work Experience

The bulk of my work experience prior to High School graduation took place on the family farm, which Daddy farmed as a tenant. That work on the farm, while valuable in later life, at the time was a necessary contribution to the family's livelihood. The above-mentioned "work" represented the few treasured times when I got "real money in my hand" for work I did.

Across the street from Auntie's apartment was an A&P grocery store. One summer, perhaps the summer of '52, when I was 14, I got my first "big time" job sacking groceries at the super market[1]. The job probably lasted two or three weeks at most, but it was a proud moment indeed, when I held that first real check with my name on it from "The Great Atlantic and Pacific Tea Company." Before that experience I had no idea what letters A&P represented. A couple of years later I would work for a few Saturdays "filling orders" at Heathman's Grocery in Nicholasville.

The next summer our next-door neighbor, Bill Jackson, got the contract to bail hay on the 600-acre Almahurst (now Ramsey) horse farm nearby. He hired me for 50 cents an hour, primarily to drive a tractor pulling a side-delivery rake. That summer it seemed like we bailed pastureland bluegrass, used for bedding, every day it didn't rain, or Bill's new John Deere automatic wire-tie bailer wasn't being repaired.

A Helpmate for Sure

While philosophically I place little, if any, stock in the "star-crossed lover" motif, my personal experience could be seen as strong evidence for that notion. The problem with the concept is that often it is used as an excuse not to "work at a marriage" and ignores the absolute necessity for couples sacrificing for one another. Barbara certainly has had to work at and sacrifice to make our marriage the joyful union it was and is. On rare occasions I may have put forth a little effort as well.

Our meeting and first date in the summer of '55 when I was 17 years of age have been described in a previous chapter. It wasn't long until we were considered a "steady couple." That was easy for me since Barbara was the only real girlfriend I ever had. Things were not quite so simple for her. While at college in Richmond a young man just out of the service had taken a serious interest in her. She hated disappointing Earnest, or Ralph, or Evert, or whatever his name was, but telling him she must that her heart had been pulled in another direction.

In September Barbara went back to Eastern for her junior year with my class ring on a chain around her neck and I started to UK. We saw each other on most weekends at church and at some high school football games. Life was blissfully happy that fall. Then came that fateful November Sunday when God said, "Who will I send and who will go for us." After telling Brother Evans about what had happened that Sunday morning, I told Barbara and my parents. In January I shared my sense of call to ministry with the Nicholasville Baptist congregation and now "everyone" knew "Buddy was planning to be a preacher."

Some of the implications of the call to ministry were obvious immediately. Since I had not been, to use Steve Martin's words, "a wild and crazy guy," my moral compass changed little though my personal devotional life became much more focused and disciplined. The most immediate change had to do with my education. Not only did the course of study need to change but I was also faced with changing institutions, which in the spring of '56 was far from settled. In addition to that uncertainty, the horizon for completing my formal education had now been almost doubled from 4 to 7 years. Finally, there was the matter of potential financial reward. I could not ignore or escape the difference in economic outlook for a career of a well-trained engineer versus that of a Baptist preacher, a difference that weighed greatly upon my mother and perhaps others.

With many of those thoughts running through my mind it was with a heavy heart I pulled up to the curb in front of Barbara's house on Brown Street one Saturday night in the spring of '56. "I need to talk to you about something before you go in,"

I began. "You know when we started going steady neither of us had any idea I might be a preacher one day. I'm going to be in school for a long time. I don't know how I'm going to pay for it. I may have to get a full-time job and go to school part-time, which will take even longer. Even when I get out of school I probably won't make much money. I know you didn't sign on for all of that and I don't want to be unfair to you. If you want to find someone else I'll understand."

When I finished there was a long silence. Finally, with a quiver in her voice Barbara spoke, "You mean you want to break up with me?"

"No, I didn't say that."

"Well, it sounded like it."

By now my voice was quivering and my eyes were tearing up. "I just don't think it would be fair to ask you to go through all the things my preparing to be a preacher would involve, to say nothing of being a preacher's wife if it should lead to that."

"Well if God wants you to be a preacher, maybe He wants me to help you get through school and one day become a preacher's wife."

The conversation continued along those lines for several minutes and ended with a long hug and kiss. When Barbara finally left the car that night we had not broken up and the dark cloud of anxiety and dread that had plagued my mind for days was replaced with joyous relief. Sixty years later Barbara's recollection of that night is vague and blurred. However, it was a traumatic moment for me and the memory of it is indelibly stamped upon my mind's eye.

From that moment on our relationship continued on a fairly steady trajectory from "you and me" into "us and we." I do not remember any real "downs" in our relationship though there certainly must have been a few minor ones.

Weekends were reserved for one another. Unlike mine, Barbara's family was small and very close. They regularly gathered for Sunday dinner at her "Mamma" Jones' who lived in a large two-story white frame house at Glass' Mill near Wilmore and about 6 miles south of Nicholasville. Mamma Jones and her first husband William Carney had four children, Marie, Eva, Lester and Russell. Lester had lost his life in an automobile accident while stationed at a California army base during WW II. Mamma was able to buy the house at Glass' Mill with money from an insurance settlement following the accident. Several years after Mr. Carney died Mamma married A. T. Jones. who had a grown son Allen.

Marie, the oldest child, husband Leo Harrod and their two children Betty Ellen and Glenda Lee who lived in Nicholasville came to Glass' Mill almost weekly for Sunday dinner. The Heathman's, Eva, "Poss" and their two daughters, Barbara and Sue Earl also came from Nicholasville. Russell, wife Martha and their daughter, Ann Russell came from Moreland near Danville about 20 miles away. Betty Ellen, the oldest granddaughter and husband Matt Gibbs came from Lexington. A. T.'s son Allen and his wife Nettie, who had no children, also came from Lexington. So, for all the holidays and on many other Sundays all 16 gathered for dinner at Mamma's. I made 17. After all what's one more among such a crowd.

After a sumptuous dinner, prepared mostly by Mamma Jones, weather permitting, the men went across the road to play croquet on a carefully constructed, well maintained, sand packed croquet diamond. Since I had played the game for years I "fit in" quickly as one of the better players. Croquet was a game my dad enjoyed and after moving to the Taylor farm we had a croquet diamond in the front lawn most of the time. My siblings and I along with some neighborhood kids played often and dad had rigged some makeshift lighting so the adults and older kids could play at night as well as on weekends. The mallets, wickets and playing surface at Glass's Mill were far superior to our inexpensive JC Higgins set from Sears Roebuck but the playing skills were the same. Needless to say, I welcomed with delightful anticipation our regular Sunday trips to Mamma Jones's.

The women did whatever women do at such gatherings. As I think back on those days it is clear that Mamma Jones and the daughters were the glue that held the extended family together. Interestingly enough all five grandchildren were girls and except for Barbara they were all called by their double names. In-laws were openly welcomed and easily assimilated into the family. In comparison to other families I have known they formed an unusually harmonious family. Those gatherings probably have influenced the value Barbara places on special occasion family dinners today along with her expectations for our daughters and their families. It also helps explain her deep disappointment when everyone is not there.

In the summer of '56 Barbara's grandmother Heathman and her Aunt Nelda took her with them on a trip to California. In Los Vegas they visited a casino where Barbara had her first and only "run-in with the law". While feeding a slot machine with coins provided by her granny a house detective asked to see her identification. Three months short of her 21st birthday she was "breaking the law." Worse still, her strait-laced grandmother was contributing to the delinquency of a minor. Somehow, they managed to avoid arrest and imprisonment and continued on their trip. During that trip Barbara found time each day to write a letter or postcard to her beloved who was waiting daily for the mailman's arrival. The reading and rereading of each word only served to deepen the longing for the trip's end and Barbara's return.

After her return there was a point one night when I said, "When we are married …"

"Who said we were getting married," she interrupted, "You haven't asked me yet."

"Well, you will, won't you?"

"Of course! You know I will."

Not a very classic or romantic proposal, but it did reflect the mutual understanding of our relationship.

By the end of summer, I had saved enough money over and above my coming Georgetown College expenses to buy a diamond ring. The shopping day was a beautiful day indeed; at least the sun was shining in my heart and mind. I had discovered she liked a single stone in a tiffany setting. After hearing a sales pitch from salesmen in several jewelry stores in Lexington and still knowing virtually nothing about diamonds I finally settled on the one that looked best to me. Though the stone was small, 1/3 carat, it looked reasonably clear and had a bright sparkle with a beautiful blue tint. He said it was a "blue diamond." I took it with the understanding they would put it in a tiffany setting and later resize it to fit Barbara's finger. Though it wasn't much as diamond engagement rings go, she has worn it faithfully and I think proudly for over 65 years because its significance had a value that could not be measured in dollars and cents.

I picked the ring up from the store a couple of days later and hid it in a drawer in my bedroom until the weekend when I planned to give it to Barbara. Though my words denied it, my behavior that week sent a loud message to my family that something was going on. It wasn't long before my sister Carol found my hiding place and came strutting to the family dinner table ring held high on her finger, flashing it for the whole family to see. Fortunately, for me they did not divulge my secret until I had given Barbara her ring. The big night was a Saturday night. Getting out of the car and going into her house that night the beam in her eye and the gleam on her finger could not be hidden. When she proudly displayed it to her father he responded with, "You've got to give it back".

"Oh no I'm not," was her firm response. "We're in love and we are going to get married. Not immediately but after I graduate."

Though he could not have been surprised he was not ready to accept the reality of what the ring meant. Thankfully, his resistance was short lived. His response was prompted not by a dislike for me but rather by the feeling of inevitable loss. It was a feeling I would know full well in another 25 years.

The summer passed quickly, and fall brought the excitement of enrolling at Georgetown. Barbara visited the campus the Saturday of Homecoming. Big Bronze Mums Corsages with blue and gold bow and ribbon streamers were the rage and I made sure she had one. We visited my room at Chambers House and attended the afternoon football game where I nearly stiff-armed her out of the stands. That experience opened Barbara's eyes to Buddy's tendency to become empathetically involved while watching critical moments of athletic competition resulting in unconscious flinches, wrenches and other minor reflex responses.

The summer of '56 would provide an unexpected opportunity to preach on 7 Sunday mornings for a small struggling Baptist church at Camp Nelson. On a few of those Sundays Barbara accompanied me offering encouragement with her presence and occasionally playing the piano for the Worship Service. I was at her house one Saturday afternoon in the spring of '57 when our Baptist Student Union director tracked me down by phone and asked if I could preach the next day for a church in Leatherwood.

"Sure, where's Leatherwood?" I responded.

"It's a coal mining camp in Eastern Kentucky, about as far back in the mountains as you can go."

He was right. It was a small community in southeast Kentucky, 30 miles from Whitesburg the closest town. Built by the Blue Diamond Mining Company, everything except the church and a boarding house belonged to the mining company. The company owned the mine where the miners worked, the houses where their families lived, and the one store that sold everything from groceries to appliances, everything.

A major flood had ravaged a number of communities in the mountains of Eastern Kentucky the previous week. I began immediately working on a sermon, "Building on the Rock," with Matt. 7:24-27 as my text. As a 19-year-old I certainly did not presume to know more about living through the crisis of a flood than they did, but I did think what Jesus had to say about the floods of life would be worth considering at that point in time.

As she would do countless times over the next 60 plus years, Barbara went with me for encouragement and support along with my sister Ann. We departed very early the next morning for the 3 ½ hour ride to Leatherwood. We ate lunch that day in the local boarding house owned by a church member and at her invitation we enjoyed a room that afternoon for "relaxing." As usual my afternoon was spent working on a sermon for the evening service. We got back to Nicholasville in the wee hours of the morning. A few weeks later I went with 8 or 10 other ministerial students on a "preaching mission" to that area of the state organized by our BSU director. I was assigned to the Leatherwood church by their request for some strange reason. My roommate, Carlos, was also on that "mission." He preached the same sermon in two different churches, one in the morning and the other in the evening, both of which he considered "very successful" because a number of people were in tears at the close of the services. I remember thinking by that standard both of my sermons were failures.

One other important occurrence in early summer was the purchase of another car, a 1950 Chevrolet 2-door coupe. A laborer on the Bell place across the road offered Daddy $100 for the Plymouth with bald tires and he took the offer. To replace it before tobacco-measuring season arrived we went car shopping in Louisville with Daddy's brother Grant, a bricklayer by trade who worked mostly in Louisville at that time. Uncle Grant and a friend of his took us to three of four car lots where we looked at "what they had" we might be able to afford. After driving 2 or 3 "possibilities" we went back to the lot that had the Chevy. Though it was 7 years old it had low mileage (under 50,000), had good tires and ran well.

The salesman asked if I would like to drive it around the block. The first time Daddy had driven the car with the salesman and me as passengers. The first test drive had been earlier in the afternoon but by the time I pulled off the lot it was completely dark with the lights of the city illuminating the main streets and neighborhoods. After a couple of blocks I made a right turn, a couple of blocks later another right turn, a third right turn and a fourth right turn onto the street where the car lot was located. It was a busy street and there were plenty of lights but where was the car lot? I thought let's try those turns again. I made the turns again but no car lot. Where was I? Finally, a big "Falls City Beer" neon sign with three flashing stars on my right caught my attention. I had seen that sign before, but it wasn't on the street with the car lot. I breathed a sigh of relief. Finally, I knew where I was. The car lot was on a street that Y-ed into the street I was traveling. What I had thought was a nice square block turned out to be a 5-sided block, a fact I had not recognized in the dark.

"It handles very nicely," was my only response to the "Where have you been?" query form several members of our party. It would be weeks before I confessed I had gotten lost, and a beer sign had been my salvation.

Daddy paid about $400 for the car, as I recall, and I had promised to pay him back "soon." It was a promise Barbara made sure I (actually we) kept sooner rather than later. As we left the lot I saw the salesman give uncle Grant a bill, a "finders" fee no doubt, which Uncle Grant in turn gave to Daddy. I proudly drove my new possession home that night and couldn't wait to show Barbara. No more trips in the old Plymouth with our fingers crossed, just hoping we would reach our destination.

Friday, August 9th, 1957, was set as our wedding date. The spring and summer had been filled with all the normal preparations for the "big day." The church was reserved, invitations were sent, the wedding party selected, flowers and decorations arranged and our new pastor, Rev. William B. Craig was enlisted to perform the ceremony. We got plenty of "Wedding Party" practice as several of our friends got married that spring and summer and we had the honor of participating in or attending those weddings.

The wedding went off just as planned, without a hitch. Barbara was radiantly beautiful as she walked down the aisle on her father's arm. It was my first glimpse of her that day and I could not have been more thrilled. Pictures were taken following the ceremony and the reception was held at Granny Heathman's house. We "hid" my "new" '50 Chevy in Granny's garage, which was easily found and decorated by our friends. We left the reception to everyone's surprise in Aunt Nelda's nearly new '56 Chevy parked in the drive, in plain view, for a 4-day honeymoon at Kentucky Dam Village on Kentucky Lake.

We returned to our first home, a 3-room upstairs apartment in Charlie and Agnes' house on Lynn Drive in Lexington. The kitchen contained a new refrigerator and stove, a wedding gift from Barbara's mom and dad along with a secondhand table and chairs we rescued from a storage room. The living room contained a big old, discarded couch that could be turned into a bed, an end table and lamp (wedding gifts), a rocking chair from Mrs. Taylor's attic, and a used black and white TV with a rabbit ears antenna from Uncle Russell and Aunt Martha who had recently bought a new one. The bedroom contained a chest of drawers from Mrs. Taylor's attic and for the first 6 weeks the bed I had used while living with my mom and dad, which they wanted and needed returned. So, the first piece of furniture we purchased was a brand-new cherry cannonball bed from the Cherry Shop in Campbellsville, KY with a new springs and mattress. It wasn't bad for a starter apartment. More important than the furnishings was the love of its occupants and their desire to sacrifice for each other's happiness.

We lived in our apartment on Lynn Dr. for almost 5 months. Charlie was gone most of the time hauling gasoline all over the state and beyond in his new diesel 18-wheel tanker truck. Agnes, Charlie's wife, and Russell, their 6-year-old son, were there by themselves most of the time after Russell got home from school. I thought things were going reasonably well until one afternoon Agnes informed me she thought she had made a mistake by renting to us. She acknowledged she was nervous and a light sleeper. We were the first couple to live in the upstairs apartment for some time and she was upset by all the noise we made. Her bedroom was directly under ours and her one specific complaint was the noise made by my shoes hitting the floor as I dropped them one at a time at irregular intervals while sitting on the unusually high new early American bed. We were able to find a nice 4-room duplex style ground- floor apartment a few blocks away on Pin Oak Drive. We moved at the end of December in a borrowed pickup truck. While looking for another apartment I tried to be more considerate, except for one night when for some unknown reason I dropped one shoe rather loudly and then softly placed the other beside it. We never knew how long Agnes lay awake that night waiting for the sound of the other shoe.

On our wedding day I not only married the girl of my dreams, but I also married a wife who would gladly help me get through school just as she had suggested might be "God's will" that night in front of her house almost 2 years earlier. For 4 of the next 5 years her schoolteacher's salary would provide most of our family's financial support. Barbara taught 6th grade at Picadome Elementary School, working hard as a first-year teacher preparing lesson plans and being the best teacher possible for kids struggling with the normal wide array of preteen problems. Though many days ended in frustration and fatigue she persevered. Thankfully, I was able to contribute something to our financial needs as a 20-hour a week clerk in the dairy department of a new Kroger store on the south side of Lexington earning $1.05 per hour. I had been recommended for the job by Mr. Craft, my Nicholasville Kroger store manager.

Near the end of October Dr. Glenn Yarborough, the college's BSU director, offered me the opportunity to preach one Sunday at the Pleasant Home Baptist Church in Owen County. He had gotten a request from a deacon named Tommy Boaz (spelled like the biblical character but pronounced Boze) for a student to supply their pulpit. Always eager to preach I accepted with an enthusiastic "yes." Once again Barbara, with more than a little trepidation, was at my side as we left Lexington early on Sunday morning for the 75-minute (65 miles) drive to Pleasant Home.

Pleasant Home Church met in a one-room wood frame building with double front doors in the center of the building located 2 miles back the unpaved Eagle Creek Lane. The building had 8 to10 rows of one-piece wooden pews on each side of a center aisle and a rough pinewood floor. At the end of the building opposite the front doors was an 8-inch-high podium containing a pulpit and 2 upholstered chairs, one for the pastor and the other for the song leader. A piano sat on the left side of the podium and an antique pump organ was on the right. White muslin curtains were hung on 2 clothesline wires stretched across the width of the building. Two other curtains were on wires stretched on either side of the center aisle. When pulled from both sides and the back where they normally hung they provided line-of-sight screens for the 4 Sunday School classes; men, women, youth, and children. A coal burning stove near the front on the piano side heated the building in the winter.

Some 25 people gathered that morning at 10:00 for "Sunday School" and "Church" (the worship service) which followed. Deacon Lonnie Poland and his wife along with their two children hosted us in their home for Sunday dinner. Their oldest daughter Evelyn and her husband Tommy Boaz were also there. The meal was a superb country dinner consisting of 2 meats, several vegetables, homemade rolls and cornbread, and freshly baked pies for dessert. It was delicious by any standard. That afternoon as we visited we got the "low down" on everyone at church that morning and naturally we gladly shared our backgrounds. Since the house had no running water we relieved ourselves in the two-hole outhouse discretely screened by a few shrubs 20 yards or so from the house. It was equipped with the traditional Sears Roebuck catalogue and a fresh roll of toilet paper for their guests I presumed.

At the conclusion of the service that night I was asked to wait in the car for a few minutes where I hoped they were discussing how much of the days offering to give the preacher for his expenses and an honorarium. Some 10 or 15 minutes later Tommy came to the car and said, "We just voted to call you as our pastor if you will accept. Our salary isn't much, $25 per week, but it's all we can afford."

I was shocked, to say the least. The thought they would call me as their pastor that night had never entered my mind. I looked at Barbara who shrugged as if to say, "It's up to you."

I accepted their offer on the spot without even so much as a "Let me pray about it."

"If you want me to be your pastor I'll do the best I can. As you know, I'm not ordained, but I have been licensed by the Nicholasville Baptist Church and I suppose they will ordain me."

"That's fine with us. Can you be with us next Sunday?"

"Sure!"

"Both of you come back inside with me and I'll tell the church we have a new pastor."

Barbara was now a pastor's wife. In addition to attending all the services, she would play the piano or organ, help in Bible School, critique sermons, cut stencils for Sunday Bulletins, type sermon outlines as well as term papers and eat meals in homes with highly questionable sanitary standards. A sheet of notebook paper with each Sunday of the year listed was posted on the inside front door. Church members could volunteer to take the pastor and his wife home for Sunday meals by placing their name beside one of the Sundays. Tommy explained that on Sundays no one signed up we would go to their relatively new home in Warsaw which had running water, or we would go to the Poland's. We were never disappointed when we saw the sign-up sheet was blank for that particular Sunday. Staying in houses without running water presented Barbara with one of her greatest challenges, as a pastor's wife but she accepted it like a trooper.

I also got a wife who was a good cook and would become a superb cook. She enjoyed cooking and read cookbooks for fun. There have been few weeks in my life when we did not have a dish we had never eaten before. I weighed 150 the day we married and by the time we celebrated our first anniversary I had gained 20 pounds.

Barbara was an excellent organizer and a very good household manager. The house was always neat, never in disarray. No matter how early she left for work the sink was never left with dirty dishes and the beds were made every morning. Meals were planned and groceries bought with careful attention to nutrition and frugality. Without knowing it I had a "low maintenance" wife who not only spent little on herself and but also would become an excellent seamstress making clothes for both her and our three daughters. Beyond "helping me get through school" she would make it possible for that low preacher's salary to provide adequately for the family.

In retrospect there is no way I could have been wise enough or even lucky enough to have selected a wife so perfectly suited to be my lover, comforter, encourager, counselor, partner, helpmate and wife. She was and continues to be nothing less than a special "Gift of God."

Preparing to be a Christian Minister

As I alluded to earlier, my enrollment in the College of Engineering at UK had been more by default than a carefully weighted decision. I do not ever recall a time when there was a discussion of my doing anything other than going to college when I graduated from high school. I had made reasonably "good grades" in school, perhaps a little better than average, but never very close to the "top of the class," except in math. To be honest "making straight A's" was never a priority. It certainly was not considered to be worth the effort of "studying beyond the classroom" even if "straight A's" might have been attainable. The only high school activities that seemed worth extra effort were playing on the football team, being on the debate team, and being in speech and drama events.

Like most boys in my circle of friends I enjoyed playing several sports, i.e. softball, basketball and football, however the thought of being an athlete was quickly squashed. I "went out" for the basketball team my freshman year in high school and "warmed the bench" on the "B" team, playing briefly in 2 or 3 games. One day in practice my coach said, "McGohon you dribble, pass, and shoot pretty good, but you've got one problem though."

"What's that coach?"

"You run too long in the same place."

That accurate assessment of my athleticism ended all thoughts of a basketball career except for some pickup games and an occasional game of "horse."

My football "career" was a little more rewarding and lasted somewhat longer. In a small high school with perhaps 50 to 60 male students in all four grades and a strong focus on basketball, fielding a normal football team was impossible. Because there were at least eight schools within a 50-mile radius with similar issues, Wilmore High School was able to participate in a 6-man football league, similar to today's 7-on-7 summer contests. There was a center and 2 ends on the line along with a quarterback and 2 halfbacks in the backfield. Perhaps the two most significant rule changes were (1) all players were eligible pass receivers and (2) a first down required 15 yards.

During my junior and senior years, I was one of the 15 or so boys on the football team. I was a reserve with some playing time my junior year and the starting center on offence my senior year. Football practice was held for 60 to 90 minutes after school each day except on "game day." Since we lived about 7 miles from school getting home after practice sometimes was a challenge. David, a teammate and good friend commuted in his own car each day from his home in Lexington. His normal route took him within 2.5 miles of my home so I usually road with him the first part of the journey and then walked or hitchhiked the rest of the way. The joy and privilege of playing made the difficulty of getting home from practice seem like a minor inconvenience.

Because some of our better athletes played both basketball and football we had a good team. Our team was undefeated my junior year and also in my senior year until the final game, which was against Perryville, a team we had defeated earlier in the season. The league championship game was played at Perryville in a downpour. Near the end of the first half I got a slight concussion in a muddy pileup and had to leave the game. I begged the coach to let me play in the second half thinking I could somehow make the difference between victory and defeat. I insisted I knew all the plays if only he would give me a chance. But, my repeated question, "What's the score?" coupled with my inability to remember whether we were on offense or defense convinced the coach that for my sake and the team's I was where I belonged, on the sideline.

The reward for all of my sterling athletic accomplishments was a "football letter" and a beautiful green athletic jacket trimmed in gold with gold leather sleeves on which to wear the impressive green "W". Sixty years later that trophy worn often in those teen years, though now tattered and torn, still hangs proudly in my closet as a reminder of a tiny bit of athletic glory I once enjoyed even if I did "run too long in the same place."

Growing up, living and working on a farm made vocational agriculture a natural course of study and FFA (Future Farmers of America) an accompanying club activity, though being a future farmer was never a serious consideration. We were taught good agriculture practices and conducted various farming projects. One year I raised 1/3 acre of strawberries and made a nice little profit from my labor. Several times my project was caring for sheep. I helped shear their wool and showed lambs in the Central Kentucky Livestock Show at Bluegrass Stockyard. Daddy helped me pick the best lamb in the herd to show. We never won but usually finished in the top half of the 30-40 participants. The winning lamb was sold at auction and usually was purchased by an elite restaurant paying several times the normal price for advertising purposes. We also learned proper parliamentary procedures used to conduct FFA meetings. Little did I know at the time how valuable that knowledge would be one day for presiding at church business meetings, as chairman of the Alabama Baptist State Board of Missions, and even as a Director of Missions refereeing a church squabble.

At the beginning of my freshman year in High School Jim Young, a recent graduate from Asbury College, was hired to teach English at Wilmore High School. Fortunately, in addition to his regular teaching duties he had a strong interest in the extra circular activities of speech and drama. In my senior year he left his position at the high school to teach at Asbury College. (From his annual Christmas letter, I learned he earned a PhD degree in Drama from the University of Michigan, taught at Taylor University, the University of

Wisconsin-Madison, and became chair of the theater department at the University of Massachusetts in Amherst. The last 23 years of his career were spent as professor of Communications at Wheaton College).

In my sophomore year Mr. Young made participation in regional High School speech and drama competitions available for the first time to interested students at Wilmore High as an extra circular activity. I decided to compete in the "Oratorical Declamation" contest, a memorized 3 to 5-minute speech initially given by a famous orator i.e. Patrick Henry's "…give me liberty or give me death" speech. I knew the speech perfectly and had practiced it several times before a mirror at home. Needless to say, as I stood that day in a large classroom on the campus of Eastern Kentucky University in Richmond to give my first-ever public presentation the butterflies were not only in my stomach but all over my body.

The audience, perhaps 40 tops, was made up of other contestants, a few parents and friends, and 3 judges. My voice was a little squeaky as I began and the longer I spoke the dryer my mouth and the tighter my vocal cords became. Less than 60 seconds into the speech I opened my mouth and not a single sound came out. It was as though my vocal cords had frozen in place. I remember lowering my head, stepping back, taking a deep breath and thinking "It's all over now, there's no chance to win anything." When I finally raised my head and looked back at the audience my vocal cords along with the rest of my body had relaxed at least enough to go on. I started over and completed the speech for the most part as I had planned. With such a traumatic beginning I have often wondered why I ever tried anything similar to that again.

Though I could not have known it at the time this humiliating experience would be the beginning of a lifetime of public speaking. Indeed, the sharing of that experience would prove to be an encouragement to others struggling with "stage fright" at the thought of making a presentation before an audience.

Wilmore High formed its first debate team my junior year and I participated for the next 2 years. The second of those years we prepared for and debated the topic; "Resolved that the president of the United States be elected by a direct vote of the people." The fact that we had to know both the pros and cons of the issue and be prepared to debate either side of the issue, sometimes with only a few minutes notice, provided an excellent civics lesson in the American political system. It also sharpened our skills in logically organizing our thoughts and speaking extemporaneously in rebuttal to counter the arguments of the opposing team.

In the regional speech festival that spring I participated in the "Extemporaneous Speaking" event in addition to being on the debate team. During my senior year I participated in the "Dramatic Monologue" contest earning a superior rating and was a member of the drama team that presented a one act play in the drama competition. Though no academic credit was given for any of these activities I found the challenge to be enjoyable, exciting and at some level quite fulfilling. While all of these activities were enjoyable and would later be a major factor in my college education they in no way influenced its beginning.

I enrolled in the College of Engineering at the University of Kentucky in the fall of 1955 with little knowledge of what an engineer did other than "build things." Neither did I have any idea of how many different fields of engineering there were. Math had been my easiest and favorite subject in both elementary and high school. When coupled with an innate curiosity of how things worked the suggestion at some time by someone "Buddy, you'd make a good engineer!" stuck.

In September of '55, the enrollment at UK totaled 7,861, 1,872 of whom were freshmen and 76% of those were male. Enrollment in the College of Engineering totaled 1,236 students, 4 of whom were women. My 18-semester hour class load included English Composition (3), Adv. Algebra (3), Trigonometry (3), Engineering Drawing (2), Chemistry for Engineers (4), Air Force ROTC (2) and Physical Ed (1). Without an academic advisor I must have simply used the course of study suggested in the school catalogue for incoming engineering students. In reality there was little if anything new in my Algebra class; my seemingly innate messiness was a serious disadvantage in Engineering Drawing (my only D ever); and never having darkened the doors of a chemistry lab proved to be a serious liability in that class. In spite of those minor challenges I found my first semester of classes at the university enjoyable. Until that fateful November Sunday morning at Nicholasville Baptist Church, the thought of being something other than an engineer never consciously crossed my mind.

Having acknowledged my "call" to Christian ministry as a preacher and a pastor, which in my mind at that time were one and the same, I was now compelled to reexamine or thoughtfully examine for the first time the purpose and direction of my college education. What kind of college education did I need to be a preacher/minister? If I were to be a Baptist preacher would I not need to go to a Baptist college? Had not all of our Youth Revival teams, and our part-time church staff members been students at Georgetown College, the oldest and largest Baptist College in the state? Since Georgetown was only some15 miles north of Lexington that seemed like the only logical choice.

Changing colleges, however, presented a couple of problems, time and money. I had heard that tuition at Georgetown, a private college, was over $1,000 per semester and that did not include room and board. Climbing that mountain would take some time and at least a minor miracle. Beyond that, with the end of my first semester only weeks away, changing schools in the middle of a school year seemed out of the question. Thus, changing from

College of Engineering to the College of Arts and Sciences at UK, seemingly my only reasonable option at the moment, became my first step down the path of preparing for the ministry. English Comp, ROTC and Phys. Ed. remained on my schedule but everything else changed. The new 3-hour courses (most of them required) included World History, Psychology, Sociology, and an elective Speech course, which I thought would help me prepare for the ministry. In retrospect, each of these "new" courses proved helpful in providing a valuable foundation for understanding people, including myself, along with the world in which I was to live and minister.

Even changing colleges at UK in the middle of a year was at least a minor challenge. First, I had to find a faculty advisor who would sign off on the courses I had chosen and then I had to find classes that were still open. Registration in those days was a "Zoo" to put it mildly. Located throughout Memorial Coliseum, UK's basketball arena at the time, were tables with a limited number of registration cards for every class taught at the University that semester. The freshmen were the last to register and the freshmen changing colleges along with incoming freshmen were the last of the last to register. If by the time you found the table with the class you wanted to take and if a card was left you got the class. If that class was full, you hoped there was another section of the same course usually taught at a different time that had one card left. Of course, this meant you had to rework your schedule.

One of my memories of that day was seeing a young lady sitting in the bleachers crying. Having finished my registration, I went over to see if I could help. She had been there all afternoon and had succeeded in getting only two classes she wanted. I found a way to help her get one more class. What she did beyond that I don't know. At the end of the day I wound up taking two classes that met on Tuesdays and Thursdays which meant I had to find a way to Lexington and back five days a week. The first semester all my classes had been on Monday, Wednesday and Friday, which was ideal. It took long days but certainly helped with travel.

I liked my first semester English professor and was able to get him for the second semester, but this time for a Tuesday/Thursday class. As the second semester rolled around he had learned my plan to "be a preacher" was the motivation for changing class sections. He found that most interesting and reminded me often of the importance of a minister using correct English. He marked my errors, usually spelling and punctuation, with large red circles and would occasionally add "good thoughts but way too many errors." It may have been his way of trying to be helpful, but I didn't think so at the time. On one occasion when the class was discussing Hemmingway's <u>For Whom the Bell Tolls,</u> he called on me to give a minister's perspective of the morals of Hemmingway's leading character. Though such challenges were at times unpleasant and embarrassing, especially when I could not give good coherent answers, they forced me to think about some of the implications of my faith and recognize my decision could have negative consequences in the eyes of some.

The other professor I remember from that semester was my ROTC captain. When he discovered I was planning to enter the ministry he asked me to stop by his office. When I did he congratulated me and encouraged me to continue down that path. He said, "The Air Force always needs good chaplains. When you finish your ministerial training let me know and I'll do what I can to help you negotiated the ropes of enlistment and get a good assignment." I told him I liked what I had seen of the Air Force that year and we'd see. If anyone else at UK encouraged me in my new direction that semester it didn't stick in my memory bank.

Thankfully, there were other sources of encouragement for which I shall forever be grateful. Members of the Nicholasville Baptist Church were a source of immense encouragement. With the departure of Brother Pete Evans as pastor, the church called as its interim pastor Dr. William Tedford, a young and relatively new professor at Georgetown College. His term of service for the Nicholasville church though brief was a monumental blessing for me. His encouragement and helpfulness, upon learning of my decision to enter the ministry, proved to be a crucial link in my transition from UK to Georgetown.

Even while concluding my second semester at UK I began, with Dr. Tedford's help, looking for a way to overcome the seemingly impossible financial barrier of enrolling at Georgetown College. In retrospect, the "Hand of God" was all over that process from the beginning.

First, there was the matter of almost $900 in additional annual tuition, $450 per semester. Then there would be additional expense for room and board. I had commuted the 12 miles to UK mostly by hitch hiking and occasionally driving the family car. Georgetown was almost 20 miles north of the UK campus, making a daily commute to school of some 30 miles from my home on Keene Pike through Lexington traffic highly improbable if not downright impossible. So, I would need $400 to live on campus, bringing my total needs to an additional $850 per semester.

"Don't major in religion," Dr. Tedford advised, "You'll get that in the seminary. Use your college work to learn what you may need but won't get in the seminary." That proved to be excellent advice. To begin with Georgetown had an outstanding Speech and Drama department and offered a scholarship of $150 per semester to Speech and Drama majors who had received a superior rating in state speech contests for high school students. Then I discovered a ministerial student could get a $100 scholarship per semester. Wow, with $250 in scholarships, half of my tuition for the first semester, I was well on my way. In July along came another surprise. Mrs. Hare's Sunday School Class (a class of the oldest ladies in the Nicholasville church) notified me they were sending $500 to Georgetown to assist with my college expenses for the coming year. How incredible, tuition for the fall semester was now in hand along with most of the dorm fee. I would later learn that the class member who suggested the sponsorship and may have given most of the money for it was Mrs. Sally Taylor, owner of the farm where my father was the tenant and the house where we lived.

A summer job of measuring tobacco for the US Government's Agricultural Stabilization Cooperative (ASC program) also came through. In order to keep the price of tobacco at an adequate level, farmers had voted to participate in a program limiting the amount of tobacco they would plant. Each farm, even very small ones, had an assigned allotment that varied each year depending on the "supply and demand" from previous years. My job was to measure the amount of tobacco the farmer had planted and plot those measurements on a 3' x 3' aerial photograph furnished by the ASC office. Back in the office a telemeter would trace the outline of the planted area, accurately measure the various angles and determine the acreage planted. If they had planted more than their allotment we would return to the farm, measure off the excess acreage planted and witness the destruction of that part of the crop. (Most farmers intentionally over planted so they could destroy the worst of their crop, often less than one tenth of an acre).

Compensation for the job was based on the amount of work done. The one drawback at the beginning of the job was the lack of a vehicle for traveling to the various farms. After a week or so of using the family car my father paid $95 for an old beat-up 1946 4-door Plymouth for my use. The driver's side floorboard had a rusted-out hole about the size of a man's fist, which we covered with an out-of-date license plate. The good news was the old car served me well for over a year. At the end of that time my father sold it to a neighbor for $100. Until this day to my knowledge it is still the only car anyone in our family ever sold for a profit.

It soon became obvious the only way to measure more than 2 or 3 farms a day and make a decent amount of money was to make appointments with the farmers in advance and plan a few days ahead where possible. Once the tobacco had been measured and farmers notified of the results, the destruction phase began. By starting early and working late I easily became the top producer in the office that summer. By saving nearly all of my earnings I was able to take care of the remainder of my room and books for the fall semester as well as have a little money left over for food and a few extra expenses.

Of course, this was only enough for one semester. In mid-January a second semester began and after doing all my calculations I was about $500 short. I had heard that if you were having financial difficulty the school's financial officer would sometimes help. So, I went to that office hoping a loan or something else could be arranged. When the clerk looked up my account she said, "Your account is up-to-date, and you even have a small surplus. It looks like a few days ago you had a $500 deposit from the Hare Sunday School Class. Somebody's looking out for you." How true! It seemed as though there was an unseen plan in place that was unfolding week-by-week as I moved toward the goal of preparing for a life of Christian ministry.

Campus life at Georgetown for me was at best limited. While on campus, five days and four night a week, my focus was on STUDY, STUDY, STUDY! (Except for the day that began with a "W"). I lived in "Chambers House," a large two-story older frame house a couple of blocks from the main campus. The college bought the house to supplement on campus male student housing. A wonderfully kind and gracious housemother lived in a ground floor apartment. A large living room on that level served as an all-purpose "meeting room". Thirteen young men, mostly freshmen, lived in 6 upstairs bedrooms, 3 on each side of a small hall. The bedrooms were served by 2 baths, one on each side, equipped with 2 commodes and 2 shower stalls. Hot water was often a scarcity, but that seldom proved to be an issue for this early rising country boy.

I slept in Ole Chambers House Monday through Thursday nights for the 9 months of my sophomore year. On Monday I left our family home near Nicholasville a little before 7:00 in my "usually trusty" 1946 4-door Plymouth in time to arrive for my 8 o'clock class. I brought with me each week a supply of milk and eggs from the farm which when coupled with bacon and Post Toasties purchased at the local A&P grocery, plus a forbidden hotplate, made for a good breakfast 4 mornings a week. Except for early fall and late spring, a ledge outside my window provided sufficient refrigeration for the milk and bacon. My typical Monday afternoon trip to the A&P allowed me to purchase in addition to bacon and cornflakes peanut butter, crackers and occasionally a few slices of bologna for my daily lunch usually eaten in my room. On most days my evening meal consisted of a hot freshly fried hamburger from the Student Center Grill.

Ah, but that day beginning with a "W" was different. On Wednesday when my last class was over my trusty little Plymouth headed south out of Georgetown through Lexington and east to Richmond, a journey of 40 miles. There I spent a delightful evening with the love of my life who was completing her senior year at Eastern Kentucky University. The evening always included dinner at a wonderful restaurant near the campus that catered to college students. Barbara's meal ticket sure came in handy. Often, we would go to a vesper service provided by the campus Baptist Student Union and occasionally to a drive-in movie at near-by Berea. We'd sit and talk until 9:30, her dorm curfew, then I'd make my way back to G-town. On Fridays following my 2 o'clock class I headed back to Nicholasville.

I don't think Barbara's dad knew at the time he was providing my one good weekday meal. A few years later I did get up the nerve to thank him. Since we spent the weekends in Nicholasville "courting" (hanging out) either at a church activity or on Saturday nights at her house watching TV (my family didn't have one), what little time I was at Georgetown I had to study.

As hard as it is to believe now, I got by most weeks on $5. Three dollars went for food, $1.50 spent at the A&P and $1.50 for hamburgers at the campus grill Monday, Tuesday, and Thursday nights. The remaining $2 was spent on gas for the car that at the time cost between 20 to 25 cents a gallon. Though the 4 tires on the Plymouth were bald as a bowling ball there was no money to replace them. I became adept at changing flat tires. One Wednesday afternoon I had a flat on the way to Richmond. A lot of our dating time that night was spent finding a service station that would patch my now flat spare tire. A good thing too, for on the way back to Georgetown that night I had another flat tire, which I changed by feel and the light of passing cars.

Barbara and I got engaged officially about halfway through my sophomore and her senior school years. We were married in August after she had earned her degree and I had completed my first year at Georgetown. Our first home was in Lexington, a three-room upstairs apartment in the home of Gladys and Charley and their 6-year-old son, Russell. The house was near Picadome Elementary School in Lexington where Barbara got her first job teaching 6th grade. I commuted to Georgetown the next school year. (See chapter "A Helpmate for Sure.")

When I began my class work at Georgetown a major in Speech and Drama with an emphasis in Speech was a no-brainer. It would include classes in phonics, radio, public speaking, drama, directing, and a personally guided study of Great American Speeches supervised by the Department Head. English, my weakest academic subject at this point, was chosen for a minor field of study. I took my UK English professor's critique to heart and sought to shore up this glaring deficiency. Not only did my composition and grammar improve but since most of college English consists of literature courses my mind was also opened to the great authors of English and American Literature. The writings of the great minds of our culture would prove to be fertile seedbeds for countless sermonic ideas and illustrations in years to come. Tragically, I never became a good speller, a weakness the Lord compensated for through a very good spelling wife and gifted ministry assistants.

The decision to use my academic electives for education courses that would satisfy the requirements for a teacher's certificate in secondary education again proved to be a fortuitous one. At some point the idea had taken root in my mind that the Lord might call me to be a church planter in a pioneer mission area in which case I would need to support my family with employment outside the church. Also, given the impact teachers had on my life I considered teaching to be a high and holy calling. Though I would never serve as a church planter the discipline of lesson planning and the experience of student teaching would carry over into my work as a minister.

I did get that secondary teacher's certificate and taught courses in Speech, English and Remedial Reading at Shelby County High School during the 1960-61 school year, the year our Beth was born. I would also do some substitute teaching in the local schools during my first pastorate out of the seminary at New Salem Baptist Church in Lowndes County Mississippi. So once again the unseen hand of the Lord was at work but as is often the case it was best seen and understood in retrospect.

The desire to get as much education as possible so as to get on with the "main job," pastoring a church "full-time," provided the impetus to take at least 18 hours of course work every semester. This course load coupled with one summer of Student Teaching and one correspondence course enable me to complete the work for my BA degree in January of 1959 3 ½ years after beginning in the fall of '55. While graduation activities would not come until the following May beginning my seminary education couldn't wait. Thus, I matriculated (a fancy name for enrolled) as a student at The Southern Baptist Theological Seminary in Louisville, Kentucky and began classes two weeks before I took my last test in Philosophy at Georgetown. Technically, a degree from an accredited College or University was a prerequisite for matriculating in the Bachelor of Divinity program but I convinced the registrar I was going to complete my BA degree work in two weeks, so he said, "If you are that anxious, have at it!" It was a hectic two weeks but well worth the inconvenience for now I could focus full time on studying the Bible and preparing for the ministry I loved and felt called to fulfill.

At that time Southern Baptists had 5 other seminaries; Southeastern at Wake Forest, New Orleans, Southwestern at Fort Worth, Golden Gate near San Francisco and newly opened Midwestern at Kansas City. Southern at Louisville was the only one I ever considered attending. It was the seminary all of my previous pastors had attended. It was also the oldest and most prestigious, though I don't think I even knew that at the time. Practically, it was the only Seminary I could attend and continue my pastorate at Pleasant Home, and it was also the only Seminary I could attend while completing my work at Georgetown.

In the summer of 1958 Barbara and I moved from Lexington to Shelbyville, almost exactly halfway between Louisville and Georgetown so I could attend college in the fall of '58 and seminary in the spring of '59 while she taught in the same school the entire school year. She got a 3rd grade teaching position at Southside Elementary School in the Shelbyville City School System. Shelbyville proved to be such an ideal location that we lived in Shelby County for the next four years until I completed my Seminary training. Barbara taught 3rd grade at Southside for 3 of those 4 years.

Once again, we moved into another upstairs apartment of a large 2-story red brick on Main Street owned by Mr. & Mrs. Fielding Ballard who lived downstairs. Mr. Ballard, sick when we moved in, died a couple of months later. Early on we got to meet the entire Ballard family of at least 5 children, all of whom had attained positions of unusual prominence. One son was the local hospital administrator; another son had taken over his father's insurance business; a son-in-law was president of the local bank; a second son-in-law owned a jewelry story and an upscale antique gallery; and a third son-in-law was head of the chemistry department at the University of Virginia.

We could not have asked for a better landlord than Mrs. Ballard. She was the ideal gracious southern lady. Her lot extended the full width of the block giving her a large back yard with a well-kept flower garden she tended. She preferred spending time in her backyard to regular housework so she had a full-time maid who cooked and cleaned. On one occasion we received an invitation to join her for lunch served sharp at 12:30 p.m. It was a full four-course meal served on fine china with sterling silverware. The maid was summoned by Mrs. Ballard with the ringing of a small silver bell to serve each course at the appropriate time. We later concluded what was most unusual for us was probably an everyday occurrence for Mrs. Ballard.

My first year at Southern was exciting and rewarding. Again, I was grateful for the council of Dr. Tedford. Seminary courses were not only "in depth," but outstanding professors made the scriptures come alive. More than once in my introductory New Testament class I became so enthralled with the lecture that I would suddenly realize several minutes had elapsed since the last note was taken. Though the required reading in some classes was a load it was quite interesting to read highly competent scholars' differing opinions on various biblical passages.

The seminary's educational goal was to provide effective ministers for congregations by giving students the tools to interpret scripture rather than indoctrinate them in a "correct" theology. On one occasion between classes two of the most respected professors, Dale Moody and Wayne Ward, got into a lively discussion about a theological issue on which they disagreed. Before it had ended eavesdropping students, who had skipped their regular classes to hear the impromptu debate, filled the small post office and adjoining hallways. I was disappointed to discover that not all Southern Baptist Seminaries were as tolerant of differing theological views or supportive of this approach to theological education. Once again, I was blessed by God's grace with a dimension in my education I did not knowingly seek.

The range of courses was broad. While basic courses in Greek and Hebrew did not make us thoroughly competent in the biblical languages, they provided valuable help for understanding scholarly discussion of complex textural issues. The study of individual books of the Bible was complemented by courses in archeology and church history. Practical courses in church administration, homiletics (preaching) and pastoral care were added to courses in biblical and historical theology. While seminary training did not give me all the answers to the questions I would face as a pastor it gave me a foundation on which to build a lifetime of further study and ministry.

I first met "Pappy" Saunders on a hot afternoon in the summer of 1959. "How hot was it?" you ask. Well, it was so hot in our upstairs apartment in Mrs. Ballard's red brick house that Barbara came home one afternoon to find the candle on the fireplace mantle had wilted and fallen over still in its holder. That afternoon I walked down the stairs to our side-doorway entrance wondering who in the world could be ringing our doorbell. The short older gentleman standing on the landing outside the door introduced himself has H. G. Saunders, chairman of the pastor search committee of Buffalo Lick Baptist Church. "I understand you are a student at the Baptist Seminary in Louisville," he began. "If you are interested I would like to talk with you a few minutes about our church?"

It seems their former pastor, George Horton upon his graduation from the seminary in May had resigned their church to become a full-time pastor of a church in Tennessee. My name had come to the committee from a Buffalo Lick church member who had been impressed by a prayer I offered at the midweek prayer service at First Baptist Church, Shelbyville. Barbara and I began attending that church's Wednesday night service when we moved to Shelbyville partly because that was Mrs. Ballard's church and partly because the pastor, Rev. Raymond Lawrence, had a daughter in Barbara's 5th grade class at Southside Elementary School. Brother Lawrence, wishing to encourage a young seminary student-pastor, would occasionally call on me to lead in prayer.

Before inviting me to preach a "trial" sermon, they "checked me out" through Seminary Professor Dr. J. J. Owens who often served as their interim preacher between seminary student pastors. At Mr. Saunders' suggestion, I stopped by Dr. Owens office to get his assessment of the church and, I discovered later, "to be interviewed" by him. The church was double the size, had double the salary, and was 50 miles closer than Pleasant Home so it didn't take a lot of praying to discern this "opportunity of service" had come from the Lord and so it proved to be.

Buffalo Lick Baptist Church was located near Bagdad in Shelby County. The church had a long history of being served by seminary students. Former pastors had gone on to become seminary professors and one a seminary president. Altus Newell, one of my successors, would eventually pastor Birmingham's Dawson Memorial Baptist Church for a short time. However, I think I was the only pastor to live on the "church field" rather than commute from Louisville. Though the church was located 7 miles east of town several faithful members lived in Shelbyville. Living on the church field meant having the privilege of attending all the church meetings, being able to visit the homes of church members for social events as well as in times of crisis. I was available 24/7 for hospital visits, funerals, ball games and sharing in the life of the community.

One day a few weeks after beginning my tenure at the church, I got a phone call from a Mr. Lawson asking if at my convenience I would mind stopping by his men's clothing store on Main Street. When I arrived and introduced myself he explained the reason for his request. His mother's eye had caught the brief article in the local newspaper announcing the arrival of a new pastor at Buffalo Lick Baptist Church. She recognized the name McGohon, and she wanted to meet the young man who owned it.

Leaving the store in the hands of a clerk, he took me to his home, a fine two-story brick house. We climbed the stairs to a bedroom on the second floor where I met his bedridden mother. After several minutes of polite conversation, she told me the reason for her request to meet me. She had a document entitled "Past Recollections" she wanted to give me. It was written in 1889 by Elizabeth McGuire relating her memory of events described by her grandfather, Mark McGohon Jr. It told of his early life, his coming to America from Scotland, of being a revolutionary soldier and being an early settler at Fort Harrod, Kentucky's first permanent settlement.

I knew, at the time, that Mark McGohon Jr. was my great-great-great-grandfather and there was a McGohon cabin in the restored Fort Harrod at Harrodsburg, KY. He died in 1848 at the age of 98 and his remains are now buried in the 'Pioneer Cemetery' at the fort. Reading this first-hand account helped "bring him to life" for me and greatly enhanced my appreciation for my heritage.

A photocopy of that document can be found at the end of this memoir. I do not remember how Mrs. Lawson said she got the document she gave me. I understand that Elizabeth Moreland Wishard, a great-granddaughter of Mark Jr., wrote a biography of her father, Dr. William Henry Wishard which contains a chapter entitled "A Revolutionary Romance" about incidents in Mark Jr.'s life "as recorded in the account or her Aunt Elizabeth McGuire."[1]

Three or four months after accepting Buffalo Lick's pastorate we moved from Mrs. Ballard's upstairs apartment into a nice but small 4-room house in Shelbyville owned by one of the church members. I was now through college and near the midway point of seminary. I had a fine supportive congregation to serve, and Barbara was enjoying her second year of teaching. Shelbyville finally seemed like home. It seemed like the right time to start our family. A study of the seminary catalogue revealed a path to pause my seminary education for the coming two semesters. Upon returning I could complete a full semester's work in 2 summers by taking an extra course during a regular term. I would still finish in the summer of 1962, 3½ years after I began seminary and 7 years after beginning college.

Shelby County was consolidating 3 small community schools into one County-wide High School in a new location just east of Shelbyville. They needed teachers, even inexperienced ones who might leave after only a year, so I was hired. With a major in Speech and a minor in English I was hired to teach freshman English, remedial reading, coach the speech and debate teams for students interested in those activities and anything else the principal might assign. English went reasonably well. Half the students in Remedial Reading by then had given up on school and learning. It was the first-time speech, drama and debate activities had been offered in a county school, so I had to recruit my students, but that period was a real blast.

By summer we moved again, this time to a small house in the country about 2 miles from Buffalo Lick church. It was a cozy 4-room house with a small bath that had only a shower. When we put down the little 3-piece bath set consisting of a seat cover, rug and the horseshoe shaped commode mat, the bath had wall-to-wall carpet. The house was located about a quarter of a mile from the paved highway on a gravel road that led to the house of our landlord, Mr. Blades.

We were living in the Blades' house in the country when our first daughter Beth came into the world. We had gone home for dinner after the Morning Service that Sunday. Early in the afternoon Barbara began having contractions and by 4:30 we were on our way to the hospital in Shelbyville. Upon arriving at the hospital Barbara was quickly swallowed up into the hospital's interior and I was left alone in a general waiting area. I had no idea what to expect but I had heard tons of stories about long hours of labor and delivery. Consequently, when someone in a nurses' uniform appeared at the waiting room window about 6:00 p.m. I approached her with what I thought was a reasonable question.

"I'm the pastor of a church," I began, "about 7 miles from here and I was wondering if I might have time to go preach at the 7:00 o'clock evening worship service?"

Her response was quick and sharp with the unmistakable tone of a charge nurse, "You don't need to go anywhere except back over to that chair and sit down. That baby is going to be here before long and you need to wait, right here."

The truth is Barbara was doing something that night far more important than any sermon, or group of sermons for that matter, I would ever preach. My prayers and presence in that hospital waiting room were the only contribution needed from me that night. The idea of a prospective father in a delivery room was a generation or 2 in the future. Actually, I would not even be allowed to touch Beth until I held her while Barbara got into the car to go home from the hospital a week later. My role that night of faithful waiting husband and soon-to-be father was paramount.

The first time I saw Beth in the hospital nursery she looked so perfect. Her almost olive complexion was free of wrinkles and incredibly smooth for a newborn. Looking at her there along with 4 or 5 other babies I felt a tinge of remorse for the other parents who must surely be comparing their babies to Beth. Caring for her when we got home was fun. I soon had the drill down. Get up for her 2 o'clock feeding, go to the kitchen and get the bottle out of the frig, put it in a pan of water on the stove to get the chill off, go back to the baby bed and change her diaper, back to the kitchen to test the temperature of the milk by shaking a few drops on my wrist, now finally to the rocking chair where with baby nestled in the cook of my arm she took her bottle until she fell asleep. Occasionally both of us went to sleep and Barbara had to get up and put both of her "babies" back to bed.

The next 8 months of pastoring, teaching and being the father of the prettiest baby alive passed quickly. Barbara had lots of company at church as 3 other young mothers gave birth within a few weeks' time. I was asked on several occasions if crying babies during my sermon bothered me? My typical and accurate response was, "Only if she's mine."

A couple of moments from my Shelby County teaching experience were particularly memorable. One Saturday I took a team of students to the adjoining Henry County for a speech and drama festival.[2] A snowstorm put an early end to the contests, about 10 a.m., and we barely got back to Shelbyville by nightfall. Church members Boyd and Juanita Green who lived in Shelbyville put me up for the night along with several of the students who couldn't get home. A trip on foot to Shoney's restaurant, plus stories and games in front of a blazing fire, will be long remembered by several high school students as well as their young teacher. Fortunately, Barbara and Beth had gone to Nicholasville for the day that Saturday and were safe and sound with her parents. There were no church services anywhere in that area the next day.

The second moment came on the morning of May 5, 1961. I listened anxiously with my class to the radio as Alan Shepherd became the first American astronaut to rocket into space. His suborbital flight would stay in space for a mere seven minutes before falling back into the ocean, but it would be the first step to overtaking Russia in the race to space.

In the spring of '61 we moved from the country to a larger and more adequate house on the outskirts of Shelbyville so Barbara could be closer to the school where she would teach the following school year. The house was at the end of a dead-end street of modest but well-kept owner-occupied homes. Mrs. Belk, a senior adult widow lived three houses up the street and kept Beth in her home while Barbara taught school that year. Her granddaughter Martha Lane, whose father owned one of the two funeral homes in town, would soon marry Bill Collins, a G-town classmate and younger brother to Mary Margaret, the wife of my first cousin Donnie McGohon. Martha Lane would eventually become Kentucky's first female governor.

During my last year of college and for my entire seminary experience I had the privilege of serving as pastor of a church. This provided not only some necessary income but also an opportunity to apply, test and evaluate theological concepts being taught. Without practical application theological study can become a purely esoteric exercise or just so much gobble-de-gook. On the other hand, simply learning the how-to-do-it of ministry without an adequate theological foundation can lead to either stale rote practice of once meaningful traditions on one extreme or thoughtlessly adopting the latest apparently successful fad at the other.

Being a student-pastor also made it possible to "double-dip," using lecture and study time as preparation for preaching especially since most of my preaching was from notes rather than manuscripts. It also gave a practical focus to pastoral care and counseling classes. Beyond that, the opportunity to have Seminary professors lead weekend Bible Studies or speak at special events in my church proved priceless. Those weekends provided an opportunity for valuable interaction with favorite professors outside the classroom. Their on-site critiques of my ministry were quite helpful and usually affirming.

On one occasion, Dr. W. W. Adams, a brilliant New Testament professor nearing retirement age, came to Buffalo Lick to lead a weekend Bible Conference. Maintaining a beautiful rose garden at his Louisville home for the pleasure of his nearly invalid wife was his primary hobby. During his weekend visit he asked if one of the dairymen in the church could provide him with some manure for his roses. Of course, the farmer was more than willing to grant his wish. On Sunday afternoon he filled the trunk of his car with 3 burlap sacks of fresh manure to take back to Louisville for his roses. A couple of days later he told our class he had spent the weekend at Buffalo Lick. "When I left, Ole McGohon gave me a trunk full of manure, said he was paying me in kind!" he bellowed gleefully.

Even the forty-minute (30 miles) commute twice a day usually in a carpool with 2 or 3 other student pastors living in the Shelbyville area had its benefits. While we seldom had the same classes, we shared many similar experiences of both elation and frustration. Earl Wilson was a natural born humorist. He had been a successful young entrepreneur owning and operating a trailer park in Knoxville before responding to God's call to the ministry. He never forgot a funny joke or story and when he got on a roll everything he said was funny. He preached a revival for me in Vernon and after a long pastorate in Knoxville eventually became Executive Director of the Tennessee Baptist Foundation.

Marshall Phillips and his wife Dorsey became good friends who upon graduation from the seminary became career missionaries serving in Tanzania. Then there was Bill Morris who was from Alabama and after seminary returned to pastor churches in the Huntsville area. Bill was 6 foot 6 and weighed 300 pounds if he weighed an ounce. He drove a big Desoto and one snowy morning during rush hour a few miles short of the campus Bill had to stop rather quickly to avoid a collision with the car in front of us. The less fortunate guy behind us slid into our rear end. He jumped out of his car and in red-faced furry came running up to the Desoto. Bill could not jump out of a car; rather he more or less unfolded as he got out. By the time Bill finished unfolding and stood towering over his 5'8", 150 lb. adversary the fellow's demeanor had undergone an amazing transformation. "Uh, uh" he stammered, "it doesn't look like either car has been damaged so I think we can both just go on our way, if that's okay with you." Well, there hadn't been any damage and we needed to get on to class. Thus, God's grace, Bill's forbearance and the other motorist's wisdom won the day and there was no "incident."

Living off campus though was not without its drawbacks. We seldom participated in campus social life and most of my fellow students I only knew from sharing classes with them. I also missed the opportunity to spend extra time in an outstanding seminary library housed in a new 3-story building completed in my first year as a student. At the conclusion of my last class in July of 1962, having fulfilled all my degree requirements I walked from the Library's front steps onto the large grassy quad, threw my briefcase in the air and shouted, "Hallelujah!" After 7 long years the goal of formal institutionalized preparation for ministry had been realized, at least for now, and full-time pastoral ministry could soon begin.

Leaving "My Ole Kentucky Home"

G aining a seminary degree, important as it was, proved to be only one step among many in my education for the ministry. Some of the most meaningful lessons would come from the first two churches I served out of seminary, New Salem in Caledonia, Mississippi and First Baptist in Vernon, Alabama.

Wanting to become a fulltime pastor as soon as possible I contacted "Prof" Johnson, head of the Seminary's placement office, several months prior to completing the requirements for graduation at the end of July. I updated my resume and expressed to him my desire for fulltime pastoral ministry. During the Spring of '62, Ken Day, an employee of the Michigan Baptist Convention, spoke in a chapel service about the need of Michigan churches for seminary trained pastors. I expressed an interest in the possibility of serving a church in Michigan and began praying earnestly for the Lord's direction. In the weeks that followed I exchanged several letters and phone calls with Rev. Day.

Meanwhile, I also had several conversations with a fellow student, Marion Sherrill who was serving a church in his hometown of Flint, Michigan. Each Monday he drove to Louisville, attended classes, slept in a one room apartment during the week and drove back to Flint the following Friday. Near the end of April, Day sent word that he had arranged for me to preach in two churches in the Detroit area on a Sunday in early May. I was to preach in the morning service at one church and in the evening service at the other church. Both churches were seeking a pastor. I was to ride to Michigan and back to Louisville with Marion and the two churches would share responsibility for "entertaining" their pulpit guest on Saturday and Sunday.

I made arrangements for a preacher to supply my pulpit at Buffalo Lick on the appointed Sunday. When the fateful Friday morning arrived, with suitcase packed and in hand, I kissed Barbara "good-bye," and headed for Louisville. Having deposited my bag in Marion's room prior to our first class, I was sitting on his bed talking about the trip that lay before us when his phone rang. Ken Day was calling to express his regrets for an unfortunate mix-up. There had been a misunderstanding about the date and each of the churches where I was to preach had made other arrangements for their pulpits that Sunday. He promised to get back in touch as soon as he could set up another engagement.

I prayerfully awaited a letter or a call about another arrangement for a Sunday perhaps later in May or June or July, but there was no letter or call from Michigan. While waiting for word from Michigan I continued checking with Prof Johnson for other opportunities. As early summer arrived I began contacting school systems in hopes of finding a teaching position and perhaps remaining at Buffalo Lick as its bi-vocational pastor. First, I contacted Shelby County where I had taught a year earlier, then the Shelbyville city system and then the nearby Franklin County system. All told me there were no openings for someone with my credentials. To say I was shocked was an understatement.

In late July Prof Johnson call to report he might have something of interest to me. He had received a request from a pulpit committee in Mississippi looking for a pastor about 40 years of age with a rural background. Well, at least I had a rural background. The church was near Caledonia, a small rural community on the Mississippi/Alabama state line some 15 miles north of Columbus. Having given no thought to serving in that region of the country and with an impression of the deep South based primarily on the racial tension regularly reported on the nightly news my initial response was negative.

"It wouldn't hurt you to go look at it," Prof. Johnson responded, "They will take care of your expenses and give you an honorarium, so you could go on to New Orleans for a mini vacation." It didn't sound like a very spiritual endeavor, but after talking it over, Barbara and I decided to take the church up on their offer and at least "look it over."

Little did we know at the time how life changing that first trip to Mississippi and the Deep South would be. In the spring of '62 we had traded in our old two-tone yellow and black Mercury, an embarrassment for Barbara to be seen in it from the day I bought it, for a nearly new beautiful '61 powder blue Pontiac. So at least we were setting out on our adventure in style. The route, before there was an I-65, took us past the state capital building in downtown Nashville and down the median of a 4-lane highway leading into Columbia, Tenn. lined with crape myrtles in full glorious bloom. It was the first such view for this Kentucky farm boy.

Whether it was our youth, the adrenaline, or both, we arrived in Columbus, Mississippi at the home of our weekend host, Wayne and Elaine West, with little feeling of fatigue and eager to explore New Salem and nearby Caledonia. For the evening meal Wayne, the search committee chairman, and Elaine treated us to an exquisite charcoal-grilled steak dinner. As I watched, Wayne shared his deepest secrets to charcoal grilling a steak.

The congregation I preached to on Sunday numbered close to 100. After lunch with the search committee, we toured the nice brick pastorium adjacent to the church. Without exception, the church members were warmly welcoming and complimentary. Following lunch, Wayne and the committee assured me that though I was younger than they had expected, they were sure the congregation was pleased with what they had seen and heard. The church would take the official vote at the evening worship service to call me as their pastor, a vote they were sure would be positive.

Before midafternoon we were off to New Orleans for the rest of our "vacation" with an understanding I would call Wayne collect that night to get the official word. Wow, what had started out for us as a casual exploration had quickly morphed into one of life's major decision. We stopped at a motel just short of New Orleans for the night. I made a call to Wayne. The church had voted unanimous to call Buddy to be their pastor and looked forward to having him and Barbara living in their pastorium by the first of September. The committee wanted to know our response as soon as practicable, but before next Sunday, if possible.

Monday morning, we crossed the Lake Pontchartrain causeway, marveling at the sites as we made our way into the world-renowned Crescent City. We drove down Canal Street and watched the streetcar turn onto Saint Charles Avenue. Parking the car near Jackson Square we got out and wandered around with no particular destination in mind. We meandered into the French Quarter, looked at menus on two or three restaurant doorways and moved on. With a weighty decision neither of us had anticipated resting squarely on our shoulders, the city famous for its Mardi Gras parades held little attraction or distraction for this young couple from Nicholasville, Kentucky.

Without so much as even sampling the famous New Orleans cuisine, except for a sack of pralines, we were in the car and on our way out of the city by noon. Crossing the Mississippi river, we headed down highway 90 toward Mobile with windows down and the ocean breeze blowing through our hair (air conditioning was a luxury back then). We drove along what were then the sparsely populated beautiful white sand beaches of the Mississippi gulf shore.

Somewhere between Gulfport and Biloxi, about 2 in the afternoon, we stopped at a quaint seaside restaurant for a delicious seafood meal. As we sat at a window table facing the gulf we had the dining area to ourselves except for one or two patrons at a counter and a couple of waitresses. Our entrée was shrimp as I recall, but our sharpest memory is of the end of the meal. As we sat lingering, I took some lemon wedges, squeezed them into a glass of water, added some sugar and made a glass of lemonade. Barbara could not help but see the amused laughter of the waitresses observing the antics of their country-bumpkin customer. Though it happened 60 years ago it remains one of those idyllic moments indelibly engraved on our mind's eye. On more than one occasion in later years we drove down that highway hoping to once again eat in that restaurant, but it had disappeared.

By noon Tuesday we were racing our way northward through Alabama toward Kentucky. We had left our one-year-old Beth in the care of Granny Mae and Papa Poss and though we knew she was well Barbara could hardly wait to get back to her baby. Though "what to do?" had been the consuming focus of our conversation for two days. I now remember only a few of the specific issues we discussed. The people had been very warm and friendly and seemed eager for us to come to Mississippi. The educational level of the congregation seemed above average for a rural or small-town church. There were several teachers, a couple of business owners and farmers, most of whom were landowners.

Sixty years later there is no memory of a discussion at that time of either the emotional difficulty of moving almost 500 miles from the families that had nurtured us all our lives, or the cultural differences between Central Kentucky and Mississippi. Even if we had thought of them at the time I doubt we could have discussed them objectively.

The major concern at that time, apart from "Was it God's will?" was could we make it financially? They had offered a salary of $300 per month plus a house ("pastorium") with utilities. Any health insurance or retirement benefits would be deducted from the salary. There was no local travel allowance, but there was a $300 Convention allowance as an encouragement for the pastor to attend the annual SBC and State conventions. We had been making it on Barbara's $300 monthly salary and using half of my pastoral salary for rent and utilities. In summary, our annual income would be reduced by about $1,300, but Barbara could stay home with the children (by then Amy was well on the way), I could follow "my calling" full time, and surely "God would provide." This was certainly not a door we had sought to open, but one "God seemed to be opening."

Somewhere near Tuscaloosa we stopped to make another phone call to Wayne West. "Yes, Wayne we accept the church's call to become the pastor of New Salem Baptist Church, Caledonia, Mississippi." We were to rent a U-Haul truck and load it on our end. They would unload it when we arrived and pay all the rent and gas expenses. In the 5 years of our marriage we had already moved 5 times and paid all the expenses involved each time, so this sounded like a good deal.

U-Haul loaded and headed south, I left Shelbyville brimming with excitement and anticipation that last week in August of 1962 bound for Caledonia. Barbara, Beth and Carol, my sister, were following in the Pontiac. The thought of never living in Kentucky again never crossed our minds. It was an unexamined and unvoiced assumption that the move to Mississippi was simply the first step in a career that would at some point lead back home to Kentucky. If for some reason the financial or social challenges of our venture were too demanding we could always come back home to Kentucky.

To describe September of '62 as a HOT month in Mississippi would be an understatement in anyone's lexicon. To be sure, the weather was extremely hot, but racial tensions had reached a boiling point as well. James Meredith, a black citizen of Mississippi, who was also an Air Force veteran with 8 years of service, had applied for admission to Ole Miss in May of '61 to complete his college degree. Since all the public schools in Mississippi were segregated, as was true for most of the South, his application was denied. After over a year of multiple court decisions and appeals, the US Supreme Court upheld a 5th US District Court decision that the denial of Meredith's admission to the University was unconstitutional. Mississippi governor Ross Barnett and the state legislature, refusing to follow the court order, blocked the enrollment of the black student. As the standoff escalated, opponents of integration began gathering at the campus to help block the enrollment.

On September 29th, US Attorney General Robert Kennedy ordered 500 US Marshals to Oxford to accompany Meredith as he enrolled. The Mississippi Highway Patrol was withdrawn to avoid a confrontation between the two opposing law enforcement entities. That night a riot broke out, cars and buildings were burned, and two men were killed. President Kennedy federalized the Mississippi National Guard, placing them under US Army control and sent Federal troops to restore order to the campus. On Oct. 1st, with Federal troops in place, classes resumed on campus and Ole Miss had its first black student.

Meanwhile back in Caledonia, exactly 100 miles southeast of Oxford, New Salem's new young pastor was trying desperately to comprehend his role in this new culture in which he found himself. The events in Oxford made the nightly news across the nation, but in Caledonia those events were a daily obsession. As tensions built, wild rumors began to circulate. At our September deacons meeting, my first at the church, the deacon chairman, a retired vocational ag teacher, reported that a retired general from North Carolina was on his way to Oxford to take command of the volunteer resistance. He announced he was leaving Saturday morning in his pickup for Oxford, rifle and ammo in hand. Anyone wishing to go with him was more than welcome. I was thankful he didn't go, but the frustration, anger and animosity he expressed would provide the unsettling undercurrent for my short two-year pastorate. It would also provide the context in which many pastors, young and old, would wrestle with their conscience and the cultural ramifications of their faith. How can a person be God's prophet calling a congregation to righteousness behavior and at the same time be God's loving shepherd ministering to a congregation struggling with all the normal issues of life? That was the inescapable dilemma.

As I began, getting to know the families in the congregation, as well as getting to know the community was priority one. I spent most of the mornings in a small study at the church less than 50 yards from the house preparing and planning the church's program for the coming year. There were 2 messages to prepare for each Sunday and a Wednesday night Bible study. Afternoons I spent visiting. Parishioners in the two Columbus hospitals and those who were homebound took priority. That was followed by driving through the community, often on dusty unpaved roads, meeting and visiting with the various families of the church in their homes. Often on

Sundays we were invited to member's homes for Sunday dinner. Warm personal relationships developed rather quickly and with all this visiting came the reputation of being a "good caring young pastor." Those relationships made the congregation more tolerant of their young pastor's "radical" views on race relations, but those relationships also served to heighten the stress and turmoil of my own inner struggle.

Since Barbara was 4 months pregnant with Amy when we moved, finding a doctor became another early priority. Someone suggested Dr. Platt would make us a good family doctor. With some hesitancy and much anxiety, especially on Barbara's part, we drove to Columbus for her first visit. Dr. Platt was well past middle age, somewhat dour, and on that day lacking a comforting bedside manner. When Barbara asked Mrs. Platt, who was also his nurse, if we could pay a portion of our bill each visit as we had done in Kentucky, the seemingly curt answer was, "You'll have to ask Dr. Platt."

Only then did we learn Dr. Platt treated Baptist pastors and their families without charge. Barbara got the impression Mrs. Platt thought we surely knew this and had come to them for the free treatment. Of course, we had not, but that suspicion seemed to cast a shadow over the doctor/patient relationship. Barbara's prenatal care was adequate even if at times it seemed more like an necessary trial to be endured. Shortly after nightfall on Monday, January 28, 1963, the labor contractions became regular enough and strong enough to call Dr. Platt. "Come on in and I'll meet you at the hospital," were his words.

The trip to Columbus that night went quickly for me, partly because I was able to pick up WHAS's broadcast of the UK-Georgia Tech basketball game. Though the doctor had been alerted to Barbara's rather quick delivery of our first child, when we got to the hospital there was no Dr. Platt. About an hour after we arrived I saw him come sauntering down the hall and entering the door to Barbara's room. In less than two minutes he came out of that same door in a trot saying, "We're ready to go." A few minutes later Barbara gave birth to our second beautiful daughter, Amy Marie.

Our two years at New Salem became the occasion for another life-changing event for the McGohon family. As good fortune would have it, sister Carol, while waiting for her fall classes at UK to begin, happily assisted her big brother's family with the tasks of moving and getting settled in far off Caledonia. That Sunday at church the pastor's pretty college-age sister garnered more attention that the new pastor, at least from her young peers. A would-be matchmaker suggested to a young engineering student at Mississippi State and the son of a leading family in the church, he should ask the young visitor for a date. "I can't." he replied, "She's got a ring on her finger," meaning she is either engaged or has a steady. Somehow that comment reached the ear of Sis and the next time he saw her the rings were gone. Two years later at the Nicholasville Baptist Church I was officiating at the couple's wedding.

The church's addition of a convention allowance as a church sponsored benefit not only encouraged my participation in the denominational life of the Southern Baptists, but it also marked the beginning of our family's exploration of our United States. We went to Atlantic City, New Jersey for the SBC in June of '63 and to Detroit in '64. Travel was usually on a bare bones budget. In Atlantic City, we went one evening to the Knife and Fork, a restaurant that had valet parking and an entrée menu beginning at $7.00. Before the waitress could take our order, we picked up Amy, apologized for our restless child, and made a hasty exit. No way could we spend our food allowance for 3 days on one meal. By the time I retired, we had visited 49 of the 50 states. I think we missed North Dakota.

Our stay in Caledonia also brought us the Christmas of '63, perhaps the most exciting and memorable of our life. When our first Christmas in Caledonia rolled around, we thought it unwise for our 8th month pregnant Barbara to make the 500-mile trip back to Nicholasville, so we spent our first Christmas ever away from our beloved Ole Kentucky home. Thankfully, Barbara's family came to Mississippi, and we enjoyed Christmas with them even if we were not in Kentucky.

By the time Christmas of '63 got here we were determined not to spend another Christmas away from "home." That year Christmas day came on Wednesday which meant we could travel on Monday, spend the entire week in Kentucky and return to Mississippi on Friday or Saturday in plenty of time for church services on Sunday. When we got home from church on Sunday night, we had nearly everything packed and ready to leave bright and early Monday morning. A cold steady rain was falling outside as we sat down in our warm den to watch the evening news. The excited weatherman topped the news that evening with a forecast of "Snow for Mississippi." A cold front was moving in from the west, and in fact, snow was already falling in Memphis.

What to do? Even if it didn't snow in Mississippi it would surely come to Tennessee and Kentucky, making travel for the next couple of days difficult, if not impossible. If we left now, we reasoned, maybe we could beat the cold front and the snow to Kentucky. In less than 30 minutes, suitcases and boxes of presents in the trunk, and the Pontiac with an 11-month-old baby, her 3-year-old sister and her wide-eyed parents was headed north. Just north of Sulligent, Alabama the rain began to be mixed with snowflakes. The snow covered the ground and was sticking to the road in Hamilton. A car was having a difficult time on a hill near Russellville, but we were able to pull to the left in some fresh snow and keep on moving. The snow was 3 inches deep in Florence. In Columbia. Tennessee slowly turning a corner we exchanged stares and grins with the passengers of a car headed south, each probably wondering, "What are those idiots doing out on a night like this?"

The Christmas lights of downtown Nashville covered with 6 inches of snow at 3:00 a.m. were the most beautiful we had ever seen. The big hill north of Nashville, now my most pressing worry, had been cindered by the time we arrived. Eight inches had fallen in Bowling Green as we continued our trek north. We found a little restaurant with 2 or 3 cars in front just before leaving Elizabethtown where we finally stopped for a little nourishment and to stretch our weary legs. We got back into our car for the final leg of our journey in time to hear the radio announcer report that Highway 31, from Bowling Green to Elizabethtown, the highway we had just travelled, had been closed to all traffic.

"They are here!" was the shout from Granny Mae's lips that greeted the weary travelers as they pulled to a stop in front of the Nicholasville house on Brown Street a little before 11:00 a.m. The normal 10-hour trip had taken at least 15 long treacherous hours without even a minor mishap. In retrospect, it was a foolhardy decision to leave Caledonia with 2 small children under such circumstances, yet in spite of our bad decision the Heavenly Father guided and protected us.

For more than another decade every Christmas would be celebrated back "home" in Kentucky. Luggage racks and on a few occasions even a big box would be strapped on top of the car to hold both Santa's and the family's gifts. Not until we were living in Birmingham and the girls were getting bicycles for Christmas was the annual pilgrimage back to our Ole Kentucky home interrupted. Barbara's parents made their first Christmas visit to Birmingham after our move to Clairmont Ave., finally inaugurating a new chapter of observing Christmas as a family in Sweet Home Alabama. Still, we would go back to Kentucky during the Christmas season for 28 more years, as long as Granny Rie, my mother, lived.

Racial tension in the South and especially Mississippi continued to escalate following the assassination of President Kennedy. Three civil rights workers, were murdered in early 1964. A voter registration drive was organized for the coming summer. The summer also saw "freedom riders" moving from city to city attempting to enter or be turned away from Sunday morning services at all-white churches throughout the state.

That year following Easter Sunday, as I had done before, I preached a series of messages from the Book of Acts. When I came to chapter 10, Peter's encounter with a vision from God calling him to set aside his prejudice against gentiles by eating and having fellowship with a gentile, I felt compelled to preach on that text. Though I had preached several messages on God's love for all people and our need to love one another, this passage hit the issue head on. I carefully prepared a manuscript. Copies of the message were mimeographed and made available to the congregation at the close of the service. If I was to be fired, which I thought was very possible, I wanted to be fired for what I actually had said, not what somebody misunderstood me to say.

At the close of the service, I stood at the door as usual greeting the worshipers as they left the building. A few, but not many, picked up a copy of the message. A few thanked me for addressing a difficult subject. Grace M. said, "Brother Buddy, I don't mind worshiping with them, but I don't think I could ask one to eat Sunday dinner at my table. I'll have to pray about that." Though I was uncomfortable and anxious about what the future might hold, most church members seemed relatively unconcerned about their young pastor's thoughts or occasional comments on the subject.

I made increasingly earnest prayers asking the Lord to move me back north, preferably to Kentucky. I didn't come south to cause trouble or tear up a church. And, if the truth be known, I had little hope of changing anybody's attitude or action on the matter. At their July meeting the deacons decided the time had come for a plan of action in case "troublemakers" should come to the church. Ushers were to be stationed at the door each Sunday with instructions to deny entrance to any blacks or "racial agitators" even though they may be white. The rationale offered was the motivation of such visitors. Blacks and agitators would be coming to disrupt true worship, not to participate in it. Ironically, at this point, the church had no elected ushers. One man was charged with enlisting 4 men to collect the offering, at the appropriate time, a task usually performed while the congregation sang the offertory hymn and fell to whoever happened to be wearing a dress coat that Sunday. Ignoring the pleas of their pastor, the motion was passed and would be passed on to the church's monthly business meeting for official action two nights later.

The Wednesday night business meeting proceeded as usual with the pastor serving as moderator. The Deacons' secretary made the deacons' report that concluded with the recommendation to instruct the ushers to deny entrance to blacks and agitators. Now, in that church, the deacons had a tradition of making recommendations but not making either the motion or second to the motion that their recommendation be adopted. Also, though all seven deacons had been at the Monday night meeting, only the secretary and one other deacon made it to the Wednesday night business meeting, which was attended by between 20 and 25 adult church members. No sooner had the deacon secretary sat down than his wife, sitting a couple of pews in front of him, without standing said in a clear strong voice, "I'll tell you what we ought to do, bring them in and sit them on the front pew. They need the Gospel worse than anybody."

After two or three other comments, as moderator I reminded them we needed a motion to adopt the recommendation before we discussed it. After a few moments of additional discussion, the church treasurer stood and made the appropriate motion. There was more discussion. Even though I was aware that such discussion was not in keeping with Roberts Rules of Order, I could find no polite way to interrupt the spontaneous discussion taking place. Finally, I yielded the moderator's gravel to another church member and made another plea to not close the church doors to anyone who may come to worship with us even though their motives may appear questionable to us. "Have not all of us at some time entered these doors with less that pure or noble motives?" was the crux of my plea. Having made my point, I assumed my role as moderator once again and asked for a second to the motion. More discussion.

At this point, a young husband of a devout and very active wife, who was also the father of 5 children, a leader of the church's Sunday night program, a son of the former church patriarch and the younger brother of the deacon secretary, slowly stood and with measured deliberation spoke.

"You all have known me all my life. I was born here, I went to school here, and every day I carry your mail. I don't want to go to school with Ni...s, I don't want to eat with them, and I don't think I want to go to church with them, but I sure would hate for us to do something here tonight that would displease our Lord." Having uttered only those few words he sat down

Following a prolonged silence, I asked, "Do I hear a second to the motion?"

Again, Silence!

"Hearing no second I declare the motion dies for the lack of a second."

"I move we adjourn!" someone said.

"Second the motion" came an immediate response.

The vote to adjourn passed without opposition. And so, the most stressful and maybe most important church business meeting I ever presided over came to an end. By the grace of God, and the courageous act of an honest, truly devout young Christian man trying his best to follow Jesus, an all-white, primarily rural church in racially charged Mississippi during the summer of 1964 refused to close its doors to anyone who wished to join them in the worship of their Lord. The decision was never publicized, and I was never under any illusion that this decision represented the will of the majority of church members, but it did represent the will of a large majority of those attending that business meeting.

Early Friday morning, Murry showed up on our front porch. It seems the treasurer who had made the motion at the business meeting had come to him with a petition that the pastor be fired. "I told him I wasn't going to sign it nor would other church members I had talked to. Go on back home and forget about it."

He apparently did just that, for that was the only comment I remember anyone making to me about that business meeting. However, my anxiety level continued to rise as did my desire to find a pastorate outside the deep south.

Earlier that year I had conducted the funeral of a young boy who had died in an accident. Though the family was not active in our church they were friends of a New Salem family and asked me to be their minister in their hour of tragic need. Attending that funeral was a member of First Baptist Vernon, Alabama, whose pastor had just resigned to become a Southern Baptist foreign missionary. This member suggested to the church's pastor search committee that they consider New Salem's young pastor in their search. On at least 2 different occasions in early summer members from Vernon attended a service unannounced. Jack Hankins, committee chairman, called and asked if I would be willing to meet with the committee at my convenience to discuss the possibility of coming to their church. Mostly out of curiosity on my part, the meeting was scheduled for a Monday night a couple weeks hence at our home. Believe it or not, all 5 members of the search committee arrived for the meeting on the Monday following the business meeting just described. After introductions and a few minutes of casual conversation, the committee broached the matter of the reason for their visit. When the chairman concluded his initial remarks, my response went something like this. "I'm sorry I did not call you sooner, for I fear I have wasted your time. I don't think I'm interested in coming to Vernon and I am quite sure you do not really want me to be your pastor."

I proceeded to tell them exactly what had transpired the previous week at New Salem. I explained my understanding of the biblical and Christian position on the matter of racial equality. My desire as a pastor was to build up churches and not to disrupt them or cause dissention. After I finished there was a period of silence and then several comments by various members. Earl Glenn, a young physician, began speaking and concluded with, "Buddy I would tell you this. We expect our pastor to be ahead of us for only then can he lead us. The only thing we ask is that you not get so far in front of us that we cannot see you." Shortly afterwards the meeting was adjourned with no follow-up response discussed or arranged.

Two to three weeks later as I walked from the church to the house a car pulled up into the parking area in front of the church and out stepped Jack Hankins. We chatted for several minutes before he asked, "Well, have you changed your mind?"

"About what?" I asked.

"Do you think you could live with us? Our committee is convinced you are the man God wants to be our pastor."

After more prayer and soul searching, we could only conclude God must be calling us north; 25 miles north of Caledonia, out of Mississippi and to Vernon, the county seat of Lamar County, Alabama. In the ensuing years, we often revisited that decision wondering if we had been too timid to pray specifically enough, or if God's grace and mercy is also accompanied by a gigantic and intriguing sense of humor, or maybe both.

In our 9 years at Vernon I seemed to be on a roller coaster ride of certainty vs. uncertainty about Vernon being the place where God wanted us to be. When doors of opportunity were opened, or at least cracked, to relocate, the timing or place seemed to be wrong. When those opportunities came everything would be going great in the church and I was feeling fulfilled. When I became dissatisfied and ready to leave there was no place to go.

On one occasion, while on vacation back in Kentucky, I preached at a church in Dayton, Ohio in view of a call to be their pastor. It had appealed to my desire to minister in a "pioneer" mission area where there were a large number of unchurched people. During our weekend there I discovered that nearly all of the families in the church were from the mountains of eastern Kentucky, eastern Tennessee or West Virginia. I began to feel I was in an enclave of Appalachian culture in the middle of Dayton. The wife of the Search Committee chairman prepared a lovely Sunday dinner for her family, the committee and the prospective pastor and wife. At some point during the dinner conversation I asked, "Are there many native Ohioans in the church?"

"Naw!" was the hostess' immediate response, "Not many buckeyes around! I guess our daughter-in-law is the only native buckeye we have, but she doesn't act like 'em!" A pastor with a heart for reaching native buckeyes and a church content to have none would have been a mismatch from the beginning.

Three years into the Vernon ministry I began to feel the need for a mini sabbatical. I mentioned this to Jack, and he offered to float the idea to some other leaders. The result was a month (4 weeks and 3 Sundays) off in June of '67 to spend at Southern Seminary in Louisville auditing classes or doing whatever I wanted. The seminary had an apartment on campus normally reserved for furloughing foreign missionaries empty and offered it to us at no charge. We were free to visit Nicholasville on weekends. Barbara and the girls might even spend an extra day or two there during the week. Occasionally, we would picnic in nearby Cherokee Park. I was free to go to class in the mornings and read in the library in the afternoons or evening.

The 6-day Arab/Israeli war broke out that month. My eschatology class was taught by Dale Moody who had just returned from teaching a year at the Hebrew University in Jerusalem and was a vocal proponent of the Israeli side of the conflict. My Old Testament class in Post Exilic Prophets was taught by J. J. Owens, a Hebrew language scholar who had at one time lived for a year with a group of Arab Bedouins in Jordan and he was equally vocal on the Arab side. It was indeed a wonderful renewing and restoring month.

On the Monday of my last week at the seminary I received a call for a man from Frankfort, Ky. asking to meet with me the following day about the possibility of becoming their church's pastor. He had been given my name by a mutual friend, Brother Craig, my mentor. The next day he arrived with another gentleman, the church's deacon chairman. Their pastor had just left, and they were charged with getting a preacher to fill their pulpit for the coming Sunday. A pastor search committee had not been formed, but they were certain one or both of them would be on it when it was formed. If I would come and supply their pulpit I would have "my foot in the door" when the actual search began. As we discussed the matter I expressed my interest in the fairly new, rapidly growing suburban church. But, I did not feel right about asking Vernon who had so graciously provided me with a mini sabbatical to get a preacher for a 4th Sunday so I could "get in front of" another church.

They said they understood my position, admired my integrity and would get back in touch with me. The search committee was formed. They got my resume and visited Craig at his home in Lexington to discuss in detail my qualifications and the strengths I would bring to their church. Craig later told me they left his house that night with firm plans to send a delegation to Vernon the following Sunday to hear me preach. He was astonished to learn from our phone conversation the next week that they didn't show up.

The day following the meeting at his home, Craig learned later, a lady on the search committee got a letter from a pastor who had preached a revival in their church a few months earlier. In the letter, he told the committee how God had revealed to him he was to be their next pastor. The committee made the recommendation and the church who in turn called the man to be their pastor. A little over a year later they asked him to leave. A troubled church was not where I needed to be at that point in my life. Once again God was taking care of me, and I knew it not.

I preached in Corbin, Ky. once for a committee from a church across the state line in Tennessee, even though it held no interest for me. The biggest open door of all came when a search committee from the church in Lexington where my mentor had served interviewed me at a home in Nicholasville. It was the church to which my sister and her family belonged. As we shared visions and dreams, I also shared a concern about denying my sister's family a real pastor if I should come. By the time the interview ended, the hostess for our meeting, a longtime friend and secretary for the church in Lexington told me the committee was disappointed I did not seem to want to be their pastor. I suppose the one thing lacking for me was any clear sense of God's direction and that deficiency must have been apparent to them as well.

If we had known the day we left for Caledonia we would never again live in Kentucky we probably would not have moved from our Ole Kentucky Home. But we walked the path our Heavenly Father seemingly had for us and found His blessing bountiful and his grace more than sufficient.

Shepherding a Congregation

Vernon (population 1500 in '60 and 1900 in '70 and 90% white) was a small county seat town with two main streets, highway 17 running north-south and highway 18 east-west. The courthouse took up the town square. Most businesses, several owned by church members, were located around or near the courthouse. There were 4 main denominational churches; Church of Christ being the largest, then First Baptist, Freewill Baptists and Methodist in that order. There were 2 smaller independent Pentecostal churches and 1 very small African American Methodist congregation. Many residents attended smaller rural congregations in communities where they had lived before moving to town.

The Ministry in Vernon had a delightful "honeymoon" period. Church members were eager to meet the new pastor and his family. A number of members invited us into their homes for Sunday dinner following the morning worship service. Members with businesses, seldom overrun with customers, invited me to come by and visit with them. One of the businesses, an old-time dry goods store that sold a little bit of everything except groceries, was owned by Mrs. Clerman and managed by her son and only salesclerk, Sonny. As we chatted one day Sonny introduced me to a local customer as his pastor and added, "You need to come to church some Sunday and hear him, he's a dog-gone good preacher." After a few more flattering comments he offered, "He does have one fault though. I've noticed that sometimes he cusses (pause) especially when he gets drunk." I now had a "cut up" friend for all my days in Vernon.

First Baptist Vernon was the fourth church to "call" me to be their pastor. I served Pleasant Home for about 20 months, Buffalo Lick for 3 years and New Salem for 2 years. In reality, I now realize I was never the pastoral leader of any of those first 3 churches. At best, I was their regular preacher and the minister who officiated at some of their weddings and funerals, provided the family involved did not have a stronger attachment to another minister. It wasn't that I didn't want to be a caring "shepherd of the flock," because I really desired to serve them in that way. That privilege, however, is not bestowed by a vote to "call", rather it is earned through years of compassionate ministry.

During the three-weeks that lapsed between the Sunday Vernon voted to call me to become their pastor and the time we were able to move into their pastorium, Mr. Christian died of a heart attack. He was the search committee's oldest member, and I was told, my biggest supporter. I know he was the prime mover in making the church's pastorium ready for his new pastor's family. I was asked to preach at his funeral, and so my ministry began by providing pastoral care for one of the leading families of the church.

Within the year tragedy struck again. Susan, one of the church's most active youth, a beautiful high school senior, who occasionally baby sat our girls, was killed in a car accident on highway 18 between Vernon and Columbus, Miss. Our family grieved, the youth group grieved, indeed, the whole church family grieved with and gave support to Stella, Susan's single mom.

During those early days at Vernon, Jack Hankins, the search committee chairman, made it a point to introduce his new pastor to all the community leaders. He was owner and editor of the county paper, The Lamar Democrat, and a member of the Alabama House of Representatives. When the legislature convened he took me to Montgomery and introduced me to members of the legislature including Albert Brewer, Speaker of the House, and Tom Bevel, majority floor leader. He quickly became a confidante I could trust for sound advice. I quickly recognized the value of running by Jack ideas for improving or changing things in the church for his thoughts on the matter. In that first year, as we discussed an item I wanted to see in the proposed budget for the coming year, he suggested I discuss the matter with another deacon he mentioned by name.

As fortune or fate would have it, the Sunday I preached my "trial sermon" and the church called me to be their pastor, this particular deacon, a man in his mid 50's,' was out of town on his honeymoon, having married the leader of the church's Woman's Missionary Union. The former pastor who had resigned to become an SBC Foreign Missionary to Spain performed their wedding. According to Jack this deacon took pride in being seen as one of the church's more respected leaders. He suggested I make an appointment with him at his office to discuss the matter. He also, suggested this deacon would be pleased if I asked him to present the idea at the next deacons meeting. I did just that. He did just what Jack thought he would, and I had another friend among the deacons, at least for a time. Identifying and enlisting key congregational influencers in formulating and implementing plans, plus making sure they got appropriate credit were important leadership principles I learned gradually and followed consistently over time.

Like New Salem Vernon owned a home for their pastor about half a block down the street from the church. However, it was not as "nice" as New Salem's home, a fact the search committee discovered for themselves the night they came to our New Salem home. Committee members quickly called attention to the inadequacy of their pastorium and to their intention to build a new one. We would be the first family to live in it. It was a promise that took some wrangling, an occasional misunderstanding, a few hurt feelings, and almost 3 years to keep, but keep it they did. In the meantime, they painted their present house and made it as pleasing as possible.

One of the early hurdles for the church was financial. The church had no building fund or room in a tight budget to make payments on a loan. The church needed to increase its budget and income in at least three areas: its dismal support for its meager educational program, its support for missions, especially since the beloved former pastor was now a foreign missionary, and to set aside some resources for a new pastorium. Striving to add all three of these items at once gave almost everyone (except Mrs. B. C.) something they believed in and made them open to supporting their first ever organized stewardship emphasis. Mrs. B. C., who lived in a nice 2-story brick house 3 houses to the right of ours came strolling down the sidewalk one day to express her opposition, "You know Dr. Glean, the biggest giver in the church is moving to Tuscaloosa. If anything, you ought to be cutting the budget instead of raising it." I knew she had a point, but I also knew we didn't have to spend what we didn't raise.

A large number of church members agreed to serve on various committees. Several agreed to give stewardship testimonies, including Mrs. Jennie Butler, one of the least affluent members, but by far the most sacrificial supported of missions I have ever known. She lived in a trailer at the end of our street with her disabled husband and alcoholic army veteran son. The income from a few laying hens she kept in her backyard was carefully saved week by week until the December Foreign Mission offering was collected. A class of widows "Mrs. Jennie" taught usually led the church on the giving chart.

During the stewardship emphasis church members were asked to pledge to tithe or at least increase the amount of their normal gift but they were not asked to estimate the amount of their gift. On Demonstration Sunday when everyone was asked to bring a week's tithe the church's offering was by far the largest one Sunday budget offering it had ever received and the church went on to exceed its largest ever annual budget for the year.

The success of that stewardship emphasis opened the door for moving forward with plans for a new pastorium. Al, *(not actual name)* a deacon and local community leader, gladly agreed to spearhead the project and chair the 5-member Building Committee. A couple of years earlier he had completed the construction of a beautiful new brick house for his family, which he happily made available for touring at the slightest provocation. This experience, the committee would soon learn, made him "the leading expert" on planning, constructing and furnishing a house for the church's pastor, even though an electrical contractor and the county home demonstration agent were also on the committee.

As the planning got underway in early summer Al decided the church's present house needed to be "put up for sale," convinced it would take months if not years to sell in Vernon's slow real estate market. By the middle of summer, they had an offer nearly matching their asking price. The chairman along with the chairman of trustees handled the negotiations which included giving possession to the new owner the first of September without any plan for housing the pastor and his family while the new pastorium was under construction. To complicate matters further Barbara was 7 months pregnant with our third child, Alisa. Needless-to-say, the chairman, rather than being praised for a shrewd business deal, was roundly criticized for his lack of attention to the needs of the pastor's family.

While disconnecting the window air conditioner Barbara's father brought us the first summer we lived at New Salem, the chairman said, "Oh no, you can't do that, the air conditioner goes with the house.

"This air conditioner doesn't belong to the church, it belongs to us," I said.

"Well, nobody knew that. It was fastened to the house, so it goes with the house. Anyway, you are going to have central air in the new house, so you won't need it." Barbara couldn't believe such a cavalier attitude about something that had symbolic significance to her.

Fortunately, a few months earlier the church had bought a vacant house adjoining its property to the south for future expansion. The Sunday School was growing and a couple of rooms in the house even now were being used for Youth Sunday School classes. It was decided that with a few needed plumbing repairs in the kitchen and bathroom along with some paint the house could be made livable again. A lot of folks pitched in and by September 1 we were in our "new temporary" quarters across the street and about 100 yards north of our previous house.

Barbara, 8 months pregnant now, had all those decisions about where to put stuff that didn't have a place in this smaller house, what to do about the windows, the glass-pained doors, and on and on. Robert, the electrical contractor, offered to replace a light fixture in the front room so we could have more and better lighting. The chairman, upon learning of the improvement, suggested the old fixture was a desirable antique and Robert only wanted it for himself. Hearing about the chairman's comment, Robert immediately reinstalled the old fixture, and to my knowledge, the relationship between these two men was never completely mended.

The house plan chosen followed the style and footprint of the chairman's house though somewhat smaller and less ornate. The problem of location was solved when the president of the local bank offered to donate a lot adjacent to her house on the north end of town. Another church deacon, Alford, a building contractor gave the low bid for constructing the house, however to my dismay and distress, several points of contention would still arise. One was over the brick. When the contract was signed, only a financial allowance was given for the brick since the exact brick had not been chosen. One day as Robert and I were on our way to the golf course we began talking about the brick in some of the newer houses along the way. One house that stood out had a light cream colored, almost white, brick.

"That's pretty," I said, "It's different, makes the house stand out."

"I like that too," Robert said, "I think it would be just right for our new pastorium."

"It's probably over the allowance," I remarked. "We'll see", was Robert's response.

Early in the process I concluded I did not need to attend the building committee's meetings, so I have no idea how most of the committee's decisions were made. I only know that one day a brick company truck pulled up in front of the pastorium construction site and unloaded several pallets of white brick. I was later told that white brick was the one thing Robert insisted on, and though I cannot be sure, I strongly suspect he personally paid for the difference between their cost and the contract allowance.

Initially, as matters of personal preference arose like the location of a few wall plugs or the washer and dryer outlets, Alford asked Barbara where to put them. As the house was nearing completion, I asked Alford if he could put two rods in the closet of the bedroom Beth and Amy would share, one above the other and nearer the floor than normal. Alford responded, "I've been told to follow the blueprints and specifications exactly. Any changes must be authorized by the committee chairman. So, I'll have to do it like this for now, but after the dust settles, I'll come back and fix it like you all want it."

As the day of completion drew near, plans for an Open House and a joyous celebration began to take shape. The building committee chairman had a plan. As soon as the house was completed, while everything was pristine, the building committee would host an open house for the church and the keys to the house would be presented by the chairman of the building committee to the chairman of deacons. As he soon discovered, the building committee chairman was out on that limb all by himself. The building committee refused to go along as did others who heard about the idea. The church had built this house for its pastor and his family. They would move in, arrange and decorate with the help of ladies in the church and welcome guests. Members of one of Alabama's premiere rose clubs, saw to furnishing it with beautiful rose arrangements throughout. It was a joy indeed on that May Sunday afternoon to welcome members of the community at large and especially members of the church into their new pastorium.

After over 8 months in our "temporary quarters" we were finally settled into a beautiful new 3-bedroom, 2-bath house on a lovely large, wooded lot. The main level had 1600 sq. ft. and the lower level had a 600-sq. ft. furnished guest bedroom and bath and a 2-car garage. We would enjoy that house for 6 good years and were blessed to entertain family and some wonderful pastor friends in that guest bedroom, including, Bill Craig, Earl Wilson, Raymond and Eula Lawrence, Hudson Baggett, and S. R. Woodson, to mention a few.

A few weeks after the open house I decided to try some fence-mending with the building committee chairman. We had a good relationship prior to the building of the pastorium, and I was hopeful of restoring that relationship. I knew his feelings had been hurt by the ultimate resolution of some the disagreements within the committee and for some reason much of his anger seemed to be directed at me personally. So, on a Saturday morning when I thought both of us would have some relaxed time I called and asked if I could come by. "Sure, I'm at the office by myself catching up on a few things, come on by."

When I arrived, he welcomed me in and suggested I take the chair across the desk from him. After a few moments of chit-chat, I indicated the purpose of my call ending with something to the effect, "If I have done anything to offend you I'm sorry and would like to make it right if I can."

"Well, to begin with you've never been interested in the church. Since the day you came the only thing you've been interested in is getting that new house built. You don't know the first thing about leading or working with people. From the time I took this job you've done nothing but criticize and interfere. Selling that old pastorium was a good day's work, but you and your special friends have done nothing but criticize me for a little personal inconvenience. If it hadn't been for me your special friend would have walked off with a valuable chandelier."

With the listing of each new grievance his voice grew louder and his face redder. Some 10 minutes later he paused to catch his breath and there was a moment of silence. After a couple of failed attempts to offer some unemotional rational response to his rant it occurred to me that the best thing for me at this time was to say nothing more.

"Well say something, don't just sit there smiling like a Jackass."

"I don't know of anything to say right now that would be helpful to either one of us. So, I think I'll go on back home for now and perhaps there will be a better time in the future to resume this conversation." Since that was a discussion neither of us wanted to have it never took place.

Reflecting on that event there was much that a young pastor could and did learn the hard way. For one thing, I personalized the issue entirely too early. I let it become a conflict between the two of us rather than seeking to understand the deeper issues with which he was struggling. Second, I tried to do too much too quickly myself. When wounds are deep time is often our best ally. Beyond that, a third party both conflicted individuals trust can bring balance and insight to the situation. The next church I pastored got a less defensive pastor and a better conflict manager. Finally, wisely or not, I resolved to never again let a personal benefit to me become an issue for which I would contend. Before leaving Vernon, our family would suffer because I did not let our needs be known more clearly. During our last year in Vernon, to make ends meet, Barbara found it necessary to go back to teaching school, this time the second grade in Sulligent. Following our departure, the church found it necessary to increase their salary and benefit package by 25% to attract their next pastor. Several church friends later apologized for not being more proactive in addressing our financial needs.

I wish I could say that for me, and the building committee chairman bygones became bygones, but that was not to be. The spring following the completion of the pastorium I received a call from the chairman of deacons, Zeb, (*not actual name*) asking if I could meet with the deacons on the coming Thursday to discuss a matter of mutual concern. The meeting began with the deacon chairman reading a resolution commending me for my preaching and pastoral care for the congregation that had led to significant church growth. However, to keep things going in a positive direction they would like for the pastor to agree in the future not to discuss anything of a controversial nature with anyone inside or outside the church family until first discussing it with the deacons.

It seems that the Al's wife had heard at the local beauty shop First Baptist Church was inviting the small black church "up on the hill" to join them for Bible School. Al was infuriated, first, that his church might have an integrated Bible School, and second, that someone at the beauty shop knew about it before he did. He had requested a called meeting of the deacons without the pastor's knowledge or presence to plan their confrontation of the pastor. Only Al and the chairman of deacons, Zeb, knew the real purpose of the meeting. The other deacons were told the pastor was unable to be present, which they considered technically truthful since I didn't know about it and thus was "unable" to be there.

When confronted with the resolution I first explain what had actually happened. During a Sunday afternoon planning meeting with our Bible School faculty the matter of reaching more children for Bible School was discussed. Since the public schools were fully integrated by now one faculty member suggested the black children be invited to join us. Someone else observed that the black children would be more likely to attend a Bible School in their own building rather than come to the intimidating "big" First Baptist Church. I asked if anyone there would be willing and able to help teach if we had a Bible School at their church on a Saturday. Immediately half a dozen hands went up.

The next step was to arrange a meeting with the Methodist pastor to determine if their church would have any interest in working with us since the black church was a Methodist Church. The Methodist pastor, Joe Rush, was very interested in a joint sponsorship though he had reservations about how many of their people could help. In the meantime, I also had a conversation with Ed Allen, a trusted friend, church member and county school superintendent, who I asked if he had any thoughts or advice on the matter. He thought it was a good idea and it had his support.

I concluded, "I assume in this resolution the 'people inside the church' has reference to the Bible School faculty and Ed Allen, and the reference to 'people outside the church' is to Bro. Joe Rush. This approach was entirely appropriate. If the response of any of these people had been negative there would have been nothing to bring to the deacons. Beyond that, how can I possibly know in advance all of the matters each and every deacon may consider controversial. The assumption here is that I do not respect the advice or council of the deacons. I can only offer you 4 years of ministry with you and ask if there is one example where I have disrespected the deacons or tried to do an "end run" to accomplish something against your wishes. To sign this document would be an admission of wrongdoing in fact or motive which I cannot do."

Zeb and Al kept insisting that to fail to agree to the resolution showed a lack of respect for the deacons. By now several of the deacons were expressing support for their pastor and questioning why such a resolution was ever drafted. After several tears were shed and prayers offered the pastor arose and said, "I've done all I know to do. If you want to bring the resolution before the church and the church adopts it then I'll have to decide on my future as your pastor. Otherwise I have nothing more to say on the matter." With that I left the meeting and drove home. Some 30 minutes later as I was sharing with Barbara what had happened our doorbell rang and there stood 2 of our younger deacons. With a warm embrace and tearful eyes, they apologized for not being more forceful in my defense and promised the rest of the deacons had no idea what was going on behind the scenes. They explained, after I left the meeting quickly adjourned with nothing further being said. They felt sure the issue would never come up again. And it didn't.

Regretfully, in the remaining five years of my ministry these two men missed few opportunities to criticize or cast aspersions on me or my ministry. At one regular deacons' meeting while I was at an SBC meeting these men gave an extensive litany of the pastors short comings. I was told Mr. Brock, the manager of the town's one manufacturing industry, the local garment plant, interrupted, "I've been a Baptist deacon in churches in three states and this is the worse deacons meeting I have ever attended. Deacons are supposed to support and encourage their pastor. If you don't want to support your pastor you ought to get off the deacon board." No wonder I hated to see Mr. Brock leave Vernon and move back to Bremen, Ga.

A climactic event came a couple of years later on a Sunday evening as the budget committee made its annual budget presentation to the church. The recommendation included an increase in the pastor's auto allowance. Al offered the observation that the new amount proposed by the committee sounded too high to him. He drove all over the county and did not use his car that much, implying the pastor was not being totally truthful. Zeb chimed in with "It seems awfully high to me too."

From the back of the room one of the older and highly respected members offered, "I move we amend the budget by removing a set amount for auto allowance and ask the pastor to submit a monthly mileage log and pay him the rate allowed by the federal government." Before the matter was voted on someone else asked, "What about his convention allowance, shouldn't we reimburse him for his actual expenses?" By the time the vote was taken I had received substantial increases in both budget items. For the first time the opposition of these two men had taken place in a public forum. Dr. Davis, a highly respected new deacon, came by the house that night and assured me the church members knew exactly what they were doing. "This year when you go the SBC convention if the room you are in doesn't have a color TV check out and find one that does." The next time Al and Zeb were eligible for election as deacons the church chose other men by-passed both of them. Perhaps an unbiased observer may have seen these events somewhat differently, but their impact of me at the time was significant. Hopefully, it in someway shaped my ministry for the good.

Few church members, I am now convinced, wish to quarrel over who will "run" the church and, unless provoked to do otherwise, are more than willing to leave that to the few who seem to enjoy running things. I was both amazed and a little distressed to learn that my two nemeses had become bosom buddies of my successor and regained prominent leadership roles in the church. Upon my successor's resignation a young man was called who did not curry their favor. Once again, these two men became their pastor's antagonists. Following this pastor's departure under pressure, about 20 families withdrew from the church and organized another Baptist church in Vernon. Sadly, most of those families were close personal friends and strong supporters while I was their pastor. They concluded that peace and tranquility among like-minded worshipers was to be preferred to the almost constant turmoil of the previous 15 years.

Those 8 months in "temporary quarters' were certainly not uneventful ones. The arrival of our third daughter, Alisa, early on a Thursday morning, about 1:30 a.m., as I recall, brought great joy to our family. Dr. Glenn had moved to Tuscaloosa and Dr. Davis had not yet arrived so the Sulligent doctors, Dr. Haig Wright and Dr. Bill Box, provided Barbara's prenatal care. The Lamar County Hospital in Vernon was a small rural hospital staffed with local nurses most of whom we knew personally. During her hospital stay of 5 days or so Barbara and Alisa got the best of attention. The baby nursery was located adjacent to the nurse's station so when the nurses were not busy caring for other patients, they took turns rocking the new baby and curling her hair. I also found time to do my share of rocking as well.

Like most small towns Vernon offered the benefits of a caring community. Both the church and the community embraced our family, and we formed many lasting friendships. One spring day when Alisa was 3, just before noon, I got a call from Barbara with a note of desperation in her voice, "I can't find Alisa! "

I hurried home and we began looking and calling. We searched around the house and then into the large overgrown wooded area behind the house. A couple of neighbors heard us calling and joined the search. About 5 minutes later a police car pulled into the edge of the woods. Before another 10 minutes had passed a National Guard truck pulled up and I learned the local National Guard unit had been called out. Two High School classes, one Vo. Ag. and the other P.E., were dismissed to join the search. The local garment plant manager, Mr. Brock, sent a crew to help with the search. About 1:15 a siren sounded, "She's been found!" To my amazement people by the scores began to emerge from the woods. I later concluded at least 75 people had been involved in the search. Alisa, following our neighbor's dog, had wandered into the woods. Becoming entangled in some honeysuckle vines and briers she just sat down. The dog she following into the woods stayed by her side until a national guardsman picked her up.

It was in July of that same year, 1970, the call came from my mother that Daddy was in the hospital in Lexington. Arrangements were made for the coming Sunday; the green Pontiac station wagon was loaded, and we were bound for Kentucky. Problems with stomach ulcers had plagued dad for as long as I can remember. He might occasionally see a doctor, but his usual remedy was warm milk and crackers or toast. This time the new ulcer plus scar tissue from previous incidents had completely closed the duodenum where the stomach empties into the small intestines. Surgery was the only answer. One of Lexington's leading surgeons performed the surgery early in the week and "all went well." Dad was scheduled to go home by the end of the week, but his fever came up a little on Thursday and even more on Friday. I called the Vernon church deacon chairman and explained I needed to say a little longer than expected. His response, "Sure, stay as long as you need."

They began running cultures on Friday and through the weekend hoping to determine the source of the infection. An antibiotic was added to the fight. I spent a lot of time with dad that weekend, trying to keep his lips moist with lemon swabs and reassuring him. On Tuesday, the doctor came in to say the cultures had not given them a lot of help, but they were doing everything they could. As the doctor left for the first time in my life I saw fright in my father's eyes. It lasted only for a moment before he closed his eyes. When he opened them again that look of fright was gone. From that point on though, he grew progressively weaker. Late Friday afternoon, July 31, 1970, he went home to be the with the Lord.

Following the funeral, the surgeon asked the family to meet with him in his office for a review of what the autopsy revealed. With tears in his eyes he told mother how very sorry he was. Had he used an older surgical procedure of bypassing the duodenum dad would not have died. It seems that in using a newer procedure of removing the scar tissue that had built up over the years, he unknowingly pricked the pancreas. As pancreatic fluid leaked into the abdominal cavity it became infected, which led to acute peritonitis from which he was unable to recover.

I knew in my mind my dad was mortal. I had done funerals for younger men, but to die 2 weeks before his 59th birthday, when he was seemingly in good health two weeks earlier, was hard to rationalize. How many times had I told him "Everything will be alright?" I could spiritualize it and say ultimately it really was "alright," but that's not what I meant at the time. Beyond that, I have never known anyone more unprepared to face the future without their mate than my mother. She was too young to draw social security. She had never learned to drive. She had never worked outside the home. In 5 months, she would have to move from the tenant house that had been her home for the last 22 years. Finally, when all of dad's tools, machinery and interest in the livestock was sold slightly more than $20,000 was left standing between her and abject poverty. How she negotiated that future for 35 years is more a story of the love and care of my 2 sisters, Ann and Carol, than mine.

The people in Vernon were terrific upon learning of dad's death. Four couples, Sue and Henry Allen, Jean and James Weeks, Martha and Robert Covington, and Jane and Jim Burnett, were in Nicholasville by Saturday, two of them having driven most of Friday night. Two of them stayed for the funeral on Monday. I could never express my gratitude for the support they gave their pastor in his hour of need, but I have never forgotten that act of sacrificial grace. Dr. Wayne Oats, my seminary professor, said, "pastors have a 'be there' ministry. You don't have to say anything or do anything but being there is everything." My friends drove that point home to me in a powerful way that weekend. I was now assured that in years to come my greatest contribution to a family in moments of crisis, regardless of how horrific or tragic the circumstances, would not my words but my presence as a caring minister of Jesus Christ.

It was in Vernon my dream for lay renewal began to be realized. Dr. Davis accompanied me to a Christian Life Conference in Atlanta. He, Henry Benton and Ed Gosa also joined me at one of Dr. Findley Edge's Vineyard Conferences at Southern Seminary. Harold Shirley, whose Huntsville church was noted for its strides in lay renewal, guided a weekend retreat for our deacons at Pat Bertram's camp in Winston County. Unfortunately, as some laymen became more focused on their spiritual development as well as that of the church, the gap seemed to widen between them and those church leaders with a more traditional focus.

It was in Vernon that my buddy Robert got me hooked on golf, a sport I would never master, but enjoy the rest of my life. One spring day at his country club's small course between Winfield and Hamilton I was playing with Dr. Haig Wright, the crusty Army surgeon who delivered Alisa. The second hole, a short par 3 over a pond to the green, was quite a challenge that day. After 3 tee shots found the pond, Dr. Wright stepped to my side and asked with solemn seriousness, "Preacher, would you like for me to say a few appropriate words?"

A second temptation I found irresistible was the urge to own a classic car, one I would enjoy driving and might grow in value with age. In the early 70's a friend let me drive his spiffy '65 Mustang 2+2 fastback. I was smitten, but by then their growing popularity put them beyond my price range, if not out of my mind.   Then, one day I spied it, on the Sulligent Ford dealer's used car lot. James Hill, a Baptist deacon, was reluctant to even make me a price.

"You don't need that car," he said. "The motor is shot, the transmission needs work, the tires are slick and I'm not sure it would get you back to Vernon."

"I'm looking for something I can work on," I pleaded.

"If your heart is set on it I'll let you have it for what I've got in it. But don't say I didn't warn you."

Tommy had just moved back to Vernon and opened a garage in an old building next door to the church. Previously, the head mechanic at a Ford dealership on Long Island, New York, Tommy offered to let me work on the Mustang in his garage and give advice as needed. I found a 289 engine with a 4-barrel carburetor at a junk yard near Jasper. I rebuild the transportation. To be exact, I took the transmission apart, Tommy put it back together.

While at Sixty-Street the Mustang got a new paint job. At South Avondale, under the watchful eye of Sherrell Maples, I cut out some body rust, patched up a few dents and scars and gave it another new paint job. In Montgomery it was idolized but used sparingly. Eventually, I lost interest in skinning my knuckles. With no place in Birmingham to put an extra car at last I parted with my 35-year obsession. My neighbor, Greg, was thrilled to add my once treasured Mustang to his 2 Corvette collection and had it running like new \again before we moved.

It was in Vernon that Beth as she was leaving for her first day in kindergarten said to Amy, "When I get home this afternoon, I'll teach you to read." In Vernon, Beth and Amy took piano lessons from Joy Steincross, the Sulligent pastor's wife, and later from a piano teacher in Belk, near Fayette. And it was in Vernon, as a 6th grader, Beth marched in the high school band.

It was during our last summer in Vernon that our family took the vacation of a lifetime, a three-week trip to Portland, Oregon, site of the '73 SBC. Two months earlier we had traded in the green Pontiac station wagon for a new blue AMC Matador station wagon. Its maiden voyage was west through Arkansas, Oklahoma, Texas, the Grand Canyon, up California's San Joaquin Valley to Yosemite National Park and finally into Portland. After the convention we came back through Idaho, Montana, Yellowstone, Wyoming, South Dakota, Iowa, Illinois, and finally, lighting for a couple of days in

Kentucky. What an adventure and what a way to bring our 9-year Vernon pastorate, the longest in the church's history, to a close.

Finding My Way - With the Help of Many

I soon discovered, as have many others before me, finding my way as a young pastor involved much more than earning a couple of degrees in college and seminary. Good mentors were essential. Thankfully, at strategic times God seemingly placed mentors in my life who proved to be immeasurable blessings. While there were more than I will be able to mention, a few stand out. Bill Craig taught me more about being a pastor than I can ever put into words. In the early summer of 1956, six months after I understood God was calling me to be a preacher, following the rather brief interim of Dr. Tedford, God led the Rev. William B. Craig to the pastorate of the Nicholasville Baptist Church. His philosophy of ministry made an imprint on me at both the conscious and subconscious levels. Unknowingly, I latched onto many of his phrases, mannerism and even attitudes. After preaching at the Nicholasville church one Sunday many years later, a lady commented, "You remind me so much of Brother Craig." She meant it as a complement, and I felt flattered.

In the summer of '57 Brother Craig encouraged a small Baptist congregation at Camp Nelson, 7 miles south of Nicholasville, to invite me to preach for several Sundays. It was the first time I had preached anywhere more than once. On Friday, August 9, 1957, he officiated at the marriage ceremony of two young church members, Barbara Heathman and Buddy McGohon. In the fall of that year Pleasant Home Baptist Church called me to be their pastor and requested my ordination. In response to that request Brother Craig convened an "Ordaining Council" of 7 experienced Baptist ministers to consider my worthiness for ordination to the Gospel Ministry. Meeting in a conference room at Lexington's Central Baptist Hospital Brother Craig guided me through the minefield of questions about my call to ministry, my understanding of the Bible and of Baptist doctrine. At the conclusion of that hour-long "inquisition" they voted to recommended my ordination, which took place November 17, 1957, at a Sunday evening worship service of the Nicholasville Baptist Church. As I sat on the front pew Brother Craig gave a "Charge to the Candidate" and with members from the Pleasant Home church in attendance Rev. John R. Wells, Director of Missions for the Elkhorn Baptist Association,[1] gave a "Charge to the Church."

Bill Craig was reared in an upper middle-class family in Louisville, Ky. His parents owned and operated a substantial nursery and florist business. When he came home from the Air Force, following WW II, he resumed working in the family's nursery and landscaping business. His wife Doris, an accomplished pianist, prior to their marriage was the accompanist for a team of professional musicians on their concert tour of South America. Craig owned an interest in a couple of thoroughbred racehorses and frequented Churchill Downs in those early days.

Following his "Call to Ministry" he left the nursery business and enrolled at Southern Seminary in Louisville. He completed the 3-year course of study for a Bachelor of Divinity degree but lacking a BA or BS from an accredited college, he was only awarded a Diploma in Theology degree. He had a brilliant mind and became a favorite of several seminary professors. Following a 7-year tenure at the Nicholasville church he was asked to lead an experimental, bi-racial, inner-city church renewal project sponsored by the Seminary, the local Baptist association, the SBC's Home Mission Board and Louisville's Third Baptist Church.

Brother Craig's deep devotion to God and His Church was expressed through his joyful imaginative entrepreneurial spirit. He was an avid motorcyclist, owning a Harley Electro Glide, and a Honda Gold Wing. He regularly rode through the Smokey Mountains and attended rallies in Daytona Beach, Florida. At one time, during the 60's and 70's, he was chaplain to a motorcycle "gang" in Louisville. He often told jokes on himself, his family, and the church. He loved poking fun at people he considered overly pious for taking themselves too seriously.

Throughout most of the 20th Century, the week-long revival, with a guest preacher and guest musician, was an annual program highlight for the vast majority of Southern Baptist churches. I invited Brother Craig to be the revival preacher in four of the six churches I served as pastor, New Salem and South Avondale being the two exceptions, and he was deeply loved by almost everyone. At Pleasant Home in addition to preaching and loving people he gave me some shrubs and told me where and how to plant them to beautify the front of the church. The members fed us fried chicken several times that week and on the last night of the revival he thanked the church and said, "As I came in tonight I think I heard a rooster, who has contributed several sons to the ministry this week, perched on top of a fencepost crowing, "Is he gone, is he gone?"

At a revival in Vernon Craig teased Barbara and me mercilessly and joked with the congregation all week long. He stayed in our home in the furnished guest bedroom of the new pastorium. The revival's hospitality committee had made arrangements that week for individual church members to bring food to our house for breakfast and lunch. Other members would entertain us in their homes for the evening meal. Most nights at the service Craig would brag on the evening meal but then comment on how "skimpy" the breakfast and lunch meals were. "I heard a knock on the door," he would say. "Barbara would go to the door and return with a nice tray or dish, but that's the last I'd ever saw of that tray or what was on it." Of course, this was hilariously funny to everyone in the congregation, except Barbara.

By week's end several people thought it would be a good idea to turn the tables on this jokester. A plan was devised for me to bring Brother Craig by the Bank of Vernon on Friday afternoon at closing time, 3:00 p.m. As the last customer left and the door was locked one of the tellers escorted Craig behind the tellers' cage, ostensibly to show him something about her operation. Just then a loud alarm sounded and suddenly the chief of police with a drawn gun emerged from a back room, followed closely by the county district attorney.

"Who are you and what are you doing here?" the Chief barked at Craig whose face for a few short seconds reflected total shock and bewilderment. A picture of that moment would have been "priceless." Oh, to have had a phone with a video camera back in that day! Craig soon recognized the district attorney to be a regular revival attender, as were the teller, the bank VP and others. But it was an experience he would not soon forget. For years to come, folks in Vernon gleefully talked about the revival preacher who was caught red-handed trying to rob the bank.

Several "preacher types" succumb to the temptation of taking themselves too seriously. Being unable to laugh at themselves, they miss the obvious humor in much of life. Not so with Brother Craig. I usually publicized revivals by placing pictures of the revival preacher and featured musicians in the local paper and on flyers distributed around the neighborhood. I always asked Brother Craig several weeks prior to the revival for a publicity picture. One year when racial tensions were high in Mississippi and Alabama, he sent me a picture from his Third Baptist Church days in Louisville of 3 black children clinging to his neck and leg. On that occasion, a usable picture followed a few days later.

On another occasion, however, in response to a second request for a photo he sent a picture of an organ grinder's monkey in a bright red captain's coat and hat. No other picture followed, so the main revival publicity went picture-less that year. However, with the help of deacon Bill Grauel, a professional printer, I had about 25 flyers printed with the monkey's picture and Craig's name prominently displayed underneath. They were posted liberally around the entrance to the building I would guide Craig through when he arrived. A number of years later, after he had retired, while visiting his Lexington home, he got out a box of memorabilia. To my surprise he produced a copy of the flyer with the monkey's picture along with a copy of the Lamar Democrat's article on the "Local Bank Heist." Unfortunately, I had failed to save copies of either incident.

The revival with the monkey's picture was also the year he rode his Harley Electra Glide from Lexington to Birmingham. He was a hit with all the teenage guys. He told several motorcycle stories during the week. In one, he told of being caught in thunderstorm while riding through Georgia on his way back to Lexington from a motorcycle rally in Daytona Florida. "People often ask me what happens when you are on a long road trip, and it starts raining. Well, you get wet of course. On that occasion after it quit raining I stopped by a local drugstore where a nice young lady asked if she could help me. 'Do you have any talcum power?' I asked. With a nod and motioned of her hand, she said, 'Walk this way.' 'My dear if I could walk that way I wouldn't need the talcum powder.'"

While his personality and style were never something I tried to imitate, these episodes are shared to call attention to his authenticity as an individual blessed by God and very "comfortable in his own skin." The freedom from conformity he exhibited, he graciously extended to others. This was a trait I admired and hopefully took root in my life, at least in some small measure.

One Sunday morning, just prior to an opening revival service, we were sitting in my office at church when the telephone rang. An active church member asked if I could perform a wedding ceremony for his daughter that afternoon. Her fiancée was in town on a brief "leave" from military service and was going back to his base the next day. I explained I had a well-known, long standing, policy that I did not perform marriage ceremonies for couples without the opportunity to counsel with them prior to the wedding. It was an idea I had picked up in a seminary class and had made it my own. I reasoned that making an exception to the policy might lead other couples to think it was only a "suggestion" rather than a "serious policy" and treat it casually. I did, however, offer the name of another minister in the county who had no such policy and would be glad to marry them.

I hung up the phone and turned back to Brother Craig confident I had made a tough but wise decision. As we talked about the situation for a few moments he suddenly asked, "Who did you help today? You've got a young couple who are probable in trouble and need some help. You've got a mother and father who are in trouble and looking for some help from their pastor. Who did you help today?"

"In my own experience," he continued, "I've found that following policies may be the easiest way out of some tough situations, but people are more important than policies. It seems to me; Jesus always came down on the side of helping people!"

Wow!! I don't know how I would have heard that from anyone else, but I needed to hear it and hearing it from him made a difference. It was a tough, but good, lesson that certainly changed the tenor and, to some degree, the direction of my ministry.

As long as he lived Brother Craig was my mentor and pastor. Though he was a great "Man of God," he was certainly not perfect. In the latter years of a successful pastorate he had a disillusioning experience. In one of our conversations during this period he commented, "I sometimes wonder if a lot of so called 'church leaders' aren't hypocrites, faking the Christianity bit. When I was in the nursery business a group of us guys would stop by a local bar after work for a drink and to unwind for a few minutes. One of the guys was a judge, another was an attorney and a couple of others were guys I met at the track. There was more honest dialogue and genuine concern for one another in that group than I've seen displayed by a lot of church people I've known."

Hurt, frustrated and disappointed at the lack of support he had expected, but not received, from some trusted "church friends," he went through several months of depression and darkness. With more than adequate financial resources, he retired to a small nursery farm, inherited from his parents, near Louisville. He eventually began to find healing and wholeness in a small Episcopal fellowship nearby. I was permitted the privilege of walking beside this beloved mentor who had been God's conduit of so many blessings to me. In time, he returned to Lexington and eventually was called to pastor an inner-city, non-denominational church that met in an abandoned movie theater. The church prospered under his ministry, and he thrived spiritually in the waning days of his life. Conducting his funeral service was a treasured honor and privilege. The church, he formerly pastored and where he had been disappointed, was packed as hundreds came to pay tribute to a genuine "Man of God" the Heavenly Father had used to bless their lives.

Of course, Bill Craig was not the only person God used to mentor me at crucial periods of my life. While at New Salem in Caledonia, I was blessed by the examples of Dr. S. R. Woodson, pastor of First Baptist Church, Columbus, Mississippi and Dr. Dewey Roach, Professor of Philosophy and Religion at Mississippi State College for Women who for some unknown reason befriended me. Their influence continued when I moved to Vernon.

Dr. Charles Davis, pastor of First Baptist Church at Fayette, and later president of Fayette Junior College, was a spiritual giant God brought across my path. Ironically, our paths first crossed at Buffalo Lick. He was a Southern Baptist Missionary to Venezuela at the time, home on furlough, who was assigned to speak at Buffalo Lick during a World Missions Conference. Shortly after speaking at Buffalo Lick he returned to the mission field for a second term of service. Unfortunately, that term was cut short by his wife's illness. Following his wife's recovery, the Foreign Board decided it was unwise, for health reasons, to reappoint the family as SBC missionaries to a foreign field. Since he was an excellent preacher and a devoted Servant of the Lord, the First Baptist Church at Fayette, AL was excited to have him as their pastor, and the church thrived under his leadership.

We got together occasionally for lunch and at least once for golf. That was the time he told me of attending a social event in Venezuela with a number of handsomely paid Americans workers in the oil industry. An oil executive wife was ecstatic about her new hobby, golf. She described joining an exclusive golf club, buying an expensive set of golf clubs, and purchasing a designer golf outfit. She was thrilled with the way she looked and how the whole experience made her feel. Then with a small frown on her brow she said, "Actually, it would be a perfect game if I could just learn to hit that *-+#* little white ball."

Though the Davises' enjoyed Fayette, adjusting to the idea they were not supposed to be in Venezuela evaded them. When the Foreign Mission Board again refused their request for appointment, they decided God was calling them to "go on faith." Charles resigned his pastorate, raised some financial support and set out for Venezuela. They stayed 6 months. He would later tell me, "It was a disaster almost from the beginning." Neither the place they planned to work, nor the people with whom they planned to work, turned out to be what they had been led to believe. Once again, his wife got sick, leaving them no choice but to return to the States. But return to what?

The newly founded Fayette Junior College (now Brewer State Junior College) was looking for its first president to get it off the ground. The state senator who had lobbied hard for the college was a member of First Baptist Fayette and a dear friend of the Davises. He had kept in regular contact with them during their "Venezuela fiasco." Jimmy B. convinced both the state "powers that be" and the Davises the college presidency must be God's plan. At any rate, it was a great fit. He served as president of the college for 10 years from 1969-79.

During one of my spiritual low points while serving at Vernon I stopped by Charles' office one day. As he listened to my concerns, the specifics of which I now have no memory, he said it sounded like I need a little break. "What if for the next month you let me come and preach for you on Sunday Evening as my gift to you and the church? You can just sit with your wife and family in the congregation and worship. Do you think your folks would have any objection?"

The answer to that question seemed obvious. The congregation relished hearing a fresh inspirational series of messages from an outstanding preacher. I enjoyed relaxing on Sunday afternoons and worshiping with my family on Sunday Evening, with no leadership responsibilities. At the conclusion of the 4th, and last service, I "walked forward" to thank Dr. Davis and offer myself to God and the congregation as a renewed and rededicated pastor-servant.

Then there was Dr. Hudson Baggett, a former professor at Samford University, and for 20 years editor of The Alabama Baptist paper. He became a trusted counselor, good friend and always advocate for many years. His recommendation would ultimately lead to my becoming pastor of the South Avondale church.

Dr. Dotson Nelson, Pastor of the Mountain Brook Baptist Church would also become a friend and encourager, especially during my days in Birmingham. He became my "field supervisor" for my work on the Doctor of Ministry Degree from Southern Seminary. Once or twice a month, for almost two years, I spent a 60 to 90-minute session with him. His wisdom and affirmation gave a needed boost to my confidence as a pastor, and it was his encouragement that ultimately led to my serving two terms as chairman of the Alabama Baptist State Board of Missions. His council was also important in my accepting the opportunity to become Director of Missions for the Montgomery Baptist Association.

In addition to the many ministers who served as mentors in my spiritual pilgrimage, I am forever indebted to many devout and wise laypersons God brought into my life. I mention only a few of those individuals, from my earlier days. In truth there were surely dozens, probably hundreds of similar cases sprinkled through more than a half century of ministry.

A couple of months before my 20th birthday the Pleasant Home Baptist Church in Owen County, Kentucky called me to be their pastor. Without a doubt, I learned more from that small congregation than they ever learned from me. I learned the value of visiting church members in their homes. Tommy Boaz, our 30-year-old deacon, offered to visit with me and introduce me to all the church members living in the community, some of whom seldom came to church. Following Sunday dinner, either at his house or at the home of the Polands, his in-laws, Tommy often interrupted my unannounced afternoon plans for relaxation with, "Who would you like to visit this afternoon?" Or, "I hear so and so hasn't been doing well, do you want to go by and check on them." In less than 6 months I knew every member of the church, had expressed my concern for each one and had offered to be available if they should ever need me. Tommy helped me understand that being a good pastor involved caring for people, as well as preaching sermons.

Tommy and Lonnie Poland also taught me the value of churches working together. Fourteen, mostly small and rural churches, formed the Ten Mile Baptist Association. Only the Baptist church in Warsaw, the Gallatin County Seat, was large enough to have a full-time pastor on the field. One Sunday afternoon each month the Association sponsored an Associational Sunday School meeting for the purpose of sharing ideas and encouragement for Sunday School workers. They awarded 2 banners each month, one to the church with the most people in attendance, and the other to the church with the largest percentage of its members present. Pleasant Home usually won the latter of those banners. One Sunday morning we had 20 in Sunday School. That afternoon we won the banner with 21 in attendance, and we had 22 at the evening service.

They also taught me that a church's strength, both spiritually and financially, is more dependent on its members' commitment to Christ than their wealth. A small board, hanging on the wall to the right of the pulpit, displayed the morning's Sunday School attendance and offering. I was startled one morning when the offering, usually less than $50, was posted as over $500. In response to my inquiry about a possible mistake, Tommy informed me that Lonnie, his father-in-law and the church's other deacon, had sold his tobacco crop the previous week. He had given his tithe.

"Pappy" Saunders, the "head" deacon at Buffalo Lick Baptist Church and for many years the devoted Clerk of the Shelby Baptist Association, reinforced the value of churches and pastors working together through their local Baptist association. Attending the quarterly meetings of the Shelby Association's Executive Board with Mr. Saunders was a must for his young pastor. It was probably Pappy's influence that led the Association's Program Committee to ask his young seminary student pastor to preach the doctrinal message at an Annual Association Meeting. It was the first time I preached to a congregation that included many of my fellow pastors, leaders of other Baptist churches in the county, and even some leaders in the Kentucky Baptist Convention. The sermon on the doctrine of "Priesthood of the Believer" was well received and graciously complemented by Chauncey Daily, editor of "The Western Recorder," the Kentucky Baptist paper. Little did I realize, at the time, God was using these, and many subsequent experiences in the life of Baptist Associations, as preparation for the last two decades of my full-time active ministry.

Buffalo Lick turned out to be another extremely valuable training ground in many other areas of ministry for their young pastor. For one thing, preaching twice on Sundays and leading a Wednesday night bible study every week provided a laboratory for making practical application of theological ideas presented in the classroom. But, there was a "down-side." So many presentations each week meant that few if any of the sermons or bible studies were thoroughly prepared. Presentations were given from notes, handwritten or typed, on 1 to 2 pages, 4.25 x 5.5 inches in size. I soon discovered that an 8.5 x 11-inch sheet of paper, folded in half, was just the right size to be neatly concealed between the pages of a Bible or a typical church bulletin. The notes were in outline form with points and sub-points, often consisting of only a phrase or word, and never more than a sentence, in length. This was a form that had served well in debating and extemporaneous speaking. Unfortunately, the failure to prepare more complete manuscripts led to wandering, imprecise messages, often longer than necessary. Moreover, preaching the same message a second time, from sketchy notes, after several years had elapsed required a great deal of additional preparation. The complete list of people to whom I'm indebted continues to grow and is no doubt known only to God.

Pastoral Ministry in Urban Transition

I do not remember how the Pastor Search Committee of Birmingham's 66th Street Baptist Church got my name nor how they first contacted me. What I do remember was that my initial response was quite cautious. I was not interested in their coming to Vernon and disturbing that congregation when I wasn't thinking seriously about moving to another church. After reviewing my resume and having a couple of phone conversations, they asked if it would be possible for me to accept an invitation from a neighboring Birmingham pastor to preach at his church for a Sunday night worship service. Since I didn't want them to come to Vernon could they hear me in a neutral location. They were in no hurry, and neither was I. The best opportunity to meet each criteria turned out to be on the Sunday our Convention/Vacation -Trip-Out-West was ending. Robert Wilkerson, pastor of the First Baptist Church of Inglenook, an acquaintance but not a close friend, was also the son of a member of 66th Street. At their request he invited me to preach at his Sunday evening worship service. The committee arranged for us to spend that Sunday night in a nice Birmingham hotel before returning to Vernon the next day.

John Bell, the Chairman of the 66th Street Search Committee was a devout young man who grew up in the church. Following his graduation from Auburn, he spent 4 years in the Air Force attaining the rank of Captain. At the time, he was vice president and junior partner in a small manufacturing company that made sissy-seats and other attachments for motorcycles. With Johnny as our host we made a couple of trips to Birmingham to look over the church and the "church field." The church was adjacent to Woodlawn, a neighborhood that had already experienced a good bit of racial transition, and though most of the 66th Street church members still lived in the "church neighborhood," some had moved northeast into the Roebuck and Huffman areas of town. Johnny informed us that the church had sold its pastorium and was going to provide its next pastor with a housing allowance so he could buy his own house, build equity and live in the neighborhood of his choice. He showed us a subdivision in the Huffman area where new affordable houses were being built and new schools were among Birmingham's most progressive.

There was much about the move that was appealing and seemed to make good sense. The church was almost twice the size of Vernon. Their salary, housing allowance and benefits package was almost twice that of Vernon's. Johnny and his wife Susie were only one of several very energetic and devoted young couples in the church. Sixty-Sixth Street had a church staff consisting of a fulltime secretary, a fulltime minister of Youth and Education, and a part-time Minister of Music. Beyond that, the possibilities of growing and reaching people for Christ seemed much greater than in Vernon. The church had a bus ministry led by volunteers who brought 40 to 50 children whose parents did not attend church to Sunday School and a Children's Church worship service each Sunday. Children's Church leader, Earl Mc Kay, was also a search committee member. While the adult membership and attenders were all white, a few black children were coming through the bus ministry, a situation for which some search committee members voiced strong support.

Then there was the appeal of living and ministering in Alabama's largest city. There were times in Vernon when I felt isolated from other ministers who shared my interests and aspirations. While friendship with peers was not considered a major factor at the time the decision was made, that would prove to be one of the richest blessings of moving to Birmingham. There I became one of 30-40 ministers, mostly pastors, who attended the Baptist Ministers Conference each Monday at First Baptist Church downtown. Often as many as a dozen of us would have lunch together at a nearby Chinese Restaurant. I got to know many colleagues who passed through Birmingham and went on to other churches across the state. Most of all, lifelong and dear friendships developed with some like Otis Brooks, John Foster, Bob Curlee, Jack Farmer, and Dot Nelson, to mention a few.

In reflection, the moves to New Salem and to Vernon seemed to be guided more by divinely ordered circumstance and actually seemed against the grain of wise professional or business rationale. To use Tevye's words in Fiddler on the Roof "On the other hand," I wondered at times if the move to Birmingham could have been motivated primarily by self-serving ambition. I did wrestle with those thoughts for a while before convincing myself my basic motives were more noble and spiritual than the worse possibilities. Following a Sunday dinner meeting with the full Sixty-Sixth committee at a restaurant on the east side of Winfield, Barbara and I concluded God was indeed leading us to the Birmingham church.

A date was set for a "trial sermon" at Sixty Sixth Street and I informed the Vernon deacons of my plans. I preached on the appointed Sunday to a full house and following the worship service Barbara and I went to the home of Ethel and Blackie Anderson a couple of blocks from the church to await the results of a "secret ballot." The vote was 170 plus in favor and 3 in opposition. Later, I learned the current interim pastor's name had been on the 3 negative ballots in hopes he would remain their pastor. I announced my resignation to Vernon that Sunday evening to become effective in two or three weeks.

Johnny, true to his word, helped us find a new house on High Point Terrace ready for occupancy within the week and helped us qualify for a 90% loan. Thanks to a substantial "gift" from Barbara's parents and her 3 remaining teaching salary checks we were able to get together the $3,200 down payment and become the proud owners of our first house, a 3-

bedroom, 2-bath brick/brown frame ranch style newbie. There was still work to be done in the basement garage, and the zoysia-sprigged yard would require countless hours of weeding and care before it became an attractive lawn, but the ole farm boy was ready, willing and able.

The movers Sixty-Sixth Street engaged to move us to Birmingham arrived on a Monday and began packing our stuff, which was a first for us. They were professionals and knew how to pack well and quickly. They moved us on Tuesday and by nightfall we were ready to spend our first night in a house we could call our own. Beth, Amy, and Alisa were enrolled in Wright Elementary, a school for first through eighth grades with 4 pods of 2 grades each named after the 4 Indian tribes that had inhabited Alabama. We had hoped Beth would continue her clarinet and band activities but for some reason the Junior High Band lacked the close comfort of Vernon, and she soon gave it up. All three girls soon made friends though with other girls their age in the neighborhood as well as at church. Our first summer in Birmingham Amy joined a softball team, and at the ballpark Barbara and I quickly lost our first-name identity and became known as Amy's mom and dad.

Janis and Ben Whitten who had moved into the neighborhood, second house to our right, a year or so prior to us welcomed us warmly. They had two daughters, one a year older than Beth, the other a little older than Amy, and they were all active members of First Baptist Center Point. Ben worked for the IRS and traveled a good bit during the week and since Janis enjoyed sewing, she and Barbara soon became close friends. Before long, the Adams family moved next door on our left. John, the oldest boy, was Amy's age, but lacking her athleticism found little enjoyment playing either football or basketball with her. John eventually married Lorie Simmons who grew up in our South Avondale church. The youngest son, Jeff, was small for his age but could talk a mile a minute and had a thousand questions. Bob, the dad was Minister of Education at Roebuck Park Baptist. Our church schedules must have kept both families extremely busy because, sadly, we had little interaction except an occasional nod or wave going or coming.

Warm relationships were established with some church members but only a few lasted beyond our tenure at the church. Beth did find Mark, her one and only boyfriend and eventual husband, whose parents were devout and compassionate Christians. Mark's dad, Bill, was a printer by trade, active in his local union and our most faithful church bus captain. He spent, most Saturday mornings encouraging kids and their parents to accept Christ and start coming to church. Once Beth and Mark became a steady item I often told him I thought our couch had a growth on it. For many years Beth's best friend was Joanie Dillard a church youth from a fine Christian family. Grace Little, the church hostess and cook and her husband Bill often invited our family to their home for a cookout on holidays and their warm friendship lasted well beyond our time at the church. For me Johnny Bell and Tom Saffles became lasting friends. Johnny encouraged me to become a member of the Birmingham Tip Off Club. Tom, an usher captain at the BJJC Coliseum, asked me to usher at the SEC Basketball Tournament for several years after it started back up in Birmingham, assigning me to the Kentucky section no less.

While Amy did not make any lasting friendships during our stay at Sixty Sixth Street she and Beth were introduced during that time to the game of golf at the Roebuck Golf Course. Inexpensive Junior summer rates made it a good summer activity. Beth often played with Joanie's brother Mark who became a good amateur golfer, though I think she may have enjoyed driving the cart as much as the golf. Butch Trammell, the club pro, was of some help and Amy eventually developed a love for the game. Alisa's most memorable event, at least to her parents, happened on a Sunday morning when she developed a tummy ache. Barbara took her to see Dr. Money who was at the hospital at the time, and I went on to church. When I checked in after the worship service I discovered Alisa had appendicitis and was scheduled for surgery almost immediately. All went well and she recovered rather quickly under the attentive eye of an RN church friend, Bea Davis.

The seven-mile commute from High Point Terrace to Sixty Sixth Street, along First Avenue North, took about 20 minutes one way and was quite a change from Vernon's 5 minutes to anywhere. I rode Johnny Bell's small motorcycle to and from the church office on a few warm summer days. Actually, I was never comfortable riding the borrowed bike and when I almost wrecked one day because someone pulled out in front of me I decided that mode of transportation was too dangerous to be fun. My suspicion is that a lot of people in cars only look out for other cars and fail to see motorbikes. So, my trusty Mustang became my personal everyday car and the Matador station wagon our family car.

Edna Dudley, the church secretary for the past 20 years or more and a church member even longer, was a jewel. Her daughter, a single mom with 3 children, lived with Edna in the neighborhood and while her daughter seldom attended church, Edna was there every service along with her 3 grandchildren. Edna was not the most skilled typist or best newsletter and bulletin editor, but her knowledge of families in the church, her dependability and her desire to be helpful more than compensated for any technical deficiencies.

One of my first administrative tasks was the recruitment of Larry Gay to be our second fulltime ministerial staff member, serving as Minister of Youth and Education. Larry was completing his senior year at Samford and was planning to enter the seminary some two or three years later when his wife Susan completed her degree at Samford. They were a devout young couple whose willingness to work with and minister to youth especially, more than made up for their lack of experience and wisdom.

Larry built a strong youth program primarily with meetings on Sunday and Wednesday evenings. He organized both youth retreats and mission trips. Beth and Amy went on one especially meaningful mission trip to Indiana. One evening Larry was trying his best to prepare the youth spiritually for the mission trip. Some of the them were being more disruptive than cooperative. Finally, in frustration Larry turned to the group and yelled, "Alright, whoever's got a hair up their butt, it's time to get it out!" While I did not get a verbatim report from my children I did hear from some other parents. Fortunately, nearly all of our parents understood that the value of what was being accomplished far outweighed that momentary frustrated outburst and the event became a learning experience for everyone. [1]

When I left the stable and seemingly "stale" community of Vernon for the changing transitional neighborhood of Sixty-Sixth Street I had little idea of the leap I was taking. The Sixty Sixth Street neighborhood was located between the well-defined Woodlawn and East Lake communities. Both communities and their churches had thrived in Birmingham's growth years reaching their peak in the 1950's. Two governmental decisions and the "white flight" in response to school desegregation along with Birmingham's racial turmoil of the '60s prompted a profound and rapid transition in these neighborhoods. First, the interstate road system was routed through black and often poor neighborhoods of the city, displacing literally thousands of black families. Second, the purchase of property for the expansion of UAB's medical complex and the university displaced another large group of black families. Finally, "white flight" to the suburbs offered many of these displaced black families an opportunity to substantially upgrade their living conditions.[2] Less than 1 mile from Sixty-Sixth Street church one entire block of desirable brick houses, all less than ten years old, transitioned from a white owner to a black owner in 6 months. One of the houses on that block was the church's former pastorium. While this was an extreme example, it is reflective of the fear and accompanying panic that often lay just beneath the seemingly calm surface of everyday life.

The typical transition that occurred in 90 percent of the Sixty Sixth Street neighborhood was much slower, occurring over a span of nearly three decades from 1960 to 1990. The first major blow came around 1960 when Howard College moved its campus from East Lake to Homewood. As newer housing developments sprang up beyond Roebuck in Huffman and Center Point, younger and more affluent families moved east. The older neighborhoods became grayer and less affluent. Housing gradually transitioned from owner occupied to rental. The churches left behind for a time maintained some of their vitality drawing some younger members back to worship with mom and dad out of family loyalty. However, as their children came along they finally joined a church in the neighborhood where they lived. Consequently, the new folks moving in were different socio-economically, ethnically and racially from the older longtime members of the church.

Bridging the barriers of differing cultures in transitioning neighborhoods is extremely difficult for church members regardless of their age even when they understand what is happening and want to do something about it. When I arrived at Sixth-Sixth Street it is safe to say neither I, nor the vast majority of that congregation, had any real understanding of what was going on. Consequently, we didn't have a clue as to how the issues facing us might be addressed, even though we had a sincere desire to do so in the service of our Lord. As it happened, the remaining 30 years of my fulltime ministry and 12 years of retirement would be devoted in some measure to understanding and addressing the needs of transitioning communities and our transitioning times. In reality, every community is in some state of transition and that transition is usually occurring far more rapidly than we realize.

My first approach was to do everything we had always done that had worked in the past only perhaps a little smarter and better than I had done before. We worked at the bus ministry a little harder and with a little more organization. Of course, the parents of the bus kids were not responding, and we didn't understand or seem to have time to find out why. Maybe they just didn't care about religion, but at least we were taking care of their kids for a few hours on Sunday morning so they could sleep in or do something else. A good basketball program reached a few young men. We actually had two teams in different leagues. One team of guys, in their 30s and 40s, my team, just played to have fun. The other team of guys, in their late teens and 20's, played to win and were actually pretty good.

Revivals, vacation bible schools, lay witnessing programs and Sunday School enlargement campaigns were worked at zealously. A Pastor's Class, which I started and taught during the Sunday School hour, primarily for men and women currently not enrolled in Sunday School, was quite successful in reaching a number of unchurched adults and helping some nominal church members become active leaders. Yet, all of the gains experienced seemed temporary. More importantly, the hoped-for change in attitude and spiritual maturity of church members never seemed to materialize.

Eventually, a conscious effort was made to learn something about the characteristics of transitional communities. More and more books began to appear on the subject. In the 70's UAB began an Urban Studies Program led by Dr. Blaine Brownell. One of his seminars opened my eyes to some of the factors driving much of Birmingham's transition which I alluded to earlier. On our way to the SBC in Philadelphia in '76 Barbara and I visited Trinity Lutheran Church in Lancaster, PA, a church whose successful ministry-oriented renewal effort is described in pastor Wallace Fisher's book From

Tradition to Mission.³ Fisher was the inspiration leader of Southern Seminary's Vineyard conference I attended with 3 laymen while in Vernon. On Sunday morning we worshipped at Trinity, the oldest inland Lutheran church in America. We were joined by Nettie Jones who with her husband Allen, the stepson of Barbara's grandmother Jones, had moved from Kentucky to Lancaster some 15 years earlier with Allen's work.

In 1975 the State Convention employed Jere Allen, a former classmate from Southern Seminary, as Director of Black Church Relations. He was also asked to launch a new initiative to address the needs of churches in the inner-city and transitional communities. I became one of 15 to 20 Birmingham area pastors who began meeting monthly, often with Jere, to talk and pray about what we were experiencing and how we were trying to address our challenge. I was asked to chair the local Inner-City Committee. A proposal to bringing in an outside consultant funded by the state convention to help a church look at itself and develop a plan for the future was especially appealing. With the approval of the deacons I requested that Sixty Sixth Street be on the consultant's list for a visit in the summer of '77.

In April of '76 Jere Allen and Dr. Tom Roote, Birmingham Association Director of Missions, invited me and Ensley Baptist pastor Jack Farmer, to a weekend seminar in San Francisco on transitional community ministry sponsored by SBC's Home Mission Board. What a weekend that was! The small group of only 9 or 10 participants was led by Dr. Francis Debose, Golden Gate Seminary's Professor of Missions. The seminar began on Friday night, June 25 with a lecture by a Presbyterian Seminary professor, Dr. Lee, who stated emphatically, "As the community goes, so goes to the church." It was a statement I was unwilling to accept and challenged at the time. Thirty years later while I do not think it is universally true I am now convinced it is generally true in the typical American community.

During the weekend we visited a Saturday night Roman Catholic Pentecostal prayer and worship service; a Chinese church with 2 Saturday and 5 Sunday worship services in the same building each weekend; a church in the "Tenderloin" district with a feeding ministry to the homeless and an outreach to prostitutes; a Sunday morning service at Glide Memorial Methodist Church, the leading Gay church in San Francisco at the time; watched for perhaps an hour or more the 6th annual Gay Pride parade on Sunday afternoon; and visited on Monday with the influential Rev J. Alfred Smith, pastor of the Allen Temple Church, a large, socially and politically active African-American church in Oakland that was making a positive impact on the city of Oakland.

A number of people at that time were suggesting the social climate of San Francisco would eventually come to most regions of the United States. The thought of that being a real possibility was both frightening and challenging! I found many of the "Gay Pride" activities and the exploitive sex of the

Tenderloin district repugnant and repulsive. However, I found inspiration and hope in the compassion expressed for the hurting and disposed. Also, I was encouraged by the creativity and diversity with which various religious groups were sharing and living out the Gospel in that context. (While I still have a very limited understanding of "Gay" culture I confess my attitude evolved significantly over the following 20 years, perhaps beginning with that experience. I now believe in most cases homosexuality is not a choice, any more than heterosexuality is a choice. What we do choose is the way we behave, and sexual lust, exploitation and exhibitionism are sinful and repugnant regardless of a person's sexual orientation).

I returned to Sixty Sixth Street challenged to address the needs of our neighborhood and find more creative ways to include the newer residences of our community in our ministry efforts. Struggling with the challenge of transitional community ministry made it increasingly obvious I needed to expand my knowledge and skill in a more formal way. A relatively new Doctor of Ministry Degree, a terminal degree with a focus on the practice of ministry, being offered by Southern Seminary in Louisville[4] seemed to be my best option.

Of course, being admitted to the degree program was not automatic. Having been away from an academic environment for 14 years, I had a great deal of anxiety about meeting the entrance requirements to pursue the degree, especially the GRE score. The catalogue did not give the minimum score required, only that it would be an important consideration for admission to the program. I spent a good part of my spare time in the fall of '76 in preparation for my first try at the exam which was held on a Saturday at Samford. To my amazement I scored over 500 on the verbal half and well over 700 on the Math oriented half for a total score of almost 1300. With that score and the approval of the church I sought and received admission to the Doctor of Ministries program with my first class to begin in June of 1977.

In the fall of '76 and winter of '77 my preaching tended to focus on recognizing the needs of our neighbor, especially those who may be different from us and on becoming a neighbor to those in need. At a deacons' meeting in the early spring of '77 one of our deacons mentioned we had a problem that needed to be addressed. During the afternoon rush hour people coming up 1st Ave. South were cutting through the church's parking lot to avoid the traffic light on 66th street which created a danger for church members coming to mid-week activities. Another deacon suggested there was a problem with black boys using the basketball goals on the edge of the parking lot. One suggested solution that garnered a lot of support was putting a chain across the entry ways to the parking lot. Of course, this would necessitate taking it down on Wednesday evening, but it would stop people from using it at other times. Removing the basketball goals was suggested as a solution to "the other problem."

Finally, I asked, "In the light of what Jesus did, should protecting our property from being used by people in the neighborhood be our first priority?" Sadly, even raising that possibility seemed irrelevant and impracticable to most of those leaders. A committee of deacons, most strongly supportive of protecting our property from the neighborhood residents, was appointed to study the matter further and bring back a recommendation at next month's meeting. That night the flickering light went out on my dream that Sixty Sixth Street Baptist Church could be a church ministering to the people of its neighborhood.

Amazingly, as I wrestled with what I should do next, the following Sunday one of our members recognized a worship service visitor, Ben Campbell, as a friend she knew. She also knew he was a member of South Avondale Baptist, a church currently without a pastor. Following the worship service, she was quick to share that information with me and other church members standing nearby. I would later learn that members of the South Avondale Baptist search committee had attended other previous Sunday Morning services, unrecognized. That afternoon I received a call from the committee chairman, Bill Parham, requesting a meeting to talk about their church and determine if I might have any interest in further discussions. Could it be God was at work orchestrating another transition in our life?

A Good Fit at the Right Time

The South Avondale Search Committee got my name as a potential pastor by way of Dr. Hudson Baggett whose Alabama Baptist office was in the same building as the medical office of his good friend Dr. R. C. Green, a leading member of South Avondale. One morning over coffee Dr. Green asked Dr. Baggett if he knew of someone who would be a good fit for their church which had been without a pastor for nearly 2 years. Dr. Baggett suggested they consider Buddy McGohon.

My meeting with Mr. Parham and the search committee began a lengthy inquiry on my part into the life and makeup of the South Avondale congregation. It was, after all, another church in another transitional community that had experienced a long period of numerical decline. The church reached its zenith in 1959 near the midpoint of the 27-year pastorate of Dr. J. E. Davidson (1947-1973) with an average weekly Sunday School attendance of 615. From that point forward every year, with one exception, saw a decline from the previous year until the average attendance in 1973 was 246. Gradually members had moved out of the Avondale area, some "over the mountain," others further east. Many of the remaining families were "empty- nesters" whose children had grown up, gone off to college and moved on to careers and families in other communities, even other states.

In 1974 the associate pastor, who had been called with the understanding he would succeed Dr. Davidson, became the new pastor. In less than a year, unable to manage the stress of his assignment and unable to appropriately handle some personal problems that arose, he resigned with the support of the church leadership. Over the next two years average Sunday School attendance stabilized at between 245 and 250. In this interim period with the encouragement of interim pastor Lindy Martin the church began to focus on ministering to the community and in January of '76 launched several local ministry projects. Before long initial enthusiasm waned and the congregation yearned for a permanent full-time pastoral leader.

Though somewhat disillusioned with the response of the Sixty-Sixth Street congregation, I came to feel more intensely both the need and challenge of leading a church in a transitional community, if that church was willing to be involved in community serving ministries. Intrigued by my initial contact I wanted to gauge the church's willingness to make community ministry a major focus by asking for two important pieces of information. First, how many church leaders still lived in close proximity to the church? Rightly or wrongly, I had concluded that church leaders, including the pastor, simply by living outside the Sixty-Sixth Street neighborhood had made it more difficult for the membership as a whole to have a vital concern for the church's neighborhood. While South Avondale was much closer to

Birmingham's inner city than Sixty-Sixth Street, the church community did contain the strong residential neighborhoods of Forest Park, Crestwood and Avondale. With the help of a pin-map I was able to determine that a large percentage of the church's deacons and other key leaders still lived in these core residential neighborhoods near the church.

Second, I asked for a meeting with all the church's deacons. I wanted to know how closely their dreams and aspirations for the church aligned with mine. I began by giving each deacon a deck of 12 index cards, each card with the name of a function their pastor might be expected to perform. The functions fell into 4 broad categories (administrative leadership, spiritual guidance, pastoral care and Kingdom building leadership) with 3 functions each. Each deacon was asked to organize his cards from one to twelve based on the priority he gave to that particular function. Each deacon's selected order was then recorded one by one on a large board at the front of the room. Lastly, I shared with the group the order for each of the 12 functions I had chosen prior to the evening's meeting.

Several valuable learnings came from that activity. First, the deacons' order of priorities for their pastor differed considerably from deacon to deacon. Though they did tend to cluster in some areas, it was obvious no pastor could meet all their expectations. While I was not surprised, this proved to be an enlightening exercise for the deacons. Second, their priorities and my priorities tended to cluster in most of the same places but not all. Where there were differences it gave us an opportunity to talk briefly about those differences. Third, the exercise helped all of us realize a unified effort would require some open honest dialogue going forward. In addition, we would need to "cut each other some slack" from time to time if our relationship as pastor and people was to be fulfilling for both of us.

Finally, I made it clear I was no "messiah" or wonder worker. Nothing approaching the glory days of the 50s was likely to return, as some were inwardly hoping. One deacon later told me, my refusal to hold out that hope was what convinced him I was the man for the job. However, I assured them South Avondale could certainly be a great church with a great future if they were willing to allow God to fulfill His purpose through them.

After approximately 90 minutes I turned the meeting back over to the search committee chairman and excused myself. The meeting continued another 30 minutes or so and concluded with the deacons expressing unanimous support for the Search Committee's desire to present me to the church for a "Call" to be their next pastor. I now believe that meeting laid the foundation for my ministry at South Avondale Baptist Church, making it the most joyful and fulfilling of my pastoral ministry.

When Mr. Parham sat down with me following that meeting he asked, "How do you want to proceed? We are ready to present your name to the church as our next pastor. We can do it at a called business meeting if you wish. Preaching a 'trial sermon' will not be necessary unless you want to."

"Oh, I want to preach to the congregation" I said. "I want to experience the spirit of the congregation and feel how they respond to me in a worship setting. I also want them to do more than express their confidence in the Search Committee, I want them to express their confidence in me."

Beyond that I wanted to see how the worship attendance compared to the Sunday School average. According to Martin, a personal acquaintance, worship attendance was far greater than Sunday School attendance, sometimes reaching around 600. A friend from college days, Tom Cleveland, who had preached at the church the last few weeks agreed but estimated the worship attendance to be more like 400 - 450. When I preached that May 1st Sunday, the sanctuary was reasonably full including the balcony. I counted a few more than 300 live bodies in attendance, 350 would have required "chairs in the aisles". More impressive than the congregation's attendance was their exuberant singing and enthusiastic spirit. Following the Service our family was escorted to the home of Clell and LaVelle Wright to await dinner while the church voted unanimously to accept the Search Committee's recommendation.

In my discussions with the search committee and the deacons I mentioned a couple of personal issues we needed to work through. The first dealt with my plans to pursue the Doctor of Ministry degree at Southern Seminary. Upon explaining what the degree involved they gave their whole-hearted support even though it would require their new pastor being away from the church field for a month, two weeks after assuming his responsibilities. They saw it as a win/win for me and for the church.

The second issue revolved around the arrangements I had made through the State Convention and the Home Mission Board for a consultant to visit Sixty Sixth Street in July. Without me as their pastor Sixty Sixth Street no longer needed or wanted to have the consultant visit their church. The question was, would South Avondale want to or be willing to make the necessary preparations to participate in the program so early in my ministry. Again, they gave their complete support. Normally, I would never have considered beginning a pastorate with such unproven time-consuming endeavors. Yet, they would launch the South Avondale ministry on what would prove to be a successful trajectory. Once again God was seemingly guiding me down a path beyond my understanding at the moment. What else could I do, even with my timid faith, but follow Him?

The fulfilment we experienced during the South Avondale period of our life and ministry can be described from two perspectives, one personal and the other congregational.

Personal

Our time at South Avondale was one of immense transition and maturation for the whole family. For the family, the joy and fulfilment of that time began with the purchase of our house on Clairmont Avenue. At the beginning we continued living on High Point Terrace. The commute to church was only about 3 miles further than to Sixty Sixth Street and the girls were able to continue at their respective schools without interruption. Consequently, we were able to look for a place to live in the Avondale area with few time constraints. Mrs. Dean, a member of the search committee and a realtor, helped us begin our search for a house to buy as we waited for a buyer for our house on High Point. One day, shortly after beginning our Avondale ministry, as we drove down Clairmont Avenue we saw a For Sale sign in the yard of a split-level with white columns across the front, a double-door entry and a carport on the side.

What a beautiful house! After we drooled over it for a few days Mrs. Dean made an appointment for us to see the house. It was all we could have wanted and then some; a dining/living room combination, a large den, three bedrooms two baths upstairs, a large playroom/bedroom and bath downstairs, a patio off the den and a mountain for a private back yard. How gorgeous, but of course, it was too expensive for us, so we continued looking. Nothing we saw seemed quite right, but since our house on High Point had not sold, we were not sure exactly how much we could afford. Then Sixty Sixth Street called a pastor from out of state who needed a house immediately. They liked our High Point house and offered almost our asking price which we accepted.

The house on Clairmont was still for sale. Mrs. Dean assured us that given the location it was a good buy at the price she thought the owners would take. Barbara loved that house, but she didn't see how we could possibly afford monthly payments of almost $100 more than we were now paying. The salary package South Avondale offered was a nice increase over what we had been making and I was convinced we could manage the payments. At last Barbara agreed, the papers were signed and in October we moved into what would always be our true dream house.

From that moment forward our house became the gathering place for Christmas with Barbara's family. Her mom and dad came from Nicholasville and her sister, Sue Earl, and her family came from Nashville. There were sleeping accommodations for everyone, and each Christmas offered a delightful few days together. Following Christmas of '82, Barbara's parents, "Poss" and Eva couldn't leave when they had planned because of a big snow. That was the year Barbara and I had planned to take a group, mostly South Avondale members, to Israel with our plane scheduled to depart on Dec. 28th. Nothing else to do but catch our flight, ask "Poss" and Eva to "lock up" when the roads were safe for travel and "We'll see them in Kentucky come summer."

That house also became the focal point for some wonderful fellowship times with church groups. Shortly after we moved, we bought a big cast iron gas grill for the patio, which deacon Charles Turner, a gas company employee, installed for us. The single adult group, the apartment ministry group (mostly the same people) and several others always enjoyed coming over for a cookout. At Christmas time, we enjoyed decorating and on our first Christmas, with the help of some gracious church ladies, we had an open house for the entire church family, which we occasionally repeated. Also, every year the church staff and their spouses were invited for a festive time and Barbara's, always scrumptious, meals.

Barbara remembers these 8 years as the happiest days of our life, I think primarily, because this was the time our girls all grew into young women. Beth, always loving her privacy, immediately laid claim to the downstairs bedroom. There she carefully organized her room and clothes closet, keeping a two-week schedule of her daily attire. Though we moved during the school year the girls were able to complete the year at their respective schools uninterrupted. Since Beth was a rising senior she was allowed to complete her high school education at Huffman the following year, commuting in the car she had inherited from her aunt Nelda Heathman at her death in '76. Following high school graduation, Beth immediately enrolled in Samford University, an act made possible by her good grades, a generous tuition discount given by the school to children of Alabama Baptist ministers and her willingness to commute from home to class each day. By attending school each summer, she earned her bachelor's degree in accounting three years later. It was with button popping pride Beth's dad accepted President Leslie Wright's invitation to offer a prayer at Samford's 1982 summer graduation exercise.

Why such a hurry to graduate from college? A handsome young man was waiting at the South Avondale altar to take her hand and usher her into "a life of unending bliss." However, before that could happen her mother said she had to finish college. That young lady, without a lazy bone in her body, helped support herself with a part time job at B Dalton Book store in Century Plaza Mall while going to college full time year around. She got a smaller car when her Aunt Nelda's big gas-guzzler became too expensive to maintain. Though that ugly burnt orange color was an eye sore sitting in our driveway, the little Datsun accomplished its purpose.

On September 4th, 1982, the soft sunlight filtered through South Avondale's stained-glass windows revealing a sanctuary aglow with flowers and greenery. The ladies of the church made sure the fellowship hall was at its festive best for the reception. Now it was time for dad, with a joyful smile on his face, but a tear in the eye of his heart, to walk the beautiful bride down the aisle, past her equally beautiful mother to meet her waiting groom.

Instead of being seated with the bride's mother dad then took the place of the minister at the altar. Following a brief wedding homily, I led them in the exchange of vows and the final, "I now pronounce you husband and wife, in the name of the Father, Son and Holy Spirit." Mark kissed his bride, helped her light a unity candle and escorted her up the aisle. The wedding party departed and lastly dad, dressed in his doctoral gown and festive hood, stopped at mom's pew. With her hand in his arm they proudly exited the sanctuary, grateful that this blessed chapter in their life was closing with the promise of God's continued blessing on the newly formed family.

The transition journey from childhood to adulthood for middle daughter Amy was far from smooth but it was ultimately successful. For starters, our move to Clairmont placed us out of the Huffman school district and though Amy was able to complete her freshman year at Huffman she was required to change schools the following year. Though we were zoned for Woodlawn, she had the option of attending Ramsey, an alternative school which was open to students from any school zone in the city. However, the school was required to maintain at least a 60/40 racial balance. Because of its academic superiority to other schools in predominantly black neighborhoods, the competition among black students for admission to Ramsey was strong on the 60% side of the equation. This was most obvious on senior awards night in light of the large number of prestigious scholarships won by black students. Though the competition among white students, to fill the 40% side of the racial equation, was not as great, with Amy's good academic record she easily won admission. She made good academic progress and was tapped for National Junior Honor Society before graduation.

What was most attractive and gratifying about Ramsey for Amy though was its athletic program. She quickly made both the varsity volleyball and basketball teams and played all three years. Her volleyball team made the state tournament her last two years but ultimately lost out to the perennial powers, Bradshaw of Florence and Mc Gill-Toolen of Mobile. Barbara and I enjoyed traveling to watch her play and were thrilled when she was voted most valuable player in the 9th regional volleyball tournament.

She was the captain of her basketball team her senior year though she was the only Anglo on the team. When she came home with the news that she was the captain I asked, "How were you chosen, by the coach or the team?"

"The team voted by writing the name of the person they wanted to be captain on a piece of paper, and I got all the votes."

"You mean you voted for yourself."

"Sure, I wanted to be the captain."

I shouldn't have been surprised Amy was well liked by her teammates. She had a big heart and not a prejudiced bone in her body. If one of the girls didn't have money for snacks after practice Amy gladly shared what little money she had. When I attended Amy's games there was little doubt which parent in the stands belonged with the white girl on the floor. That year she made honorable mention for all-city basketball team. She also played that year in the Alabama Girls High School Golf Tournament, held in Montgomery, her very first golf tournament. Not a high finish, but a good beginning.

Transportation to Ramsey that first year was provided by mom or dad, but when Amy turned 16 and got her license she wanted her own "wheels." By now Beth had her Datsun and dad reluctantly offered the Mustang, but she had to be very, very careful. It was a treasured possession, which with the help of my friend Sherrill Maples, I would eventually restore to as near mint condition as we could make it. All went well until one morning during her senior year. About 30 minutes after she and Alisa had left for Ramsey they returned to the house with a startling announcement, "Daddy, we've had a little accident."

I find it hard to believe, but to this day both the girls and their mother vow that my first response was "How bad is the Mustang hurt?" As it turned out the damage to the Mustang was minimal and easily repaired. Oh, the girls were alright too, which was obvious at first glance.

Shortly after basketball season when she had a little spare time Amy got a part time job at KFC at Eastwood Mall. She worked hard, saved her money and before long had money to buy her first car, an old nearly worn-out Buick.

The last few months prior to and following Amy's high school graduation Barbara and I made a number of suggestions for colleges we could visit. There was Samford where Beth was going. "Not interested!" How about Montevallo? "Not Interested!" What about UAB? "Not interested!" Only one school was ever considered by Amy, The University of Alabama. "Roll Tide Roll!" We helped her move in, paid her tuition for the next four years, and she took it from there. She was independent, self-reliant and determined to succeed, which she ultimately did with flying colors.

Unfortunately, our move to Clairmont was most difficult for Alisa. During her four years at Wright Elementary, by the school's design, she was able to progress at her own pace, which was somewhat faster than the typical fourth grade student. When she enrolled in the fifth grade at Comer elementary school, only ½ mile from our house, she was assigned to an already-in-progress class. Her older teacher insisted that all class members study the same material together and move forward at the same pace. Naturally, repeating material she already knew was extremely boring to Alisa. We scheduled a conference with the teacher and asked her to consider giving Alisa some more challenging material, but to no avail. She knew how she wanted to conduct her class and there was no changing her mind. Alisa's parents considered that a nearly wasted year, at least from an academic perspective. She completed her 6th grade at Comer before moving to Holman Jr. High on the north side of Crestwood Boulevard for her 7th grade.

In the spring of 1980 Alisa won Holman's spelling bee and went on to win her district which included 7 other schools. Orrie Irwin, an Avondale deacon, upon hearing of her accomplishment rewarded her and her dad with an afternoon fishing trip to his place on Logan Martin Lake. Though our hooks were avoided by every fish in the lake, the gesture was appreciated.

Alisa found Holman to be a much more enjoyable experience than Comer, but still her full capabilities were not challenged. In a conference with one of her teachers at the end of her 7th grade year the teacher mentioned the possibility of skipping the 8th grade and moving on to her freshman year in High School. With an Oct. 5 birthday, she was one of the oldest kids in her class; plus feeling she had wasted her 5th grade year and being confident of her academic ability, mom and dad readily agreed to the advancement.

While she made the academic leap successfully it was, considering everything, a greater challenge than we recognized at the time. For one thing, Ramsey's academic standards were among the highest in the city which ultimately led to Alisa's straight "A" record taking a mild, but disappointing hit. Without a doubt, in some measure, this contributed to her unhappiness during her freshman year. Beyond that, the social challenges she faced in going from being one of the oldest in her class to being one of the youngest, may have been more difficult than the academic ones. Unlike Amy, now a senior, she did not seem to find a comfortable niche and the year concluded with her having found few, if any, real friends.

With Amy no longer at Ramsey, Alisa wanted to transfer to Woodlawn, the school for which she was zoned, and where she had some friends from both church and Holman Jr. High. While her academics may have suffered from the lower standards at Woodlawn, at least her social life flourished. She was selected as a cheerleader her first year. Being one of the more popular girls at school, she was runner up in the school beauty pageant her junior year.

Her days at Woodlawn, however, were not without some anxious moments for her parents. There was the day when it was her turn to drive the treasured Mustang to school. With strict instructions to go straight to school and straight home, she was unable to resist the temptation to give a nearby classmate a ride to school. As she took this "slight" detour from her "straight" route, who should she meet for an ever-so-slight fender-bender but her dear 5th grade teacher.

While the fender-bender was not her fault it did occur on a forbidden detour. Moral: while our "sins" do not always find us out so immediately, for Alisa, her day of reckoning was immediate.

Then there was the Sunday night following church Barbara and I hung out with some friends for a few minutes after church. Alisa, as usual, went out with some of the youth group. After a tiring Sunday Barbara and I kept our socializing short, headed home and went to bed early. Around 11:00 Barbara awakened me with word that Alisa wasn't home yet. I joined her in the living room where we anxiously watched every approaching headlight to see if the car would stop in front of our house to let Alisa out. When the midnight hour arrived and no Alisa, panic began to set in. As we debated which to call first, the police station, or one of the hospital emergency rooms, a familiar voice from the top of the split-level steps asked, "What are you all doing sitting in the living room this time of night?" The youth group had decided not to go out that night, and Alisa, arriving home ahead of us, had gone to her bedroom. Instead of getting in her bed she decided to lie down on the floor between her bed and the wall, where she went to sleep. Not hearing Alisa come in, her mother got up, looked in her room, and seeing an empty bed concluded the obvious. But with Alisa the obvious was not always accurate.

Never lacking for friends, Alisa accepted the invitation of a few friends on a fall Saturday to go with them to an Auburn football game. During the game, while hanging out with some other friends, she became separated from the friends with whom she rode to Auburn. Following the game, assuming Alisa had a way home, the car in which she had gone to Auburn came back to Birmingham without her. When we called the driver of the car she left in, we were told she hadn't come home with them. She must have found another ride home. Not knowing where she was or who she was with, we could do nothing but wait for her call. When the call finally came she assured us, "all was well." A friend, who was now an Auburn student, had graciously agreed to let Alisa, and maybe a few others, spend the night in his trailer.

"No indeed-eeee" I responded firmly, "Stay right where you are, and I will pick you up as quickly as I can get to Auburn." Barbara and I arrived in Auburn around midnight and called the number she had given us for specific directions as to where she could be found. Needless to say, the trip back to Birmingham was one of great relief, though not all together pleasant. I have no idea what the subject of that Sunday's sermon was. What I know is, that if some Sunday your pastor seems a little below par, it could be for any one of a hundred good reasons. The real one, you would probably never guess.

During Alisa's high school years, her gift for singing began to emerge, thanks to the attention given her by Lester Barker. Lester joined the South Avondale staff as Minister of Music and Ministries in the twilight of his career, having served in his early days several large churches, including Dawson Memorial and First Baptist, Mobile. He not only asked her to join the choir, but also, gave her some individual lessons. Occasionally, she was asked to sing the solo part in a choral piece. She entered Samford with music as her first semester major, but soon discovered she had neither the interest, nor, in her mind, the talent, to pursue music as a primary course of study.

After "majoring" in "Zeta" (ZTA sorority) for a couple of years, academic pursuits became more of a priority. Though she worked part-time in several retail establishments during the last two years of college, she finished with good grades and a degree in elementary education. It was during this time she met a young man from Atlanta, Ga., Jack (Johnny) Walker, who would become the love of her life. This father of her four children would have a multifaceted career, chasing bad guys, discipling youth, serving churches, and ultimately, developing his own business as a values-based executive coach/trainer.

The South Avondale time was one of transition and maturation for me as well. My conscious efforts to expand my theological knowledge for the first few years following seminary graduation had been sporadic at best. There were exceptions of course, like the Vineyard Conference on lay ministry renewal at Southern Seminary and a few matters that had practical application to my ministry. The pursuit of another degree, however, turned what had been a haphazard endeavor into a regular discipline, and brought a major expansion to my reading horizon.

The 4-week long seminar periods on the seminary campus for each of the three years of study proved extremely valuable. The seminars usually involved twelve or so students, all colleagues in ministry, and were guided by two professors who served as discussion facilitators. It was my first educational experience in which professors treated seminar participants as true colleagues in ministry. In one particular seminar, students were asked to prepare and present a paper about one of their ministry actions (i.e. sermon, administrative decision, counseling session, etc.) which included a theological rationale for the action. As a paper was discussed, the presenter was asked to consider inconsistencies in reasoning, unexamined motives, and often unresolved personal issues that may have been revealed or suggested. Most, if not all, of us had unrecognized or unacknowledged "hang ups" that were having a negative impact on our ministry.

One middle aged student from the Chicago area seemed to "have it all together" more so than the rest of us. He was also particularly adept at identifying underlying core issues with which his fellow classmates struggled. One day he was asked how he had developed such a keen sensitivity to these matters. "I see my shrink and unpack my emotional baggage at least once every year, whether I need it or not," was his response. Years earlier he had befriended a psychiatrist who offered to see him once a year for an annual emotional checkup. He took him up on the offer and, while some years there was more baggage than others, he reported the visit was always a profitable one. People in helping professions seem always to need helpers, especially those who think they don't.

Though I did not get my own "shrink" I did get help form a small support group in Birmingham. I teamed up with a fellow pastor who, after being hospitalized with clinical depression, wanted to address his small emotional issues before they became big ones. At his suggestion, we called ours a Yokefellow group, because it was patterned along guidelines suggested by the great Quaker theologian Elton Trueblood. The group was rather fluid over the years, never larger than five or six people at any one time. Though it was composed mostly of Baptist ministers, a Catholic priest who was a VA chaplain was a valued member of the group for a couple of years. From that time forward I was seldom without a small support group, which I used to help me debrief my emotional responses to what may be happening in my life at the time. While the groups varied in structure and intimacy, they were an invaluable independent source for feedback and support. At their best, they helped me challenge my unrealistic expectation of myself and others, as well as a few of my unwitting hypocrisies, some small, some not so small.

One Monday morning in our Yokefellow group one member ask, "Buddy, why so glum today?"

"I don't know, just Monday I guess."

"Not an acceptable answer."

After some prodding, "Well, I came home from church last night and just lay down on the den floor. After a few minutes Barbara asked why I was lying on the floor and I said, because it's as low as I can get. If I could get any lower I would."

"What happened yesterday to bring on this pity party?" one group member asked.

"Attendance was down, offering was down, can't get anybody to do anything?"

"Ah, people won't do what you want 'em to. No wonder you are feeling down. I've heard trying to be God is tough, even for preachers."

A hearty laugh, a few additional friendly verbal jabs, another's confession and we all left a little (in my case a lot) healthier spiritually, than when we arrived.

Sometimes the small group was a reading group with a provocative book as the starting place for introspective discussion. At other times, it was a fellowship group that simply enjoyed each other's company and provided encouragement and support. Sadly, a number of really quite gifted fellow ministers seemed threatened by personal transparency and openness and avoided such groups like the plague.

This was also a time for opening my eyes to the world through some international travel. In 1980 I escorted a group of church members to the Baptist World Alliance meeting in Toronto, Canada. Over the Christmas/New Year holiday '81-'82 I was accompanied by 7 other SABC members on a tour of the Holy Land and Egypt led by Dr. Jerry Vardman, a renowned biblical archeologist. The group included two seminary professors, Dr. Dale Moody and Dr. Jack McGorman, along with popular musician and

Samford Music School dean, Dr. Claude Rhea. In addition to the traditional biblical sites, we trekked through a small Egyptian village, well off the beaten path, to a long-abandoned archaeological site in the land of Goshen where Vardaman thought the supply cities of Exodus 1:11 were located. We visited a kibbutz in northern Israel near the Golan Heights. The whole experience was so stimulating I could not wait to take Barbara along with other church members on a similar tour as soon as possible. That turned out to be 2 years later in '83-'84. This group included Alisa, and we visited Greece instead of Egypt. On this trip an old Arab in the Old City of Jerusalem offered me 20 camels for my beautiful blond-haired Alias. After pondering the offer for several minutes, I turned him down. Barbara and I would make one more trip the next year again with some church members.

Vardaman who spoke fluent Arabic and knew many of the local Israelis and Arabs was the primary organizer and accompanied us on each trip. With his guidance, I bought 3 biblical period lamps. I also bought Barbara an emerald ring in a jewelry store owned by an old gentleman Jerry knew. That night we were invited to an amazing visit in his apartment above the store. He was one of the first people to recognize the value of the Dead Sea Scrolls and was an early owner of several of the scrolls. He opened a small wall safe from which he withdrew, carefully unwrapped and allowed us to view a well-protected fragment he had managed to keep from the government when they took possession of the scrolls.

Congregational Life

My work as pastor of the South Avondale congregation was guided by three foundational objectives. The first of these was to serve as "shepherd of the flock." I sought to faithfully minister to the spiritual needs of the people through preaching and pastoral care. The second objective was to lead the church members to minister to one another and to the surrounding community in the name of Christ. The third was to use the results of the consultation to develop a creative agenda that would reverse the attendance trend of the previous 15 years. Hopefully, the work on my doctoral program would enhance my skills in meeting all three of these objectives.

As was evident from my previously mentioned conversations with the church's Search Committee and Deacons, many of the church leaders and members were deeply committed to their Lord and open to at least some change before I arrived. In the ensuing years, God would bring others with similar values our way. They staffed our ministry teams, taught in our Bible study classes, cared for our children, sang in our choir and made newcomers feel welcomed and loved.

Interviews with church leaders were conducted as a part of our initial consultation. In response to our changing community, Margaret Bragdon, an older highly respected teacher of our largest ladies' Sunday School class, essentially said, "God is bringing people into our community we would never have sought. He must want us to minister and witness to them. If our church dies in the process let us die doing His will." She would become a champion of many of our pioneering efforts. They included ministering to black and white residents of a mental-health halfway house in our community, opening our doors to the first Narcotics Anonymous group in the Birmingham area and ordaining two women to the Gospel Ministry to serve as hospital chaplains.

In the fall of 1978 the church participated in a Lay Renewal Weekend lead by a team of laypeople, mostly from the Atlanta area. It fanned smoldering embers into a warm spiritual blaze. Over the next few years a number of members would become participants and leaders for weekends in other churches in Alabama and adjoining states. It also provided a spark for future mission trips to places as far away as Wyoming. Giving to mission causes both locally and abroad also increased substantially.

A competent and compatible staff was an essential component to achieving the church's renewal objectives. Though small in size, the church staff consisted of some exceptionally gifted and committed Christian servants God graciously led our way. In spite of the changing neighborhood and a higher-than-normal rate of attrition due to our aging membership, church attendance remained steady, and offerings increased significantly. Much credit for this was due to our staff. Perhaps the most noteworthy staff member, LaVelle Wright, was present when I arrived. During my tenure her title and primarily responsibility was Church Secretary, but she performed many other tasks with excellence. She was my Ministry Assistant, the church Printer, College and Career Sunday School Teacher, and Minister of Education (when that position was vacant) and an all-around "Girl Friday." In reality, she was the glue that held everything together. She knew where all the skeletons that dare not be disturbed were buried. Her faith and seemingly boundless energy could overcome almost any obstacle. She also recruited for her Sunday School class a number of Samford students who wanted to do ministry. One year at least 10 Missionary Kids were attending our Sunday School and worship services, due in large measure to her influence. In addition to seeing that I kept all my appointments, she typed my ministry dissertation to perfection before there was a computer with spell check.

Youth ministers like Nick Foster, Debbie Heard, and Ken Jacks gave our small youth group quality leadership. Our music ministry reached new heights under the part-time leadership of Samford professor Dr. Irwin Ray, who in spite of some personal flaws, enabled our choir to attain achievements beyond their wildest dreams. Robbie Head, though serving only in a part-time capacity, brought competent leadership, stability and a winsome personality to our music ministry. He would move on to a full-time music ministry position in a Montgomery church. Following Robbie's departure in '83, we placed our music and ministry programs under one umbrella and called Lester Barker to the full-time staff position of Minister of Music and Ministries. Lester, with his talent and experience as Music Minister in some of the state's largest churches, brought an exceptional level of devotion to our ministries' effort. He was a musician, teacher, leader, minister and gentleman in the fullest sense of all those terms.

Responding to a recommendation from that initial church consultation, in June of '78, the church called Phil Martin[2] to become its first full time Minister of Education. His presence along with that of Dr. Ray, who had come 6 weeks earlier, and the multi-gifted LaVelle made this staff perhaps the most talented and creative with which I served. In addition to recruiting and training lay leaders throughout the church, Phil brought an interest in and wonderful creativity to all aspects of church life. This staff team enhanced and expanded both the Advent and Lenten seasons in the church's ministry. An annual Advent brochure, highlighting the church's Advent activities and featuring suggestions for family worship times, was developed and mailed to every household in the Avondale and Forest Park communities. The brochure was a hit especially with non-Baptist families. After the first couple of years the church began receiving calls asking if they could expect another Advent mailing. Before long we were also able to budget for a community wide Easter brochure. By the early 1980s the Christmas Eve and Maundy Thursday services were our most popular services for church guests from the community.

Phil and his wife Gloria also had a keen interest in marriage enrichment. Together they spear- headed the development of a program we called MJIM (More Joy In Marriage). "Making good marriages better" was the program's advertised intent, though it may have helped some "troubled marriages" as well. Five to eight couples met in a home for a program and/or activity, often led by someone with marriage counseling training, which was followed by a light dessert. Six to eight sessions were planned for the spring and fall of each year. The program continued after Phil and Gloria moved on to Chamblee, Ga. One indicator of the program's effectiveness was a request I received, even after I had moved to Montgomery, from a couple living in Dothan asking for help in organizing a MJIM program in their new setting.

The major writing requirement of the Doctor of Ministry Degree was a detailed description of the planning, implementation and evaluation of a ministry project in my ministry setting. Giving a theological and sociological rationale along with involving members of the congregation and residents in the community were also essential elements of the project.[3] This project fit neatly into the church's commitment to minister to its surrounding community. Eight to ten church members, mostly single young adults who were apartment residents, gladly agreed to formed a core group for the purpose of reaching out to other apartment residents. When asked, "How should we begin?" their response was, "A Bible Study." I threw "cold water" on the idea as being too "churchy." Also, we had tried that a couple of years earlier with zero success. So, I surveyed a number of apartment managers asking, "What are some of the unmet needs of your residents' that we might somehow address."

Tommy managed a small complex of perhaps 30-40 apartments, one of which was his residence. As I explained to him our interest in providing a ministry simply to help hurting people, a young lady I had barely noticed, who was cleaning his kitchen to help pay her rent, paused from her work and asked, "Are you serious?"

"Yes, I am! We think Jesus wants us to help people in his name, no strings attached," I replied.

She looked me straight in the eye, raised her hand like a child in school and said, "HELP!".

I would soon discover Gilda had a basket full of needs. She was a single mom whose son had chronic asthma requiring expensive medication and frequent trips to Children's Hospital. She had left her husband, two children and a good job as a medical technician in California to follow another man to Alabama. When she refused to abort the product of their relationship, her erstwhile lover abandoned her and the baby. At the moment, a friend was helping her care for her child while she worked some nights as a bartender.

The Apartment Ministry group and numerous other church members upon learning of Gilda's needs offered helping hands. Medical bills, a good job, and nonjudgmental friendship were a few of her needs those Christian young adults set about to help address. Her once dormant faith began blossoming again, or maybe bloomed for the first time, and she reaffirmed her commitment to Christ. As her son's condition deteriorated, an asthmatic specialist at a hospital in Denver agreed to accept him as a patient. At her request, I baptized her at a Sunday evening service, before she and her son boarded a flight for Denver, with tickets provided by SABC members. Within in a few weeks she wrote back, sharing how her story of what God had done for her, in her moment of near despair, was bringing encouragement to other mothers she was meeting in her Denver hospital.

In spite of my misguided reservations, the apartment ministry group eventually concentrated their energies on a bi-weekly Bible study hosted in a different apartment each time, to which they would invite neighbors and friends. To my amazement, the Bible study often overflowed the hosting apartment and became an entry (or re-entry) point into church life for several young adults. Though their stories were not as dramatic as Gilda's their needs for a vital faith in a loving God and Christian fellowship were real and being met.

The day I arrived, I considered the church's community ministries programs its most attractive and valuable assets. The homebound ministry directed by the Olene and Hassett Lester was one of the most active ministry teams. With more than a dozen volunteers they ministered weekly to as many as three dozen homebound senior adults. They made phone calls, home visits, and took Sunday School books and worship service tapes to members on their ministry roll which included many nonchurch members. The triple L club ministered to active senior adults. The hospital ministry team provided visits and prayers for Birmingham hospital patients from out of town without a local church contact.

The various ministries were continually being strengthened and updated as needs and the giftedness of members could be matched. Annually, January was designated as Community Ministry month. Sermons and lay testimonies focused on Christian service. Special guests noted for Christian ministry performance were invited to preach. The guest list included seminary professor, Dr. Larry McSwain, nationally known church renewal leader and author Dr. Finley Edge, Kent School of Social Work Dean, Dr. Ann Davis, and Helen Fling, SBC 's WMU national president. Short presentations by various members of the congregation highlighted specific ministry needs. At the close of the worship service on the last Sunday of the month, Ministry Team Captains standing at the front of the church invited others to join them in a specific ministry. Before the benediction most active church members had "signed up" for a "beyond the walls" ministry for the coming year.

It was not unusual for someone to drop by the church office and say, "I understand this is a church that helps people. Could you help me and my family?" Before my tenure ended, on more than one occasion a large "Over-the-Mountain" sister Baptist church sent us an unsolicited substantial check to "help people."

A lot of energy and creativity in the church came from college age youth. Some, like present day college professor, Dr. Clell Wright Jr., grew up in the church. A talented musician, he devoted himself to church music. Numerous UAB and Samford students who came our way, some having grown up on the mission field, were attracted by opportunities to serve others. Students helped with after-school tutorial programs for community children and with special summer children's programs. They also came for fellowship and worship experiences with other like-minded students. Some have since devoted their lives to vocations of Christian service, while others are faithfully serving their Lord in secular vocations. Elizabeth Futral, a nationally acclaimed New York Metropolitan Opera star, sang in our choir for a time while she was a Samford student. Tony and Katrina Brooks finished seminary, were ordained, and are serving as co-pastors of a Virginia church. One couple is serving as missionaries in a predominantly Muslim country in Southeast Asia. Norfleete Day began feeling God's call to a mid-life career change which led from municipal library management to theology education and ultimately a professorship at Beeson Divinity School [4].

Generational differences existed in the congregation but they seldom, if ever, emerged as sources of conflict. Fortunately, the church had a history of respecting its leaders so when I saw an issue coming that might be controversial I made a practice of discussing it first with some key leaders. Sometimes it took more than one discussion, but I knew if the issue could be resolved among those leaders that resolution would filter down to the rest of the church. That the church was small enough for most members to know and respect one another was an important factor in the church's unity. A core of deeply committed young professionals and their families were also helpful in keeping the church on a progressive trajectory. In their number were physicians, attorneys, elementary and secondary school teachers, a public librarian, and hospital chaplains, to name a few.

From the beginning, my understanding with the deacons and church leaders was that the church would be open to all races. When a halfway house for the mentally handicapped was built in the neighborhood, the Church extended a loving hand of ministry and a warm welcome to the residents. Up to six residents, some of whom were black, became regularly attenders. As often happened, God provided by sending Charlotte Stewart [4], a gifted, compassionate and highly trained special education teacher, who started and taught a Sunday school class for the mentally challendged.

In the early 80s with little fanfare, the church became one of the few Southern Baptist churches in the state to ordain women to the ministry. Barbara Kimbrel and Karen Long had joined the church at different times. They were from different backgrounds and had experienced God's call to ministry in different ways, yet, in God's gracious economy they wound up at South Avondale at the same time sensing God's call to be a hospital chaplain. Though they received their seminary training from different institutions, they were, at the time, serving their chaplaincy internship at Montclair Baptist Hospital. Because many, if not all, hospitals required ordination as a prerequisite to employment as a fulltime chaplain, both women needed and desired ordination to be fully certified. I discussed the matter with some key leaders and then with the whole deacon body. I called attention to the scripture's lack of specific instruction in the matter and asked that the discussion not focus so much on the ordination of women but rather the ordination of Barbara and Karen. Several church members had been beneficiaries of their ministry and spoke of their compassion and effectiveness. When the time came for a formal request and action by the church, the decision to ordain Barbara and Karen was unanimous. Serving a thoughtful congregation unwilling to be bound by tradition was a blessing and a joy.

The support I received from that church and its leaders as their pastor was phenomenal. The deacons never let an anniversary go by without some special recognition and a gift. In May of 1980, the completion of my doctoral studies coincided with my anniversary as pastor. To my total surprise and amazement at a Sunday morning worship service, Dr. Larry McSwain, my major professor, appeared and on behalf of the seminary officially awarded me the Doctor of Ministry degree. He also presented me with the accompanying gown and hood, a gift from the church and its deacons. On my 8th, and what would become my last, anniversary the deacons gave me a beautiful set of golf clubs. Beyond that the individual gifts and expressions of appreciation were too numerous to list.

Finally, some concluding observations as I reflect on the earlier mentioned foundational objectives guiding my work as pastor of the South Avondale Baptist Church. First, though I have given "shepherding the flock" little specific attention it could easily be considered the major focus of my ministry at South Avondale. I loved the people of the church. Youth were counseled, marriages were performed, the sick and aged were visited, funerals were conducted, and the grieving were comforted, many times as I fought back my own tears. Countless hours were invested in preparing biblically based messages, and leading, what I trust was, inspiring worship. Second, the church's "ministry focus" was continued and enhanced to the point where members found fulfillment and joy in serving others in the name of their Lord. Their reputation as a helping congregation was authentic and earned.

Third, though the "attendance trend line" of the previous 15 years was not substantially reversed, by God's grace, the decline was at least halted. In 1977, Sunday School attendance stood at 246. Two young competent staff members were added in '78. Member confidence in the church's future seemed to rise, yet in 1979 average attendance dropped to 225, and that fall leadership positions were filled with great difficulty. Why? Had all the planning and energy expended been for naught? As I discussed the matter with staff and lay leaders we observed there had been an almost audible sigh of relief among members who had been working so hard for several years to keep the church going. They were pleased with their staff and for a change optimistic about their future. They needed and took a breather. Perhaps the new staff members also needed some time to become acclimated to their new situation. After that breather, the addition of a little "new blood," and a renewed sense of God's presence the church began to grow, if ever so slightly, even though the community continued to change. By 1985, average Sunday School attendance had climbed back near the 240 level. This may have reflected even greater strength than the 246 of 8 years earlier, when the trend of worship attendance exceeding that of the Sunday School as a measure of church strength is considered. All was accomplished by the grace of God and the faithfulness of a gallant group of saints.

Entering Denominational Ministry

A doorway for wider denominational ministry[1] opened during my days at South Avondale. I was first elected to the Executive Board of the Alabama Baptist Convention in 1972 as the member from the Lamar Baptist Association[2]. It was a seat I had to relinquish the following year when I moved to Birmingham. However, in January '73 Barbara and I attended the first annual Legislative Prayer Breakfast in Montgomery, an event hosted by the Board for all the elected state officials. The wheelchair-bound Gov. George Wallace, having barely survived an assassination attempt a year earlier, attended and strongly supported the event.

In the fall of 1977 the Alabama Baptist Convention once more elected me to its Executive Board, this time as a member from the Birmingham Baptist Association. Quite unexpectedly, at the '78 Convention meeting I was elected to the Administrative Committee of the Board. Among other responsibilities I served on, and later chaired, the Personnel sub-committee which interviewed and recommended the employment of all ministerial level Board staff. In 1980 I was elected to a second term on the board and again to its Administrative Committee. In '81 Harold Cushing, outgoing executive board chairman, was elected president of the Alabama Baptist State convention. Prior to the Board's organizational meeting following the 1981 Convention, I asked Dr. Dotson Nelson if he would allow me to nominate him for the Board's Chairmanship. He declined on the grounds that he had served as Board Chairman several years earlier. When the Board met he rose to his feet and, to my surprise, nominated me for that responsibility. Following the nomination of another candidate, I was elected by the Board to serve as its Chairman and the following year was reelected without opposition.

In 1982 Dr. George Bagley, the Board's Executive Secretary and the Convention's chief executive officer for the past 18 years, announced his intention to retire in the fall of 1983. It was my responsibility as Chairman of the Board to appoint a search committee to seek Dr. Bagley's replacement. I named Dr. Troy Morrison, a Gadsden pastor, to chair a 13-member committee on which I served as an ex officio member. After numerous meetings throughout 1983 the committee narrowed its list of candidates to three. To keep its work confidential, interviews of those 3 candidates were held at South Avondale. The committee settled on a Mobile pastor as its recommendation. I called a special meeting of the Executive Board in September to act on that recommendation. The Saturday night, before the full Board was to meet on Monday, the committee's candidate called Dr. Morrison and asked that his name be withdrawn from consideration. Morrison immediately called me and after a lengthy phone conversation we scheduled a meeting of the search committee for Monday morning, just prior to the Board's meeting. Before the Monday morning meeting we secured an agreement from Dr. Earl Potts, Dr. Bagley's associate, to serve as Interim Executive Secretary if elected. That suggestion met with the Committee's wholehearted approval and subsequently the Board's unanimous endorsement.

There was a good bit of speculation at the time as to what happened to the committee's candidate? My hunch is that another individual of some prominence wanted the position and had arranged to have his name placed in nomination as an alternative candidate. Though the committee's candidate had strong support and almost certainly would have been elected by a substantial majority of the Board, that approval likely would not have been unanimous. In my opinion, any opposition would have been minor and short lived. As it turned out, the search committee, of which I was now no longer a member, met a couple of additional times before unanimously recommending Dr. Earl Potts as the Board's permanent Executive Secretary. The Board's approval was unanimous, and Dr. Potts served the convention with distinction until his retirement in '92.

Dr. Bagley's retirement became official at the close of the Alabama Baptist Convention meeting in November of 1983, which was held in Montgomery. Appropriately, he was honored with a well-deserved recognition service for his years of service to the convention. The conclusion of that Convention also brought an end to my two terms (six years) of service on the Executive Board and my two years as its chairman. It was also at that Convention meeting I timidly dipped my toe deeper into the waters of convention politics. Since the three previous Executive Board chairmen had subsequently been elected president of the convention, I was asked by a number of friends if I would be a candidate for that position. I had reservations from the beginning, 1st, because I had never thought of myself as a convention president, and 2nd, because I lacked name recognition across the convention. However, when one of the former convention presidents offered to nominate me, with the blessing of my South Avondale deacons, I agreed. I was one of three candidates nominated. The other two candidates, both well-known across the state, were Montgomery layman Dr. Ira Myers, sitting convention Vice-President and long-time state health officer, and Rev. Wallace Henley, McElwain Baptist pastor, former religious editor of The Birmingham News and a former Richard Nixon staff member. Though the vote total was not announced publicly, I understand that of some nearly 1,000 ballots cast the approximate distribution was 29% for me, 34% for Dr. Myers, and 37% for Henley. Henley won the runoff election by a fairly wide margin, though considerably fewer ballots were cast in the run-off election. Apparently, a number of Dr. Myers' votes had come from Montgomery laymen who had come to the initial voting primarily to support him but had not remained for the runoff several hours later.

Understandably, I was disappointed at the outcome of the election, but I learned some things about myself in the process. On the positive side, I discover I had a large number of friends who thought more highly of me and my abilities than I thought of myself. I also learned to place more value on my gut-level instincts, which in this particular case dealt with the probability of my election. This also raises the prospect of a strong negative, that of allowing my ego to override my better judgment. I refused to objectively question why the person who initially offered to nominate me withdrew his offer 3 days before the convention. He had apparently heard voices I did not hear and did not trust me enough to share his best judgement, or perhaps he was fearful of being too closely identified with a "loser".

A major positive from serving as Board chairman was coming to appreciate the excellent work being done by the convention staff and agencies. There was also a growing appreciation for the difficulty of prioritizing resources, though they may be growing annually. Most importantly, I developed a better understanding of budgeting processes, which proved to be very helpful when I had similar responsibilities as executive director of an association of churches.

The conservative vs moderate controversy first surfaced openly in the Southern Baptist Convention in 1979 when an organized and well-funded group strategized and won the presidency of the convention. The ensuing battle at the SBC level continued for about eight years. During that period of time the conservative group won every election for president, always by less than 3%, sometimes less that 1%, of the total votes cast. The same battle also played out in many state conventions. Though it never caused significant disruption in the work of the Alabama convention, it was always a strong undercurrent.

My sympathies were unquestionably with the moderate group. Beginning in 1980, I sought to enlist members of my own church to attend the SBC meetings and vote their convictions, hoping that would lead to a more moderate agenda. I also met a few times with other pastors across the state who shared my convictions, hoping to blunt the impact of the conservative organization. However, when I became chairman of the Executive Board in '81, I thought it inappropriate to continue my partisan efforts. Subsequently, I sought to exercise what influence I may have had toward fostering harmony in the state convention. I made appointments I considered balanced and fair to all concerned. At the 1983 SBC convention in Pittsburgh I enlisted the help of our State Convention president in persuading Dr. Bagley not to have his name placed in nomination for presidency of the SBC. Not only would such a bid against a sitting president have failed, but I thought by forcing

Alabama Baptist pastors to choose sides it would have led to greater divisiveness in our state convention.

Such hope was naïve, for in reality most pastors had already chosen sides. Those on the conservative side were better organized and much more vocal than their opponents. After I had been in Montgomery for several years and had become friends with one of the strong conservative pastors, I was told that my defeat in the '83 State Convention was not directed at me personally. He explained that a well-developed plan was put in place to elect a conservative activist as state convention president that year. The day before the election of the convention president people in several hotel rooms were busy making calls to as many "messengers" as possible encouraging them to vote for Henley, who at that time was not widely known to be a potential candidate. He had been chosen as the conservative candidate because of his highly visible role as the Master of Ceremony for the program honoring Dr. Bagley the night before the election.

In retrospect Henley's election had little, if any, negative impact on the work of the convention. His most notable accomplishment for the conservative cause was the addition of a couple of conservative voices to the Samford Board of Trustees. On the other hand, what limited influence I may have had in the selection of two executive secretaries, Dr. Earl Potts beginning in '84 and his successor, Dr. Troy Morrison in '90, was most gratifying and proved to be quite positive for the convention. During my time on the State Board of Missions both of these men became good friends and respected colleagues. In a conversation with Dr. Potts about the Director of Missions position in the Montgomery Association he said, "I want you to know I haven't completed my staff here at the state office". While I was grateful for the apparent hint of a possible place for me on his staff, God's apparent call to the association was becoming increasingly distinct.

Mission trips became a growing part of my ministry while at South Avondale. I had always encouraged strong financial support for vocational missionaries working under responsible denominational mission boards. I had also called for all Christians to consider God's mission call on their life. When our Alabama convention adopted Wyoming as a state mission partner I began to think seriously about what South Avondale might do in that partnership. I accepted the opportunity to serve as the visiting revival preacher for a church in Casper, Wyoming with travel expenses covered by our church. The following summer, I lead about a dozen SABC members, which included Barbara and Alisa, to work for a week with a church in Cheyenne.

The most profound mission experience for me personally came in September of '83. The Nigerian convention had made a request to the Alabama Convention for an Alabama pastor to help staff their annual week-long Pastors' School in Kaduna, Nigeria. Unfortunately, the request had been overlooked when the initial assignments were made. When the oversight was discovered in early August, Dr. Potts and Harold Cushing, convention president, ask if I, as Executive Board chairman, would represent the state convention and teach the daily Bible study which would be on "Letters to the Seven Churches" (Revelation 2-3). With the enthusiastic endorsement of the South Avondale deacons and church I accepted the opportunity and hastily began preparing full manuscripts of the lectures which I would give to my assigned interpreter in advance of the presentations.

A couple weeks before I was scheduled to leave for Nigeria, I was informed by Dr. Potts that the missionary leaders at the Pastors' School were expecting two preachers from Alabama, one to teach the morning Bible study and another to preach at the evening worship time. Could I possibly do both? Since there seemed to be no other option I agreed to do the best I could. Thus, began the preparation of manuscripts of sermons, some of which I had previously preached. That task proved to be far more difficult than I had imagined, for I soon realized many of my phrases, references and illustrations would be meaningless in the culture I was addressing. Even then, my preparation proved inadequate. Indeed, most afternoons at the conference were spent rewording, rephrasing and refining the next day's presentations.

The pastors' school was a major ministry of the Nigerian Baptist Convention for the northern part of the country. Over 100 full-time students, preparing themselves to pastor churches, were enrolled in the two-year school. Most of the 300 conference attendees were graduates of the school and currently serving as full-time or bi-vocational pastors across northern Nigeria. Many conferees were alumni, who brought their entire family and were staying in small apartments as guests of a current student from their church. The students spoke the Hausa language, though many were not from the Hausa tribe, which dominates Northern Nigeria and is overwhelmingly Muslim. The other major lecturer for the week was a native Nigerian, of the Yoruba tribe, who was a professor at the Baptist Seminary at Ogbomosho. Surprisingly, he spoke English and Yoruba but not Hausa, so he too had to have a translator.

After an overnight flight from Atlanta, and an airline transfer in London's Heathrow airport, my plane landed in mid-afternoon at northern Nigeria's Kano airport. An hour later, after clearing customs, located in the small single-story terminal building, I began looking for my SBC missionary contact from the Kaduna mission station, some 150 miles to the south. The terminal began to clear as my fellow passengers met their contacts or took one of the waiting taxies. I eventually realized no "American-looking" missionary was waiting for me. For some reason he obviously had been delayed. After being pestered by a number of waiting taxi drivers, I finally chose one whose English I could understand and said, "You are my man! I need you to look after my luggage. Should my contact not arrive I will let you take me into Kano to the SIM Guest House. Do you know where it is?" (An orientation booklet had instructed mission volunteers, "In the unlikely event you need to spend the night in Kano ask for the SIM Guesthouse.")

"Oh yes, I know the place," he quickly responded.

As I waited in front of the terminal for my anticipated ride, the dwindling activity inside the terminal told me things might soon be shutting down. The orientation booklet also apprised us of the fact that the use of foreign currency was illegal. Needing to get some US dollars changed into the local Nigeria Naira, I went back inside to find a local bank outlet. To my consternation the bank outlet had closed. Back outside the sun was setting and it was now obvious my missionary contact was not coming. With some trepidation I entered the car of my taxi driver and we headed for Kano. The last half of our hour plus trip was done in darkness. In the distance I could see the lights of a soccer stadium and as we grew closer I could hear the sounds of the crowd. We turned off the main road onto ever narrowing streets and finally stopped at a compound. By the headlights of the car I could see a sign over the entrance, with the letters "ECWA".

Leaning forward and using the most distinct English at my command I said, "I am looking for the S I M Guesthouse." He said, "This is the place." As we drove past several dark and foreboding buildings the place seemed abandoned. Turning around we began retracing our route, then near the entrance a light could be seen shining through the back window of a solitary house. Asking the driver to wait, I walked up to the door and rang the bell. A couple of long minutes passed before a light went on over the door which opened revealing the beautiful smiling face of a petite lady, perhaps in her late 50s. In perfect English she said, "Hello, how can I help you?"

Wow! Seldom have I seen a more beautiful sight or heard a more reassuring sound. My anxiety level immediately was cut in half. She listened attentively as I explained my plight, including my lack of Naira to pay my waiting taxi driver. She quickly retreated back into the house and returned with Naira for the taxi fare, including his tip. This angel with hidden wings, whose name I do not remember, but claimed to be a native of Canada, would have my undying gratitude.

She asked if I'd like to come in for a cup of tea or did I want to get settled in my room. I opted for getting settled. Flashlight in hand she led the way to one of the darkened buildings and I followed with a briefcase and suitcase in tow. She opened a door and turned on the light to a spacious, but sparsely furnished room. There was a bed, a chair, a desk on one end and on the other a sink and toilet. She fetched from under the sink a 5-gallon bucket with a heating element in the bottom. The sink had "running water," but only cold. I could have all the hot water that bucket would hold and heat. Then she explained how the mosquito net above the bed unfolded, which I would certainly want to use. She also assured me that the next morning they would radio the mission station in Kaduna informing them of my presence so they could arrange for a driver to pick me up. While waiting for a driver from the mission station I would have time to exchange some money at a nearby bank and, if I wished, look around town a bit. Breakfast was between seven and eight and I was more than welcome to join all of those in the compound who came to eat.

After climbing into bed and adjusting the mosquito netting, I lay there for several minutes in the darkness, listening to the sound of the crowd at the soccer game, smelling the unique scents of Africa and wondering what tomorrow would bring. A clock from somewhere struck the hour. It was midnight. Remembering there was a six-hour time differential between Kano and Birmingham, I realized it was 6 o'clock on Wednesday night at South Avondale. The fellowship supper was ending, prayer meeting would soon begin, and those dear people would be praying for their pastor. With that thought I thanked God, relaxed, closed my eyes, and slept soundly for the next six hours.

I awoke Thursday morning to a bright clear day with a new set of sounds and odors. I made good use of my 5-gallon bucket of hot water, had a short devotion and walked out into the compound. I observed my room was in a small dormitory, one of four such buildings in the compound. The compound also contained a dining hall, the house where my Canadian missionary angel lived, an administration building and perhaps one or two more buildings. Breakfast that morning consisted of hot biscuits, scrambled eggs and bacon, no grits, and I think, some kind of molasses. I ate with a young man from Iowa who was a protestant agricultural missionary. He offered to help me find whatever I needed that day. Another young gentleman at the table said he had radioed the mission in Kaduna and told them I was there at the guesthouse. Then he added, "I don't think anyone was listening."

I walked to the bank only three or four blocks away and exchanged my money, wandered through two or three shops and went back to the compound to wait for my missionary contact. My new agricultural missionary friend from Iowa suggested we wait until noon, and if no one had come from Kaduna by then, he would take me down to the Tosha (station), find a taxi and help negotiate a fare for my trip to Kaduna.

Sadly, noon came and went but no one from Kaduna arrived. After the noon meal at the compound, my friend drove me to the "Tosha." Leaving me in the car he began talking to taxi drivers milling around the station. Soon he returned saying he had found a taxi to take me to Kaduna. He had negotiated a good price and I asked the driver if he knew the location of the Baptist mission in Kaduna. He assured me he "knew the place." He loaded my bags in the trunk, I got in the backseat, and we departed.

To say it was a harrowing ride is an understatement of gigantic proportions. Convinced every other driver on the road was a threat to his masculinity, and a foe to be defeated, my driver passed every car on the road, except a Mercedes Sedan during that 150-mile trip. Every time we passed the Mercedes that driver, similarly possessed, would pass us back. Down the 2 Lane road we sped, sometimes at 160 km/hour (if you are not good at metric conversion that's about 100 mph). We frequently passed a car using the lane of an oncoming car. The first couple of times I thought we would surely have a wreck, but the oncoming car moved over, the car we were passing moved over, and there was room for everyone. However, the sight every few miles a of wrecked, burned-out vehicle, pushed a few yards off the highway and now rusting away, was a vivid reminder that not everyone who made that trip had arrived at their intended destination. When we passed a car while meeting an oncoming car passing a car and somehow avoided a collision, I concluded God Almighty must surely want me in Kaduna.

Entering the outskirts of Kaduna, we passed what appeared to be a compound of buildings, but if there was a sign over the entrance I did not see it as we sped by. A few miles further down the road we arrived at the center of town and the driver stopped at a stately looking church building. The driver pointed at the building with the sign near the front containing the word Baptist and said, "This is the place."

"No," I responded, "This is a church building, not a compound. I'm looking for a compound with several buildings." It was then that I realized what Nigerians meant by the phrase, "I know the place." It actually meant, "I have some general, vague idea as to where the place might be, but as to its exact location, I don't have a clue." After the driver talked to a few people around the Baptist Church building he concluded the Baptist Mission compound must be somewhere else. In turning around, he got the front end of his taxi stuck in a large pothole. With the help of several men standing nearby and at least 30 minutes of pushing and pulling the taxi was finally freed from the pothole. Back on the road again, and heading out of town, we at last pulled into the entrance of the Baptist Mission compound, which we had passed on the way into town.

Upon being joyfully greeted by a couple of Southern Baptist missionaries I unloaded my luggage, paid my driver and thanked God profusely for my safe arrival. The missionaries were both surprised and greatly relieved to see me. Though they had been promised both a preacher and a teacher from Alabama to help with their conference, they had gotten no word as to who was coming or when they might arrive. They were actually astonished I had arrived by taxi all the way from Kano. The Foreign Mission Board at that time had a policy forbidding mission personnel in Nigeria from using public transportation due to its extreme danger. I was assured a car, driver and accompanying missionary would be provided for my return trip to Kano.

Payton and Helen Myers, natives of Mississippi and career FMB missionaries with over 20 years of service in Kaduna, graciously opened their home to me for the 9 days I was in Kaduna. Friday was a welcomed rest day and Saturday was devoted to some sightseeing around the town and my orientation to Kaduna. Helen, an excellent cook, in spite of her limited opportunity to purchase the necessary ingredients, did her best to satisfy the taste buds of her southern guest. A lot of her time each morning was spent dusting since the air was still permeated with very fine sand particles left over from a recent "harmattan," a dust storm that blew in off the Sahara Desert to the north. Sunday morning Peyton preached at a couple of mission points, relatively close to Kaduna. I, along with a few missionaries, worshiped with a local congregation meeting in the school auditorium. The local Nigerians extended a very cordial and friendly welcome.

Monday morning, I gave my first lecture, and that evening preached my first sermon, speaking one sentence from my manuscript and then waiting for the translator to say essentially the same thing in the Hausa language. The process proved to be quite awkward and took much longer than I had anticipated. The auditorium for both the lectures and messages was filled to capacity. Some students had brought their whole family to the conference and several of the women attended both the lectures and worship services with their husbands. Even though I got good feedback from the missionaries, I was disappointed with my efforts. That afternoon and all subsequent afternoons, with one exception, were spent in my room at the Myers' home rewriting, mostly simplifying and shorting, for the next day's presentations.

The one exception was Wednesday afternoon when I went with Payton into "the bush" to visit a "bush" church and several of its members. The last few miles we traveled along a path few vehicles ever used. Our unannounced arrival at a clearing with a few small huts was an occasion of great joy for everyone in the little village. Word soon spread to those out in the bush and before long a small crowd had gathered to welcome their missionary friend and hear what Payton had to say. One of the women with some small children at her side began preparing to cook a meal. Wood was added to an open fire. In a wooden bowl she started crushing some bean-like pellets into a pulp. Using a couple of pans, the open flame and some hot rocks, our self-appointed hostess spent the remainder of the afternoon, two hours or more, preparing an "exquisite" meal for her guest. Not to have stayed and enjoyed the fruit of her labor of love would have been unthinkable. I managed to get through most of my initial helping. Payton, on the other hand, enjoyed second helpings and commended our hostess' culinary skills. It was easy to see why Payton was admired, even revered by the people of that village. I left the "bush" people that afternoon with a great appreciation for what God was doing through the work of Payton and Helen Myers. I also left looking forward to soothing my weary body with the refreshing shower in the Myers' guest bath and pacifying my queasy stomach with the more familiar delicacies of Helen's table.

The school ended Friday morning and that afternoon a missionary driver took me on a leisure and much more enjoyable drive back to Kano. We were met by the pastor of Kano's First Baptist Church, Amos Omaresamie, an active participant in the partnership. He and I had dinner at a nice restaurant in Kano before going to the airport. Amos helped me negotiate my way through the customs ordeal and helped secure my boarding pass. Since he could go no further, he wished me God's speed and said farewell. There was one final armed guard to whom I had to show my passport and boarding pass. He hummed and hawed, asking me a lot of redundant questions, waiting for me to pass him a little bribe. (The Mission Board's orientation material had warned us, we would be asked for bribes, and strongly suggested we not bribe airport officials). When he realized no bribe was coming, he grudgingly let me pass. I learned later that suggestion was understandably ignored by many mission volunteers.

It was nearing midnight as I walked out the terminal door and onto the tarmac toward the steps leading up to that beautiful KLM Jet. As I took my seat, a smartly dressed smiling hostess handed me a hot washcloth, a small hand towel and a pillow. Taking my que from my fellow passengers, I immersed my face in the warm cloth, leaned back and uttered an audible sigh of relief. I felt as though I was back in civilization again.

We arrived in Amsterdam to a pleasant misty rain and wonderfully cooler temperature. It was there I discovered two of my fellow passengers were northern Nigerian Baptist pastors on their way to Alabama and ultimately to our state convention. Several years later I would learn, to my distress, one of them had been killed in a riot led by Muslim extremists against Christians in his northern Nigeria village. Since we had a several hours layover and my new-found Nigerian friends were not allowed to leave the terminal, I boarded the shuttle alone for downtown Amsterdam to enjoy a short solo tour and a nice European meal. Back on the plane my thoughts turned to South Avondale and the next day's message. Though the congregation may not have recognized it, their pastor had been guided through an amazing adventure on his pilgrimage of faith and would never be quite the same.

Once again, a series of events, none of which I personally initiated, led to a major change of direction in my ministry. Near the end of 1984, Tom Roote resigned as Executive of Director[3] for the Birmingham Baptist Association. Rev. Terry DeFore, the association's moderator, asked me to be one of a five-member search committee to look for a new director, provided I did not have an interest in being a candidate for the position. I assured him I did not and would be happy to serve if he so desired. The orientation to my new task and the search that followed were extremely informative as to the role and purpose of an associational Director of Missions. Halfway through our search, committee chairman, Richard Trader, asked that I consider resigning from the committee, because several members of the committee wanted to consider me for the position. I assured him I had no interest in the position and would rather remain on the committee until our work was completed. Discussing the various tasks of the Director of Missions, the needs of the Birmingham Association, and interviewing prospective candidates combined to make this a most important learning experience. In May we successfully completed our task by calling Dr. Earl Tew to be Birmingham Baptist Association's Executive Director.

In an early committee brain storming session, I had suggested Bob Franklin, Director of Missions for the Montgomery Baptist Association, be considered for our position. Two days later we learned he had just resigned to except a similar position with the Noonday Association in Marietta, Georgia. About the time our work was ending the Montgomery Association's DOM Search Committee requested I meet with them. I supposed their purpose was to discuss insights our committee had gained in our search. The meeting was scheduled for late May or early June at a restaurant near the Oxmoor exit of Highway I 65. A week or so following that meeting the Montgomery Association's Search Committee chairman, Don Williams, informed me that the committee thought I was "their man" and wanted me to seriously consider their position. He also asked for a meeting to discuss the details of their position. More as a courtesy than genuine intertest, I met with Don and his pastor Gary Burton in the courtyard of the BJCC complex. The meeting ended with my commitment to give the matter some serious thought and prayer.

Reluctant to leave the pastorate and never having desired a denominational position, I sought the council of some trusted friends. I scheduled an appointment with Dr. Dotson Nelson, Mountain Brook Baptist pastor and field supervisor for my doctoral work. He assured me I had the experience, gifts and temperament to make a good Director of Missions. Dr. Earl Potts, State Executive Director, shared similar words of encouragement. Montgomery First Baptist Church pastor, Dr. Dale Huff, a member of the search committee who had not been able to attend my earlier meeting with the committee, asked to meet with Barbara and me at Shocco Springs. He encouraged me to accept the committee's invitation and assured me of his full support.

Around the middle of July in a church near Russellville, Alabama, I conducted a Sunday School Revival for Pastor Bob Hines, who felt God's call to the ministry while I was his pastor at 66th Street. I was having some "minor" voice problems even before leaving for that series of services. By the time the meeting was over I could not speak above a whisper. Upon returning home a throat specialist diagnosed my problem as a "granuloma" on my vocal chords, a condition, he reported, occurs most frequently with singers and public speakers. The best treatment was voice rest and surgery. He went on to say that even with surgery the condition often reoccurred.

I was referred to Dr. Morton Goldfarb, another ENT specialist, for further evaluation. In early August, Goldfarb performed laser surgery on my larynx and removed a suspicious lump from my neck, which thankfully, was only some "hot" thyroid. Recovery from the surgery required two weeks of complete voice rest, and two more weeks before returning to the pulpit. I explained my health situation to Montgomery's Don Williams and suggested they continue their search in another direction. Don's response was, "We'd rather wait until you have a clearer assessment of your future. Take all the time you need for a full recovery."

South Avondale, as usual, was fully supportive. The deacons' assured me they would see to filling the pulpit for the coming month and suggested some R&R at the Gulf might be helpful. Barbara and I spent a few days at the beach and some time in Kentucky. Needless to say, that month was a period of deep soul-searching. For the first time, I was forced to consider the possibility of not being able to preach until retirement. While the role of Director of Missions required some preaching, it was not the weekly demand of being a pastor.

While we were in Kentucky, Don Williams managed to find the phone number of Barbara's parents, where we were staying, and called to check on my health. Barbara found this to be most impressive. By the end of August, I had concluded, with Barbara's blessing, God must be calling me to redirect my ministry and become the Director of Missions of the Montgomery Baptist Association. In my resignation letter to South Avondale I spoke of the personal pain of leaving that church, but I said, "I cannot ever again in good faith asked you to follow where God leads, if I do not follow my best understanding of His call on my life now." That thought was also the theme of my concluding sermon at South Avondale, a sermon based on Hebrews 11 and which I entitled "The Pilgrimage of Faith.

Churches Fulfilling Their Mission Locally

Settling into a House

In mid-September of 1985 I was employed as the Director of Missions (DOM) of the Montgomery Baptist Association[1] at a called meeting of the Association's Executive Board[2] held at First Baptist Church, Montgomery. The meeting, less than 30 minutes in length, was followed by a gracious reception with warm words of welcome and support from Board members, many of whom I already knew, especially the pastors.

Our move to Montgomery was both exciting and traumatic. The starting date of my employment was set at November 1, giving us six weeks to conclude our ministry at South Avondale and make the necessary relocation arrangements. We began by listing our much-loved Clairmont Ave. house with real-estate agent Lillian Cooley, a South Avondale member. By November we were able to move a few of our belongings into the missionary house of First Baptist Church Montgomery. This completely furnished, well located, 3-bedroom house provided a temporary home until we could find a house to buy.

We had been in Montgomery barely a month when word came on the morning of December 7th, Pearl Harbor Day, that Papa "Poss"(Barbara's dad) had died suddenly with a heart attack at the age of 73. He left his house that morning to drive his pickup to town, as he often did. He was found a few minutes later in the driveway next to the driver's door, lifeless. He had recovered from a serious heart attack ten years earlier, which had hospitalized him for a couple of weeks. This earlier attack came less than a month after his retirement from the family grocery business, to which he had faithfully devoted 6 days a week for his entire adult life. In the intervening ten years he had enjoyed time with his beloved Eva, visiting grandchildren, tinkering in his workshop and attending auctions.

Barbara remained in Nicholasville for several days after the funeral, helping her mother attend to some necessary details before they both came to Montgomery. Our family observed a somber Christmas that year in our Clarimont house before taking Granny Mae back to Nicholasville.

To our disappointment the spring produced no serious prospective buyers for "our beautiful Clairmont House." We later concluded that our listing price, suggested by our realtor, was too high for the market. In the meantime, unable to find a suitable replacement for our Clairmont "dream house," we decided to build one. With the assistance of two new friends, bank loan officer, Kay Miller, and attorney, Barry Leavell, we purchased a lot, found a builder, and launched into the wonderful adventure of building our new house. Ha! Ha! Ha

Excitement was high as the lot was cleared, the basement dug, the plumbing stubbed in, and the foundation poured, which we later discovered was a wee bit low for the sewer connection at the street. Each evening brought new joy as we watched the day's progress, that is until the day our builder, Larry, decided he had other building projects more needful of his attention than ours. When Larry finally got back to our house, the framing went up quickly and the remainder of the work continued at a sporadic pace. Eventually our frustration level was somewhat abated by our adopting a more realistic expectation for "time of completion". Larry also kept us busy with a multitude of choices about cabinets, lighting fixtures, flooring, colors etc. We were proud of our brand-new house when it was finally finished in mid-summer, but we agreed this would be 2 in 1, the first and last house we would ever build.

Amid all the excitement and frustration of building a new house and adjusting to a new job, along came an accident. While walking through a neighborhood house under construction Barbara made a misstep and broke a bone in her foot. Undaunted, with Barbara in her cast, we made our only vacation visit to brother-in-law, Terrell's, company condo at Myrtle Beach.

This proved to be only the first of a rash of accidents with which we had to contend during our first several months in Montgomery. For instance, while I was waiting in my car at a stoplight in front of the Montgomery courthouse, a man came out of the courthouse, got into his car, and without even a glance, backed into my car. On another occasion, while I was conducting a funeral in a nearby town, a woman managed to hit my car parked in the church parking lot. Then, while I was stopped on Clairmont waiting for the car in front of me to turn left, a young woman rear-ended my Mustang. Again, as Alisa was on her way to class at Samford, a car pulled out of a service station and hit her broadside. Actually, the only serious accident came when a car ran a stop light on the Atlanta Highway in Montgomery and hit Barbara in the left front fender, just missing by a couple of feet a square hit into her door. All of those auto accidents were the fault of the other driver but because they occurred within a six-month period my insurance company determined I was "accident prone" and canceled my automobile insurance policy.

On top of these minor inconveniences, we could not find a buyer for our Birmingham house. Needing some relief from two mortgage payments each month, we rented the house to tenants on two different occasions. Both instances proved difficult at best. Over 30 months would pass before the Clairmont Avenue house finally sold. If only our asking price in the beginning had been closer to what we finally took for it!!

If "smooth sailing" had been our gage for knowing we were in "God's will," 6 months into our move to Montgomery we would have concluded we had made a horrible mistake. However, I knew the transition would be difficult and thought it may take at least 3 to 4 years before we could know, with some degree of accuracy, we were on the path God had for us. That certainly proved to be the case in this situation.

Our house in Montgomery, in spite of its early headaches and design limitations, proved to be a source of great joy and blessing. Adding landscaping touches over the years was a joy, as was the back porch and workshop in the basement. It became a welcoming retreat from a work schedule that was on occasions demanding, though I was spared the interruptions and crises I often faced as a pastor. At times our house was an extension of my work, becoming the place where we entertained staff, pastors and colleagues. Annual staff Christmas parties might include as many as 10 or 12 couples for an evening meal and holiday enjoyment. While couples usually contributed a dish, Barbara's cooking was always the highlight of the dinner. With my birthday only 6 days before Christmas the gathering often included comical birthday gifts as part of the fun. The year I turned 60 I got a creative poem, a cane and some other reminders I was getting old. The year our association collected ties for pastors in our Mexico partner association I got a box of the ugliest ties imaginable, too ugly to send to anybody in Mexico you hoped would remain your friend.

Believe it or not, pastors, and especially their wives, seldom know many people outside the church they serve. This includes not knowing pastors who serve neighboring churches. We decided we might help alleviate their feelings of isolation by inviting 3 couples at a time to our house for a nice dinner and some informal fellowship. The grouping usually included people I thought would not know each other well. We would send a letter of invitation which I would follow up with a personal phone call. In one such call to a pastor friend he asked, "Who else is coming?" When I named the other two couples he said, "Don't count on me. I would love to spend the evening with you and your wife, but I have no desire to spend my day off in the company of one of the men you named." I found a replacement couple for the evening.

That "good idea" for fostering fellowship was soon put back on the shelf since neither Barbara nor I wanted guests coming to our home for a meal who would rather be somewhere else. In retrospect, I was naïve in failing to recognize the lingering depth of feelings held by some as a consequence of the convention controversy. I was grateful for my friend's willingness to trust our friendship with his true feelings, though Barbara never got over what she considered uncalled-for bluntness.

Most of all, our Montgomery House became the center of countless happy family times together, especially around the holidays. Having our daughters, their husbands and later their children, come and spend multiple nights with us were sources of immense joy. Christmas gatherings continued to include Barbara's mother, along with her sister, Sue Earl, and her family. Even following Sue Earl's untimely death, her husband, Doug, and sons,

David and Steven, were still a part of the family at Christmas and summer beach vacations for several years.

Getting Started Leading an Organization of Churches

The work as a Director of Missions (DOM) for an association of 53 churches in the capital city of the state and its surrounding area was challenging but also quite rewarding. My predecessor, Bob Franklin, was recognized as one of the outstanding Directors of Missions in the Southern Baptist Convention. Getting to know and understand the programs and people already in place was an important early task. Bob, having been a local church minister of education, had developed a well-organized program for training local church lay leaders. The association also had a history of sponsoring mission teams specializing in construction and disaster relief on projects throughout the United States. The association's strong social ministry programs included a food pantry, conversational English classes, and the resettling of war refugees from Viet Nam and Laos. Most of these programs were staffed with capable volunteers and ran effectively with little attention from me, at least initially.

There were, however, some glaring gaps that needed immediate attention. First, Bob's chief assistant, Margaret, director of the association's educational programs, resigned her MBA staff position to join Bob in Georgia. Finding her replacement was an obvious early need. Second, the Association had a history of falling far short of its budget, so the staff was continually adjusting goals and trying to raise money to make ends meet. I quickly set about the process of prioritizing adopted budget items into three categories (Essential, Helpful, and Eventual). A third long-term need was upgrading or replacing the Association's office facility. The office was located in a deteriorating church building donated to the association by a church that had disbanded. The building, in need of continual maintenance and repair, also served as the Association's Mission Center for distributing food and clothing.

I also had a personal need of rather quickly mastering the learning curve of how to be an effective director of missions for an association of Southern Baptist churches. As it turns out, that curve, though a little steeper at the beginning, was always upward and never completely mastered. I began by asking, "How did other excellent directors of missions understand and perform their task?" Aided by Larry McSwain, my doctoral professor, I identified three outstanding directors of missions of metropolitan associations. While doing much of the work of traditional SBC associations, each director approached his work differently.

I contacted each one and arranged to spend a day "looking over their shoulder." Each visit was extremely helpful. Lawrence Childes at the Mecklenburg Association in Charlotte, North Carolina, was creatively helping local churches develop customized strategic plans to deal with their changing communities. He found the best time to do this to be when the church was between pastors.

Hugh Chamblis, at Madison Association in Huntsville, Alabama, had become a recognized community leader in Huntsville. In his association, he sought to help individual pastors address their points of personal or professional need, to the extent that they would allow him. His most useful word of wisdom to me was, "I do not try to be every pastor's 'pastor'. I am every pastor's friend and a pastor to those who want me to be their pastor." In other words, don't expect to relate to every pastor the same way.

From Gerald Blackburn at the Mobile Association in Mobile, Alabama I learned the value of being present for signal events in the life of every church. Even if you were not invited to make a few remarks, though you often may be, your presence would be appreciated. Another factor common to all three directors was their focus on building and maintaining a competent staff.

Pondering what I had learned from my recent "field trips," from my 28 years of experience as a pastor, and drawing on my personal interests, I began to formulate a few short-term goals. Shortly after the first of the year, with the help of the personnel committee, I put together a search committee to help us find "the right person" to be our Church Development Director. In the meantime, I asked a young lady with seminary training to be our Interim Church Development Director. She was a skilled writer, very energetic, and ideally suited for that interim position. Unfortunately, her goal was to be the permanent Church Development Director, a goal which she had failed to share with me at the beginning. One of my prerequisites for that person was a good experience as an educational director in a larger church. I thought this would open the door to relating to the ministers of education of our larger churches as well as help our smaller churches with their educational programs. This important qualification she lacked. As I was planning to leave Montgomery for our family's first vacation in the summer of '86, she gave me an ultimatum to either employ her full-time or she would resign on the spot. I accepted her resignation and with a great deal of anxiety headed for our McGohon family vacation at the Guinn's business beach condo in South Carolina.

It would be another year before we found Bob Dempsey, a minister of education at the First Baptist Church in Campbellsville, Kentucky. Bob was looking for an opportunity to work in a denominational position. Bob recently had helped his church work through a strategy planning consultation led by Eddie Freeman. Eddie, a personal friend of mine who worked on our state convention staff, suggested Bob might be the kind of person I wanted. Bob, accompanied by his wife Martha, joined our staff in August of '87 and served Montgomery Baptists until he retired 27 years later. His skills and competencies proved to be a good complement to my own. He was low key, well organized, thoughtful, a thorough planner, somewhat introverted, but a hard worker and willing to be a pioneer.

Bob formed good relationships with the ministerial staff members of the larger churches, especially education and youth ministers, and organized many exceptional training events for both staff and lay church leaders. Under Bob's leadership, the association, in partnership with some of the larger churches, brought church growth specialists like Ron Lewis to Montgomery for customized consultations over a period of years. We came to realize that habits and traditions for both individuals and institutions are not easily changed. It usually requires continuous effort over a number of years. This continual on-site tweaking and encouragement proved to be most effective. This strategy fit well with the conviction I brought to the task that "every church along with its staff is in a unique situation and under the direction of God's Spirit must find its own way forward." The church membership and staff can often do their best work with the help of a wise and sympathetic consultant even when they did not wish to go through a full-blown strategic planning process.

Ministering to Needs in the Montgomery Community

The Baptist Center was the association's oldest and flagship social ministry. In the late '60s, the Association, led by Director of Missions, Rev. Frank Hixon, voted to embark on a ministry to the inner city of Montgomery that would add a valuable spiritual dimension to what secular groups were doing. They called Gladys Farmer [3] to lead what would be a pioneering work of its kind among Southern Baptists. The ministry collected and distributed food and clothing to people in need without regard to race or creed. Volunteers were enlisted for "Meals on Wheels." The ministry also employed summer missionaries, usually college students, to lead programs for children in "needy" areas of the community. In 1985, when I arrived, the ministry was housed in a church building that also served as the Association's office. Jim Lilly, a retired Air Force colonel, and his wife Mary were leading the ministry. Mary was the paid director and Jim worked as a volunteer helping as he had available time and the need required.

The association was also involved in a number of other social ministry activities when I arrived. A Conversational English program addressed the needs primarily of wives of international Air Force officers in training at Maxwell Air Force Base. The program was housed in First Baptist Church and had the support of volunteers from many of the association's churches. Barbara taught in that program most of the years we were in Montgomery. We also had a New Life School that sought to meet the needs of newly resettled political refugees from Laos. A Samaritan Inn Ministry sought to assist family members of out-of-town patients in one of our area hospitals with housing. Initially, the idea was to use an old downtown YWCO building but maintaining that building and providing a "24-7" attendant proved to be financially untenable. Eventually, a couple of motels near each hospital allowed us to rent unused rooms at half price (occasionally less) as we needed, and they had space. With contributions from our churches and "guests" paying modest or no fees at all, thirty years later the ministry continues serving families, often parents of newborns in Baptist Hospital's neo-natal unit.

In developing the Association's strategic plan adopted in '87, a study identified several changes that had taken place since the Baptist Center opened nearly 2 decades earlier. The Association now had a great social ministry advocate in the inner city. First Baptist Church decided against relocating from downtown and instead redoubled its efforts to minister to the inner city. In 1988, the employment of Jane Ferguson, made them the first Southern Baptist Convention church with a full time, MSW degreed, Christian social worker on its staff. First Baptist would become a valuable resource for many who had turned to the Baptist Center. This aligned well with my experience at South Avondale which had led me to believe the local church was best suited to provide a wholistic ministry to the needy. There was a need for several "Baptist Centers" located throughout the city in "areas of need" and easily accessible by "people of need" in that neighborhood. Unfortunately, the neighborhoods with the greatest needs had congregations which, though once strong, were now greatly weakened and dependent on an older senior adult membership. My vision was for a church-based "Ministry Center," in an area of need, supported by a few partner suburban churches who could provide needed volunteers and financial resources.

Making the Baptist Center Ministry transition would take time and skilled leadership. In addition, most of the ministries listed above required consistent attention and support. The recommendation in '87 to add a qualified Community Ministries Director to the Association's staff was readily approved. However, it would take 3 years to build the Association's financial base to the point we could support the proposed staff position. Finally, in March of '91, the Association called Rev. Ricky Creech who was completing his MSW degree at Southern Seminary to be our Community Ministries Director.

Ricky, his wife Donna, and their two daughters moved to Montgomery and began his work in June. When Ricky resigned in May of '95 to accept a similar position with the Birmingham Association, we had 4 fully functioning, church-based, Baptist Centers with trained directors. All the other ministries were functioning effectively and the framework for a Montgomery Police Chaplaincy program was in place. Ricky, a visionary, was creative, energetic, a good recruiter of volunteers, and a great communicator of his vision. I told him more than once, "You can think of more projects that need doing than any 2 organizations can fund." Envisioning and organizing ministries to meet human need was Ricky's great strength. Maintaining existing programs, encouraging staff and addressing ongoing problems he could do, but he thrived on the excitement and thrill of a new challenge.

Dave Morris, who had recently retired as Development Director for Huntingdon College, agreed to serve, part-time, as our interim Community Ministry Director. In addition to doing a good job, he gave us time to search for the next director God might have for us. During David's time with us, work was completed for the organization of a separate 501c3 non-profit corporation, MBA Community Ministries Inc. This new corporation would serve as the umbrella under which all of the community ministry programs would function. MBA Community Ministries Inc. made it much easier to partner with other religious groups and government agencies in projects that served the larger Montgomery community. It also made it easier to apply for grants to help fund some of the ministries. Dr. A. Earl Potts, recently retired Baptist State Executive Secretary, agreed to become the new corporate board's first chairman.

In its 1995 Annual Meeting, the association also set up a counseling ministry with Dr. Kline Johnson, recently retired head of the counseling program at Troy State University, as its director and lead counselor. This provided a much-needed referral resource for pastors and other church staff when extended counseling was warranted. We soon worked out a partnership arrangement with the Alabama Baptist Children's Home to house one of their professional counselors in our office at least two days a week.

When time came to find our next CCM director I went back to the place where we found Ricky, the Social Work School at Southern Seminary in Louisville. Debbie Nowell was finishing her MSW degree for church social work. She and her husband Harold had started their careers as Southern Baptist missionaries, serving in Nationalist China, e.g. Taiwan. After several years on the mission field, Debbie and Harold, with their three sons, returned to the States primarily for the sake of their children's education. Debbie, unable to continue her missionary career and feeling called to the field of church social work, enrolled in Southern Seminary and earned her MSW degree. Convinced she was a good fit for MBA, I recommended she be employed as our next Church Community Ministries Director.

Debbie moved to Montgomery with her family and joined our staff in May of 1996. Harold was soon called to serve one of our churches as an associate pastor and satisfactory educational arrangements were made for their children. Debbie's empathy for people in need, her relational skills, along with her gifts in recruiting and training volunteers, all proved to be just what the Association needed at that time. A native of central Kentucky, Debbie and her boys were also avid Kentucky basketball fans. This kept us in contact even after she left in the summer of 1999 to take a social ministry/teaching position at Palm Beach Atlantic University, a Baptist school in West Palm Beach, Florida. She eventually returned to Kentucky, taking an administrative position in a newly formed CBF seminary housed on the Georgetown College campus.[4]

Following Debbie Nowell's departure, Debbie Hooks, an exceptional volunteer at the Forest Park Community Center, retired from her public-school teaching position and managed much of the Community Ministry work for the next couple of years. During that time, Judy Randal, a pastor's wife with seminary training and an interest in social work, came to work as our Community Ministry assistant. She coordinated the ministry effectively after Hooks' departure and beyond my retirement. Reflecting on these events, I am amazed anew by God's ever-present guiding hand.

Building an Office Building

Finding more adequate office facilities for its staff was another long-range goal coming from the Association's '87 strategy plan.[5] Since the late '70s, the disbanded Calvary Baptist Church facilities on South Hull Street had been used by the association for its Baptist Center and for staff office space. The Sunday School rooms on the south side of the building were used as staff offices[6] and the other educational wing for the Baptist Center. The sanctuary in the middle was used for the quarterly Executive Board meetings and as storage for Baptist Center clothing and other supplies. The aging building was constantly in need of repairs and maintenance. Actually, holding the quarterly Executive Board meetings there was not all bad, since it provided a regular reminder of the need for better office facilities. In spite of that reminder, we stopped using the old sanctuary for Executive Board meetings even before the decision was made to build a new building. Rotating the Executive Board meetings among the various churches, I hoped, would increase the churches' sense of ownership of their association and give them a greater appreciation for the ministry of their sister churches.

At the association's 1987 Annual Meeting, a Facilities Study Committee was authorized. After two years of thorough study, the recommendation to build a new Associational Office Building was adopted. The building would be designed specifically to meet the association's needs and would be financed by designated gifts from concerned individuals and from the churches. The goal was to raise $150,000 from individuals and the rest from churches who would be asked to give an additional .5% of their undesignated offerings for a period of three years to a building fund. Estimated cost was to be between $350,000 and $400,000.

A lot in Colonial's Office Park on Perry Hill Road at I 85 was bought and the building was completed and proudly dedicated on May 31, 1992. There was office space for a director and 4 associates, plus room for 3 ministry assistants, a work room, a seminar room for 25, a conference room for 12, a kitchen/snack room, room for a modest but attractive Baptist Book Store[7], plus an upstairs for future expansion. Since it was a new building we engaged the services of George and Joan Ritchey to help us select the décor and all the furnishings. Modesty keeps me from saying that at the time it was the most attractive and accommodating office facility of any of the Southern Baptist Convention's 1,200 associations, but it probably was. More importantly, the new building gave visible affirmation to the value our churches placed on their cooperative ministries.

A lion's share of the credit for getting the facility built and paid for goes to John Foshee and Gene Hannah. John, a builder by trade, chaired the Building Committee. Gene, a Montgomery Baptist Hospital executive in charge of public relations and physician recruitment, chaired the Office

Facility Study Committee. Gene also volunteered to lead a Special Gifts committee of 30 laypersons seeking to raise $150,000 in individual gifts.

Gene served for two years, 1992 & 1993, as the Association's moderator. He was an ordained minister and a graduate of Southern Seminary He had been a pastor in Leeds and a Minister of Education in Montgomery's before going to work for the hospital. I was surprised to discover several years later that Gene, while a student at Southern Seminary was also pastor of my dad's Clover Bottom Baptist Church in Woodford County, Ky.

The bookstore ministry fell into our laps seemingly by accident. When I began my tenure, the annual Vacation Bible School workshop was one of the association's major training events. At the annual VBS conference, the association provided, on consignment from the Baptist Book Store in Birmingham, most of the literature, supplies, and materials that would be used for the coming year. Our secretary, Gene Haynes, would take her Suburban to Birmingham and return loaded to the brim with VBS materials. Churches picked up their VBS materials at the workshop or later at the association's office, charging them to their Baptist Book Store account. The association received 15% of the receipts for transporting the materials and providing all the clerical services involved. It was a valuable service for the churches and provided the association with a little extra revenue, usually used for office equipment or supplies.

Barbara, who had worked in our churches' Bible School for years and enjoyed working with books, volunteered to help with the clerical duties. In 1989, the Birmingham store manager agreed to expand our arrangement by letting us keep other popular study books and church supplies in our office on consignment as a service to our churches. In June, we turned an easily accessible room in the association's office into a Baptist Book Store extension. Barbara agreed to work in the "store" a few hours a week as an unpaid volunteer. Within a couple of months, the popularity of the venture allowed us to begin paying her a minimum hourly wage.

By the time we started designing a new office building, space for the Book Store became a major concern. In 1991, annual Book Store receipts were nearly $16,000 (15% of over $100,000 in total sales) and we had accumulated a balance of over $8,000 in the Book Store account. Since the Baptist Book Store was a subsidiary of the Baptist Sunday School Board in Nashville, I wrote them explaining our situation and asking if they had any plans for opening a free-standing bookstore in Montgomery. "We have no such plans for the foreseeable future," was the response I received from their regional manager. Consequently, we designed an attractive 12x24 space, just off the new building's entrance for the bookstore, anticipating revenue from the store would in time partially offset the added cost of construction. Revenues in '93, the first full year in the new location, were $22,800 on sales of $152,000.

Imagine our surprise to learn from a community realtor in mid '94 that a new Baptist Book Store was coming to Montgomery. Upon calling the Nashville office, I was referred to their regional manager. I explained our situation to him, reminded him of his letter about no store in the "foreseeable future" and suggested he come look at our store. "Oh, we've seen your store and its records. We know all about it. I came by for a visit one day with another representative."

They had come by unannounced. When I told Barbara, she remembered having seen 2 men, strangers to her, browsing around the store a few weeks earlier. Obviously, I complained vociferously, but to little avail. The regional manager agreed to employ the three ladies who worked in our store as part-time clerks in the new store. After talking with our moderator/attorney, they also gave us $15,000 as a token "goodwill" gesture. With this "goodwill" gesture we were able to remodel the bookstore space into a "Counseling Ministry" suite which proved to be a great ministry. Twenty-five years later it is still being used for that purpose. Once again, God turned what appeared to be an unfortunate situation into a blessing for many.

Barbara's tenure as bookstore clerk for the next 9 enjoyable years proved to be a ministry with manifold blessings. With her compassionate heart and ready listening ear, she became a welcome friend and counselor to her fellow clerks and customers alike. She also alerted me to happenings in some of our churches I would never have known about any other way. Beyond that, her "employee discount" made the bookstore the source of, what one of our grandchildren labeled, Grandmama's "Godish" gifts.

Churches Fulfilling Their Mission Globally

Being a Mission Encourager

I relished the task of being a mission encourager. One aspect of that task was to enhance mission awareness among the association's churches, especially as it related to the work of the Southern Baptist Convention's International and North American Mission Boards, the Alabama Baptist Convention State Board of Missions, and the work of local associations. One avenue for accomplishing this goal was a World Mission Conference promoted by the association at roughly five-year intervals. Initially, churches participated in the conference by having a different missionary speaker in both their Sunday morning and evening worship services, at additional services Monday and Tuesday evening, and at their regular Wednesday evening service.

As a pastor I had always led my church to participate in these World Mission Conferences. My first one came in 1961 while I was pastor at Buffalo Lick. However, as time went on I found it increasingly difficult to get members to attend additional week-night services. Consequently, I encouraged the Montgomery Association to make the conference a one Sunday, 4-service event (utilizing the two Sunday worship services along with the Sunday School and Church Training programs). In this event, each church would have as a featured speaker an International Board missionary, a North American Board missionary, a State Board missionary, and a local Associational Ministry spokesperson. We started the conference with an association-wide rally on Saturday where members from all the churches could meet all the missionaries and we closed the conference with a breakfast/fellowship time on Monday, primarily for the visiting missionaries. The new format was well received, and church participation increased.

In addition to enlisting its churches to participate, the association was responsible for inviting the missionaries from an availability list provided by the various boards. The association was also responsible for providing for the missionaries' expenses (room, meals, & travel) and for their honorarium. To adequately fund the expenses of the next conference without working an undue hardship of any one church, the association began setting aside several thousand dollars in each year's budget for the next conference. It was not unusual to have 30 or more International and North American missionaries participate in a World Missions Conference. Such a conference enabled members of the local churches, especially the smaller ones, to learn about the broad scope of the denomination's mission work. An added bonus for the missionaries was the enjoyment of getting to know one another and sharing some fellowship time together.

Another major emphasis of my predecessor, I thought worthy of continuing, was an annual association sponsored mission trip. Members of churches not large enough to have their own mission team were encouraged to participate. Church construction had been a major focus of many of these trips, and when I arrived the association's Missions Committee was considering a request for a team from the Shannon Park Baptist Church, in Fairbanks, Alaska. As part of an existing partnership between the Alabama State Convention and the Alaska Convention this struggling church had requested a construction team to do both "a little inside and outside" work to finish their nearly completed new building.

We accepted the challenge and sent out a request for volunteers willing to go for a week at their own expense to help with this project. When the departure date arrived, a crew of half a dozen boarded the plane headed for Fairbanks. The team included the chairman of the Missions Committee, my secretary Gene Haynes and her husband Evert, yours truly and two more hardy souls. We were met at the Fairbanks airport by Fred, driving the Shannon Park church van. Team members stayed in the home of church members. I had the privilege of staying in the home of the pastor and his wife, Mark and Diane Kisselberg, a young couple in their early thirties. The team usually had a common meal each evening around 7:00, though it seemed like the middle of the afternoon. Fred faithfully took us to the church each morning, home each night, and anywhere else we wanted to or needed to go.

Fred, in his mid 50's, had been a heavy equipment operator prior to a work-related back injury about 2 years earlier which left him permanently disabled. He had become quite despondent and had stopped attending church. However, in response to insistent pleas from his faithful church-going wife, he had agreed to drive "the bunch from Alabama" around that week. Fred made no effort to keep his disillusionment a secret. He let us know his commitment was for Monday through Friday only. On Saturday and Sunday, he was following his usual routine, fishing with his son.

Work began early Monday morning, and 10-hour workdays were the norm. Don and Evert worked on a balcony railing and ramp to the front door. I worked with a crew in the basement finishing sheetrock for Sunday School classrooms. Thursday, our day off, the church pastor took us for a sightseeing trip to Mt. Denali National Park about 4 hours away. It made for a long but gratifying day.

More than once during the week Fred asked, "Why in the world would you guys come all the way to Alaska and spend a week working on a church you will never see again?" Don laughed and teased him often, though Fred was seldom in a joking mood. Saturday morning, we finished up our work week and, to our surprise, Fred showed up to take us on a short tour of Fairbanks which included a nice wildlife museum near the airport. Sunday, we worshiped with the Shannon Park Church and some of our group shared personal testimonies during the service. Fred was there.

The church pastor, Mark, said several times during the week he wanted to take us canoeing on the Tanana River Sunday night after church. After church he seemed to be in no hurry, and I assumed it was too late to go. But, not so. He gave me a 5-gallon bucket with a top that sealed and suggested I put an outfit of dry clothes and a towel in it. He, another church member and 4 guests from Montgomery left Mark's house for the river a little after 10:00 p.m. With an experienced canoer in each group of three we made a couple of portages (where you get out and carry your canoe over a bit of land to the next pool of water). We finally reached the main river a little before midnight. My bucket of dry clothes proved to be sufficient since I fell in the water only once getting in and out of the canoe. As we floated down the river in the twilight, the sun hung just over the horizon, wildlife could be seen on either shore. Though it was mostly small creatures, no moose or big game, it was still a breathtaking experience.

Back at Mark's house, I got to bed a little after two and arose 4 hours later to get ready for our trip to the airport and back to Montgomery. To my surprise, Mark was gone. He had been called to the hospital around 3:00 that morning. While we were on the river, Fred, who was not with us, had suffered a major heart attack. Diane said they rushed him to the hospital, but Mark had just called to say he didn't make it.

On our group's way to the airport, we went by Fred's house to speak to his wife and pray with her. Though she was heartbroken, she greeted us with open arms. "Yesterday afternoon Fred told me this had been one of the best weeks of his life. For the first time he finally was at peace with his life and with God. He could not have said that a week ago. I can't tell you how grateful I am that you came to Fairbanks this week. Thank you all so much for coming."

Wow, what about that! Had God brought our small crew all the way to Alaska for this one man? Maybe! On board the plane we agreed the trip had been a special blessing for every one of us.

The following April, as a part of the partnership, Mark invited me back to be their revival preacher. This time the Montgomery team included McGhee Baptist Church Minister of Music Steve Williams and his wife Gwen who also helped with the music. I was pleased Barbara was able to go with us and meet the Kisselbergs who were our gracious hosts for the week. Another fine couple hosted Steve and Gwen. Revival attendance was good and participation enthusiastic. The Tanana river was still mostly frozen, and though we were often told to look closely we might see a moose, none appeared. However, we have a delightful and endearing memory of the sunny day when the temperature finally reached 45 degrees. Diane joyfully went through the house raising every window to its maximum height. Spring had finally come to Fairbanks, at least for her. She got a hilarious laugh seeing her Alabama guests putting on sweatshirts and sweaters to avoid being chilled to the bone.

From Fairbanks to Phoenix, what a contrast! Following a DOM conference at Glorieta, NM in the summer to '88, Barbara and I joined a Montgomery mission team of Vacation Bible School leaders at a church in Chandler, AZ. While Barbara and the other VBS leaders conducted Bible Schools in two churches, I met with various Apache associational leaders to discuss the possibility of a multi-year partnership between our two associations. Apache was an association of churches in metropolitan Phoenix's east valley which included Tempe, Mesa, Chandler, and Apache Junction. Rev. Byron Banta, their association's moderator and pastor of one of the churches where we conducted a VBS, spoke that fall at our annual meeting. At that meeting we officially approved a 4-year partnership to begin in '89.

Les Roberts, Apache Association's new Director of Missions, visited Montgomery in the winter of '88 - '89 and met with MBA's Missions Development Council to develop goals for the partnership. At that time the Phoenix East Valley area was experiencing rapid growth, adding every two years new residents equal to Montgomery's total population. In '89 a youth team of 21 visited Apache Association to work with youth and children, and a construction team of 9 men and 2 women assisted in completing a project for a church in Apache Junction.

A major goal was enlisting individual Montgomery churches to partner with individual Apache churches for prayer and other possible ways of interaction and support. Over a dozen Montgomery churches participated in that effort, sending teams to help with revivals, VBS, construction projects, church planting, and leadership development. I made 3 additional trips to the area in the following years helping with a construction project, preaching a revival, and serving as a church's strategy planning consultant. Bill and Carol Atkinson, a couple in Bryan Banta's church, hosted Barbara and me on our first trip to Chandler and they insisted I stay with them every time I came back to the Apache area. We exchanged Christmas greetings for years and on one of their rare trips east they visited us in Montgomery.

A major foreign mission partnership was launched in 1997 in Mexico. First Baptist Church of Montgomery had been working with an SBC International Mission Board missionary in the Mexican state of Sinaloa. They had planned a major area wide evangelistic effort for the fall of '97 and invited the association to join them. In the spring of '97, I agreed to join Harold Handcock, First Baptist's mission coordinator, on a planning trip to Sinaloa. As I approached the airport check-in counter with Harold I discovered, to my chagrin, I did not have my passport with me. Too late to go home and get it, I had no choice but bid Harold good-by and God's speed. The logistics of exchanging my ticket and joining Harold later during his trip proved to be impracticable. So, Sinaloa was out, at least for now. Did God have something else in mind?

A call to Larry Gay, my former Education and Youth Minister at Sixty-Sixth Street, and now a long-tenured IMB missionary in Mexico, proved to be very helpful. He suggested a partnership with the Mexican State Convention of Puebla would be worth exploring. It was a large population area with strong lay leadership and home base to a team of 3 IMB missionary couples who could offer help with the logistics. A scouting trip to Mexico with Bill Ingles, a professional photographer and member of our Mission Council, and led by Larry was arranged for May. In our visit, I discovered Pueblo also had a locally operated medical clinic which I thought could offer opportunities for involvement by our Baptist Hospital. A favorable response from the Puebla Convention's local leaders and the IMB missionaries enabled the association to officially enter into a 3 to 5-year partnership in its 1997 annual meeting.

Andrew Flagg, a Puebla-stationed IMB missionary, participated in our '98 World Mission Conference. His visit spurred already high enthusiasm among our pastors for the partnership. A number of "MBA church" to "Pueblo church" partnerships were formed, and projects conducted. A member of one of our smaller churches was a Walmart truck driver and secured a commitment from Walmart to furnish a trailer which we could fill with donations and then deliver to Pueblo. Unfortunately, few things are ever as simple as they may seem, especially in the realm of international commerce. Over a period of perhaps 6-9 months, the trailer was filled to 75% capacity with church pews, folding chairs, tables, pulpit furniture, and the like. Even a large, motorized cement mixer was donated and loaded on the trailer. It would be especially useful since nearly all buildings were cement or cement block requiring mortar.

The trailer got to the Mexican border at Nuevo Laredo where it sat for a whole year while Mexican officials argued among themselves about who had authority to admit or reject the items in the truck, all of which were correctly reported in a detailed manifesto. Finally, after a year, a new border supervisor took over and the trailer was immediately cleared to cross the border into Mexico. Unfortunately, helping the Baptist Medical clinic in Puebla did not turn out as well. To the best of my understanding, a dispute between the two countries over the credentialing of doctors resulted in Mexico placing an embargo on all USA medical supplies and personnel. The embargo deprived some of Puebla's most needy citizens of free medical supplies and treatment.

In the early summer of '99, the Flaggs and the Kennedys, two of the three IMB missionary couples in Puebla, were scheduled for stateside assignment. The third couple, the Thurmans, who had been volunteers for the last several years, were appointed as regular IMB missionaries and left for language school in Costa Rica. The IMB asked if we could furnish a full-time volunteer for Puebla. David Fleming, a single young man with a PhD from Southern Seminary, who had made a couple of mission trips to Puebla expressed an interest in the assignment. By reallocating some funds, we were able to provide a small stipend for living expenses and in May of '99, David became our liaison missionary in Puebla.

All went well for the first few months until the IMB began to hear rumblings of disagreements voiced by local church leaders over IMB priorities in the area. An IMB missionary in an adjoining state spent some time in Puebla assessing the situation. He concluded that given the absence of IMB missionaries, some of Puebla's local church leaders were attempting to use the Montgomery Association and our support of David as leverage to thwart some IMB long-term objectives. After discussing the matter with an IMB missionary by phone I concluded that for the long-term interest of the mission work in Puebla it would be best for David to come home. In early December of '99, David returned to Montgomery and further work with Puebla was postponed until IMB missionaries could be back on the field.

I, along with a layman, went back to Puebla in December of 2000 to conduct a review and bring an official closure to the partnership. Local representatives from several of our church-to-church projects gave glowing reports of what had been accomplished. One young man wept as he expressed appreciation for the work of a team from our Morningview church. In a public worship service on Sunday afternoon we presented a couple of checks for uncompleted projects and a final construction team visit was scheduled. In addition to the good that was done in Puebla and the blessing that our local participants received, one promising young musician with excellent English skills came to Montgomery and became the leader of Hispanic mission work in 2 of our churches.

When God closes one door He seems to always open another. One day in 1997, Pat Pattillo, a friend from seminary days, stopped by my office to talk about Hong Kong Baptist University. As a representative of the school's president, he was seeking to establish student exchange programs with some Baptist colleges and universities in the States. The exchange consortium included Baylor, Mercer, and Ohio University in Athens, Ohio, from the USA, along with institutions from Australia, Canada, the UK, Sweden, and the Netherlands. Students from 51 institutions participated. To help offset the extremely high cost of housing in Hong Kong, two new residence halls were under construction, one being the new NIT International House. Pat was hoping for a few churches, as a mission endeavor, to help furnish some rooms in the International House that would be set aside for participating exchange students and mission volunteers. Our Morningview church did accept the challenge and raised $12,000 to fund a guestroom in honor of their church's life-long missions champion, Becie Kirkwood.

Pat was also looking for funds and personnel to augment the University's chaplaincy program. A few years earlier, the IMB had phased out its support of Hong Kong Baptist University, including the chaplaincy program. The IMB missionary who had worked in the chaplain's office resigned from the IMB so he could remain at the University as a full-time paid faculty member. Because he now had additional faculty responsibilities, his chaplaincy post was vacant. Kang Chin-Haut, a Chinese Christian from Singapore, was the University's senior chaplain. He wanted to fill the vacated associate chaplain's slot with a native English speaker who would have a basket full of responsibilities, i.e.: working with international students mostly from Europe, Australia and the US; working with graduate and post graduate students from mainland China; organizing and teaching small English language groups; and serving as a liaison for volunteers wanting to work in Hong Kong. Moreover, such a person would need to be supported with funds from the US.

David Fleming, with his PhD degree in Old Testament and his heart for missions, seemed like an ideal fit. By December of 1999, the Baptist General Convention of Texas (non-SBC Texas Baptists) had agreed to provide a portion of the funds for such a person. Those funds, along with the MBA funds budgeted for David's work in Mexico, were enough to support David for a temporary evaluation period. If this proved to be a viable arrangement for all parties concerned, it would become a more permanent one.

In the meantime, Pattillo secured pledges from 2 Georgia churches, First Baptist Church, Gainesville, and Peachtree Baptist Church in the North Atlanta area, for the additional funding needed. The Birmingham Association, where Ricky Creech was now the Executive Director, also joined the support team. This ad hoc mission team of a state convention, 2 associations, and 2 churches supported David and his ministry at Hong Kong Baptist University for 3 full years. I served as team coordinator and treasurer for the group.

In early 2000, David flew to Hong Kong to work as a temporary assistant in the chaplain's office at Hong Kong Baptist University. Arrangements were made for me to visit Hong Kong in the Spring of 2000 for meetings with the Hong Kong Baptist University president, Dr. Daniel Tse, several faculty members, a representative of the Hong Kong Baptist Hospital, a Hong Kong Baptist Seminary faculty member, some former IMB missionaries, leaders of the Hong Kong Baptist Convention[1] and Richard Walsh, pastor of the Kowloon International Baptist Church. It was an incredible experience. Kang, a most gracious host, arranged a welcoming dinner for the evening I arrived. After a 20-hour flight and getting settled in my guest room, I'm embarrassed to report, the guest of honor dozed off more than once during that exquisite dinner.

I spent Monday, my first full day in Hong Kong, touring the University and visiting with Richard Walsh and other staff members of Kowloon Baptist

Church. It is a strong church with more than 2,000 members from more than a dozen countries. The following Sunday, I worshiped with the church in a service that included 473 in attendance on the main campus and 730 in 7 mission sites around the area. This church agreed to become a part of David's mission support team.

Frank Wells, recently retired CFO of Montgomery Baptist Hospital, flew to Hong Kong with me and we spent one morning meeting with representatives of the Hong Kong Baptist Hospital. It was a first-class western science-based hospital, the equal of anything we had in Montgomery, with minimal attention given to traditional Chinese medicine. It was rather quickly concluded that a relationship, formal or informal, would be of little value to either institution. David took Frank back to the airport Wednesday morning for his return trip to Montgomery and picked up Neal Hughes, a Montgomery pastor with a strong interest in missions and a former moderator of our association.

A breakfast meeting with IMB missionary Dr. Keith Morgan, led to an all-day Saturday visit to Macau, a former Portuguese colony across the bay from Hong Kong and now a gambling mecca. Following a McDonald's breakfast, we boarded a turbo-Jet boat that resembled the inside of a large passenger plane with reclining seats, TV etc. Following the one-hour trip across the bay we were met by our guide, Marilyn Hing, a pharmacist and IMB missionary at the Hope Medical Clinic in Macau. In addition to her clinic, we visited a temple to a fishing goddess where people lit incense candles as part of their worship. There we met a woman returning from burning incense sticks for departed ancestors. She seemed to be in some kind of trance and was weeping profusely. Later we learn, Neal Hughes, upon seeing her in the middle of that busy street in Macau, had a profound epiphany that would change the course of his life.[2]

As expected, University president Dr. Daniel Tse retired shortly after my visit to Hong Kong and was succeeded by Dr. Ng Ching-Fai, an appointee of the Chinese government's education establishment. Hopefully, his Christian ties, while not nearly as overt as Dr. Daniel's, are never-the-less genuine. In April of 2003, with the encouragement of David and Chaplain Kang Chin-Haut, Dr. Ng Ching-Fai accepted our invitation to visit Montgomery as part of his trip that included stops at some of the universities involved in the student exchange program. We welcomed him to our country and Montgomery with a banquet that included our mayor and other community dignitaries as guests.

In his three-year ministry, David touched the lives of hundreds of Hong Kong students, many from mainland China who were working on advanced degrees. In the 2001-02 school year, the Chaplain's Office reported over 150 students accepting Christ and entering discipleship programs. In addition to helping students lead Worship Services, David taught Bible studies and led several student groups on mission trips into mainland China where they connected with other Chinese Christians.

Tragically, as I write these words, the Beijing Government has severely limited freedoms previously enjoyed by the citizens of Hong Kong, especially those enjoyed by university students. Now, in 2022, it seems increasingly obvious our Hong Kong ministry was a divinely opened window of opportunity to share the Gospel. The fruitfulness of that ministry may not be known or measured for decades.

Churches Fulfilling Their Mission Uniquely

Becoming a Church Consultant

An awareness of the value of a church consultant and the possibility of my being able to provide that service I attributed to several factors. First, twenty-eight years as a pastor convinced me that no two churches are alike. Different churches serve different groups of people with very different cultural and socioeconomic backgrounds. Moreover, individual churches have members with very different gifts and resources with which to serve. Then too, churches are at different places in their life cycle. Consequently, circumstances, needs and possible solutions vary significantly from church to church.

Second, beginning in the 1950s, and perhaps earlier, our neighborhoods and our society itself began experiencing multiple levels of change and all with increasing velocity. Confronted with these rapid changes in society, many churches began losing members and some found their very existence threatened. If these churches were to serve God and the people to whom he had called them to minister changes were required. Though some pastoral and lay leaders understood the need for change, churches by their very nature tend to be conservative, thus making change not only difficult, but often very divisive. Negotiating needed change with minimal fallout can be a complex process.

Third, my successful experience with the consultation led by Jere Allen and Ezra Earl Jones in my early days at South Avondale encouraged me to believe other churches and pastors could profit from a similar process led by a competent consultant. Finally, my visit with Lawrence Childs in Charlotte's Mecklenburg Association reinforced that belief and gave me a model for how it might be done effectively during a pastoral transition period.

Early on I realized becoming a competent consultant would require a great deal of training. As it turned out, I would spend my entire 17-plus-year career as a Director of Missions training to be a better consultant. My training began by taking advantage of seminars and meetings offered by the staff of the Home Mission Board, though few if any of them had that as their primary focus. The staff at the Board's Associational Missions Division had a two-prong strategy. One prong, called Mega Focus Cities, concentrated on associations in large metropolitan areas. A few of these were in large cities of the south like Atlanta, Charlotte, Richmond, Louisville, Houston, Dallas, Fort Worth and New Orleans, to mention a few, but most were in the North, East, Mid-west and West, areas where Southern Baptists were not strong.

The Associational Missions staff sponsored semi-annual meetings of DOMs from these associations to explore creative ways of helping churches.

Though the Montgomery Association did not qualify as a Mega Cities Association, our financial strength and my interest got me an invitation to join the group, which proved quite profitable. Sadly, new SBC leadership reorganized the Board's staff in the early '90s severely limiting their work with the Associations. Several DOMs continued to meet as an informal group, but without the HMB's bright creative leaders the group eventually disbanded.

A second prong of the Associational Missions staff's strategy focused on helping churches experiencing decline, primarily because they were in rapidly changing and usually economically declining neighborhoods. They called this strategy by the acronym PACT Consultations (Project Assistance for Church in Transition). Training was offered to associational leaders interested in becoming PACT consultants, an offer both Bob Dempsey and I accepted gladly. Early in my tenure I made all our staff available to our MBA churches to serve, without charge, as strategy planning consultants. Each consultation took about 6 months and involved gathering data on the church and community, a couple of church wide meetings, small group interviews with all church members willing to be interviewed, and a comprehensive written report to the church. By January of 1996, we had conducted 33 consultations with 26 different churches in the Montgomery Association. As our work became known across the denomination, Bob and I were named by the Home Missions Board in 1993 "PACT Consultants of the Year" for the eastern United States. While my primary responsibility was to the churches of the Montgomery Association, I also was invited to assist a number of churches beyond the association prior to my retirement.[1]

In addition to taking advantage of training provided by the denomination, a lot of learning was acquired simply by doing. Obviously, I read extensively and sought training from other nationally recognized consultants. Bob and I spent a week with Lyle Schaller, the most prominent church consultant and author of the era, in a seminar at the Trueblood Yokefellow Institute in Richmond, Indiana.

I was invited by Dr. Bob Dale, Assistant Executive Director of Virginia Baptists, also a church consultant and author, to join a group of a dozen or so church innovators from across the Southeast. We had 3-day semi-annual meetings to discuss emerging trends and what each of us was doing. One member of the group, David Odom, currently on the faculty of Duke Divinity School, was at the time Chaplain at Wake Forest Baptist Hospital. In one of the first meetings of the group I attended, he shared a church consultation process he was developing to be used in churches he was serving as an interim pastor. That consultation process became the cornerstone for the Center for Congregational Health, an organization he founded which functioned originally under the umbrella of Wake Forest Hospital. It has trained hundreds of intentional interim pastors serving in multiple denominations. Because it overlapped so closely with my consultation focus

I participated in their rigorous training program featuring 2 five-day seminars separated by several months of "in the field" projects. This proved to be excellent preparation for my retirement ministry of serving churches as an Intentional Interim pastor. While continuing to train intentional interims, it has spawned a group using similar processes called The Center for Healthy Churches which has a greater focus on helping a church find a compatible pastor.

Multiple seminars led by experts with a variety of backgrounds also proved beneficial. Peter Steinke, a Lutheran minister and church consultant offered insights in how Edwin Freidman's family systems theory could be applied to the church as family. John Savage's work on reclaiming inactive church members enabled me to listen for and respond to "cries for help" from people with deep unresolved emotional pain as I conducted interviews, especially with disgruntled church members. I brought Savage to Montgomery for two 5-day intensive 40-hour workshops attended by both church staff and lay people. A Lay Mobilization Seminar led by west-coast based consultants, Sue Malory, a lay minister, and Don Simmons, a Golden Gate Seminary professor, was most helpful. I also invited them to Montgomery to train staff and lay leaders in several of our churches. Experts from whom I learned and shared valuable resources for churches with whom I consulted.

Our MBA five-year strategy planning cycle also gave me the opportunity to bring outstanding consultants into the association. George Bullard and Reggie McNeal each lead 6 months or longer planning processes. As they helped guide the association's planning process, I had the opportunity to "pick the brains" of some of the brightest minds in the nation's religious life.

In evaluating my work as a consultant, I was puzzled by the widely varying range of success churches experienced in health and/or growth as a result of the consultation. Some churches seemed to do very well following the consultation while others did not. Feedback suggested there was a need for more follow-up by our staff with the pastor after the consultation. Some pastors were more open to this than others. With more reflection, it became increasing evident that a successful consultation depended as much on the leadership skills of the pastor as on the skills of the consultant. As I explored this issue in various peer groups, there emerged a growing consensus that training in Leadership Development was woefully lacking throughout the denomination. Seminaries had focused on training prospective pastors in biblical interpretation, preaching, pastoral care and even church administration, but little or no help was offered on how to be a good or better leader. Apparently, it was hoped that leadership would be learned by osmosis or in the school of "hard knocks," which was often the case.

In January of 1993, perhaps because my consulting with churches had become more widely known, State Convention President, Rick Lance, and

Executive-Secretary, Troy Morrison, asked me to chair a New Directions Task Force authorized by the Convention in its annual meeting in November of 1992. The Task Force, composed of 36 appointed members from across the state and seven additional ex-officio members, was given two years to complete its work. In addition, the Task Force also had the assistance of all the State Board of Missions department heads and convention entity heads. In two of our early meetings I asked a leading futuristic-thinking academic, Larry McSwain, and a leading local church consultant, George Bullard, to speak to the Task Force. They discussed trends they saw in religious, denominational, and local church life, as well as society at large, which needed to be considered as we planned for a new century.

Organized into 5 work groups, the Task Force met at least quarterly and occasionally more frequently. While dozens of possible recommendations surfaced, the Task Force focused primarily on seven general directions. The two I considered most significant were 1) "a Service- Oriented Convention helping churches fulfill the Great Commission," and 2) "a Localized Organization providing Customized Services." The Task Force was followed by a Strategy Planning Committee of which I was a member. In the short term, there were two major outcomes of the whole process. One outcome was a renovated and enlarged state office building on South Boulevard, a priority of the Executive Secretary. This building was eventually traded to the Baptist Hospital for a new, smaller, and more serviceable building in Prattville. A second outcome was the creation of a new staff position on the State Board of Missions, entitled "Office of Leadership Development." Edwin Jenkins, a Birmingham pastor who had served on both the Task Force and the Strategy Planning Committee, was selected to lead this newly authorized "Office" of work. Since this had been a special interest of mine from the beginning, we worked together closely to get this new endeavor up and running.

Even before my work on the Task Force, leadership development had become a growing concern in the Dale group, the Mega Cities DOM group, and for some members of the Convention Task Force group. Leadership development was also a topic for discussion at some of our Hospital Board retreats. These groups became sources for the names of key authors writing on leadership issues i.e. Drucker, Thomas, Senge and Kanter, to name a few.

As Jenkins and I were organizing the newly authorized Office of Leadership Development, we discovered Lloyd Elder, a former head of the Sunday School Board of the SBC, had been enlisted by Belmont College in Nashville to head up the new Moench Center for Church Leadership. He put together a workbook on Practicing Servant Leadership, copyrighted in 1995. He willingly became a valuable collaborating partner as we developed our program of seminars and workshops for Alabama pastors. It was my privilege to teach in several seminars attended by a number of younger pastors from across the state.[2]

In 1999, as the Montgomery Association prepared for the new millennium, we conducted our third strategic planning process. Reggie McNeal, Director of Leadership Development for the South Carolina Baptist Convention, was selected as our consultant. During this time, Reggie was developing and sharing with us material that later appeared in his book, The Present Future, Six Tough Questions for the Church, published by Jossey-Bass. As a result, our new strategic plan refocused our leadership development thrust around the concept of Peer Leadership Learning Clusters. In the Spring of 2000, twenty-two pastors volunteered to participate in five learning clusters with 3 to 5 pastors of their choice. Most of these pastors were from moderate sized churches. I enlisted 3 pastors from our larger multi-staff churches with a weekly attendance of upward to 1,000 to form a sixth cluster. I provided guidance to each cluster to get it started and let them go from there. They chose how often they would meet, what they would discuss, and how they would handle the group's leadership. One group floundered from the beginning, but most groups did reasonably well the first year. By the second year, only 3 groups were still together. The group I enlisted and in which I participated agreed to meet bi-monthly initially, but later quarterly, and to rotate leadership from meeting to meeting. Following my retirement in January of 2004 and subsequent move to Birmingham, the group enlisted another peer to join them. Twenty years later, they are still meeting at least once a quarter, though 3 of the members are now retired and doing interim work. In 2021, I was invited back for a "reunion breakfast." Peer learning has obviously been extremely valuable for each of these individuals.

Moving Toward Racial Reconciliation

While I did not intentionally choose race relations as a significant focus of my ministry, following my graduation from seminary it was, or at least became, a concern in every place I served, and Montgomery was no exception. To be sure, my experiences in Montgomery were far more pleasant and rewarding. When I arrived on the scene, the association had 4 small, predominately black congregations. Three of these, Westside Baptist Church, Bible Missionary Baptist Church and Central Baptist Church, were all totally black though Central was technically a "Mission." The fourth, Southlawn Baptist Church, had once been all white, but by 1985, a majority of those attending were black. At the time, the church was without a pastor. Fortunately, the small white minority was committed to helping the church call a black pastor and to helping him succeed in the community that was now mostly African American. Also, the association, in cooperation with the state convention, supported a part-time black campus minister at the predominately black Alabama State University.

I counted the pastors of all four churches, Rev. Willie Graham, Rev. Eugene Zeigler, Rev. Milton Boyd, and Rev. Leroy Fountain as friends. Leroy became the pastor at Southlawn within weeks of my arrival, and his wife, Carolyn, became the campus minister at Alabama State University. As campus minister, Carolyn was on the MBA staff. Leroy and Carolyn were always in our home for Christmas and occasionally at other times. Leroy and I played golf sometimes and from time to time had lunch together. Leroy felt comfortable talking with me about racially sensitive issues and helped me broaden my perspective on both the customs and needs of the black pastors and their church members.

For years our Executive Board had met on the 3rd Monday of each quarter. When the federal government set aside the 3rd Monday in January as a national holiday in honor of Dr. Martin Luther King, Jr. I saw no reason to change our regular Executive Board meeting time. In fact, I saw it as an opportunity for more of our lay board members to attend. One day on the golf course Leroy asked me if I had thought of changing our meeting day in January to the fourth Monday. I had not and told him why. Actually, my hoped-for increase in lay member attendance at board meeting never materialized. He continued, "Have you ever thought that our Black pastors and their members might think the association's leadership was deliberately ignoring what, to them, was a very important observance?" I had not.

The next year, to the delight of our black members, the meeting date was changed. Deservedly or not, I think some came to see me as their champion. I had a standing invitation to attend their services and was always asked to speak when I showed up, which was not the case for some of our other churches. Leroy and Carolyn became good friends, and after a 10-year pastorate, he accepted a position with the Southern Baptist Convention's Annuity Board in Fort Worth, Texas. He later worked for the North American Mission Board in Atlanta and has kept in touch with me following my retirement and move to Birmingham.

Though the overwhelming majority of African American Christians in Montgomery were Baptists only a few were members of our small predominately black MBA churches, which had grown to 7 in number by 2003[3]. Virtually all of the black congregations in the city belong to either the Alabama Middle Association or the Antioch Association, the larger of the two. The leader of each association was a prominent pastor who normally served as the association's long-tenured, moderator. As I got to know these moderators I sought to assure them we had no desire to recruit any of their churches or members, and anything I could do to support them or foster better race relations I wanted to do.

The State Convention leadership, especially Dr. Potts, had worked for many years with considerable success to build a cordial relationship with as many black leaders as possible. An MBA Inter-Associational Committee composed of 6 members, 3 white and 3 black, for the purpose of fostering Inter-racial cooperation, had existed for some time but was inactive by the fall of 1985. Early in my tenure I sought to revitalize the committee with little success until Reverend G. W. Bozeman became pastor of the historically prominent Day Street Baptist Church in the early '90s. About that time, he was chosen as moderator of the Antioch Baptist Association and agreed to be a member of the Inter-Associational committee.

By the mid '90s the committee was meeting regularly to discuss possibilities for cooperative endeavors. The most successful project was a joint meeting of the three associations on Sunday evening October 16, 2000, at the Montgomery Civic Center as a prelude to the beginning of a new century of better race relations. Two years in the planning, the program theme "Many Faces – One Family" , featured pastors and choirs from all three associations. Dr. Tony Evans, a nationally known black pastor, was the featured speaker. Community leaders, both black and white, were among the 2,000 plus in attendance. In 1999, perhaps coincidentally, one of our prominent Baptist laymen, Bobby Bright, was elected mayor of Montgomery with strong biracial support and reelected in 2003 "by a landslide."

The Montgomery Baptist Hospital

In the early 1950s, the Montgomery Baptist Association under the leadership of Rev. Blunt Davidson, its Director of Missions, established a Baptist Hospital Board for the purpose of organizing, building and operating a Baptist hospital in Montgomery. The new Hospital Board was composed of some of the city's leading Baptist businessmen, several of whom were members of First Baptist Church Montgomery. Several years of persistent labor resulted in the Montgomery Baptist Hospital opening its doors to patients in 1963. Under the leadership of Taylor Morrow, the hospital soon became the leading health care facility in Montgomery.

When I came to the Association, the hospital's 21-member Board of Directors served 3-year terms and were all elected at the Annual Meeting of the Association. One third of those members were pastors. The Hospital CEO, the Medical Staff Director, and the Association's Director of Missions were also ex-officio voting members of the Board. The officers of the Board were chosen from among the business leaders on the Board, most of whom were long-tenured Board members. The Board met quarterly, mostly to hear mundane quarterly reports from the hospital's department leaders and to authorize hospital expansion projects. The Board also had an annual 2-3 day "educational retreat" for members and their spouses, initially at Callaway

Gardens and later at a gulf Beach hotel. Needless to say, the pastors on the board, along with the Director of Missions considered these retreats to be the real "plum" of Board membership.

After Mr. Morrow's retirement, the new CEO, Mike DeBoer, provided dynamic leadership for the hospital during a time of tremendous changes in healthcare, both in terms of reimbursements and the consolidation of healthcare organizations. Its name was changed to Baptist Health and though the Association continued to elect the Board, its size was gradually reduced from 21 to 15. Also, the requirement that all members belong to an MBA church was removed. This paved the way for more racial diversity and wider community involvement. DeBoer also "beefed up" the annual retreat by securing program leadership from nationally known consulting firms. Hospital medical staff leaders were invited to the Board's annual retreats now held in places like San Jose, California and Maui, Hawaii. On our trip to Maui, Jim Miller, husband of Board member Kay Miller, was a little "under the weather" one day and asked me to fill his slot on an afternoon golf outing. The Kapalua course we played is home of the PGA's first tournament of the year and includes only tour winners from the previous year. I always try to see that one on TV because I enjoy watching the pros play those amazing holes, many of which are still vivid in my memory.

Tragically, in the midst of a major hospital merging process after buying three other hospitals, Mike DeBoer was diagnosed with a malignant brain tumor in January of 2000. He died in May. The hospital never recovered. The Board elected as its new CEO Mike's recently hired assistant whose previous experience was confined almost exclusively to the Chicago area. How much that was a factor in his never being accepted by most of the medical staff of the largest of the newly acquired hospitals is a matter of speculation. At any rate, he didn't last a full year.

I considered it an honor to be asked to serve on a search committee to recommend a new CEO. The committee used a "headhunter" to narrow its choices to three candidates. After interviewing all three, we selected a man from New Orleans. I thought he gave the best interview. Regrettably, our due diligence was inadequate. Since long-time CFO Frank Wells had retired, the new CEO brought a young woman from New Orleans with him to be the new CFO. After 2 years of extremely poor management performance and flawed character revelations both were fired.

Unfortunately, by this time the hospital was in such dire financial straits the only solution to salvaging the healthcare system was entering into a management agreement with the UAB Health System of Birmingham. Sadly, the beginning of that process was authorized at the last meeting of the Board I attended prior to my retirement. I do rejoice in knowing highly qualified management, increased reimbursements (because UAB is a teaching hospital), and UAB's buying power have all contributed to making Baptist Health once again, the outstanding system we dreamed it would become.

Time to Retire

When should you think about retirement? I suppose my first thoughts about retirement revolved around the need to build a financial nest-egg that could sustain Barbara and me during a time when I could no longer earn a salary. Deep down, I probably thought I could preach until I died or at least was near death. Actually, until I came to South Avondale, I had barely made enough money "to keep body and soul together" for our family. In Caledonia and Vernon, we lived in a "pastorium," a house furnished by the church for its pastor's family. Our move to Birmingham enabled us to buy our first house, thanks to the decision of Sixth-Sixth Street church to provide their pastor a "housing allowance." We were also blessed by a generous "gift," which we always treated as a loan, from Barbara's parents enabling us to make our first down payment. Thankfully, we were able to return it rather quickly.

At South Avondale I was able to set aside a respectable, though small, percent of my salary package into my retirement account with the Southern Baptist Convention's Annuity Board. For the first fifteen years following my graduation from the seminary, my retirement contribution to that account had been the minimum $400 per year, $33.33 per month. Even with the $200 annually the State Convention added, my account total was tiny. In Montgomery, for the first time, I was able to set aside the recommended 10% of my salary for retirement and at times I even exceeded that amount. So, retirement was at least in the back of my mind for some time.

My first serious thoughts about retiring from my work came sometime in the late '90s. Following Earl Tew's retirement as the Birmingham Association's Director of Missions, I was contacted by that Association's search committee, asking if they could talk with me about the possibility of becoming their Executive Director. On the way home, following a meeting with the committee at the Vestavia Hills Country Club, I concluded that was not the Lord's will for me at that time. In a letter asking that my name be withdrawn from consideration, I suggested they needed someone to be with them longer than I thought I could work effectively. In addition, we were just into our next 5-year planning cycle at Montgomery, and I was excited about the possibilities that lay before us.

That cycle did prove to be an exciting time. We made progress in better race relations highlighted by our joint Annual Meetings at the Civic Center with Tony Evans. We also launched our peer learning cluster initiative. The mission partnership with Mexico and Hong Kong flourished with both SBC and CBF churches participating. Then, as I began planning my 2003 calendar, I recognized that planning our next 5-year cycle was at hand. For the first time, the excitement and optimism of previous years were missing. What did "put wind in my sails" was the thought of being an Intentional Interim pastor, a pastor who helped churches work through difficult problems in preparation for calling a new pastor. While I had preached a good deal in my capacity as Director of Missions, I had missed the challenge and warmth of preaching to the same congregation week after week for an extended period of time. In the spring of 2003, I attended an Intentional Interim workshop which whetted my appetite even more. Then too, the thought of moving back to Birmingham and being closer to the children and grandchildren was an enticing one, perhaps even compelling. Barbara and I took stock of the "nest egg" we had been able to put aside and concluded that by continued frugality, along with some part-time interim pastoral work, we could make ends meet.

In the summer of '03, I told the Personnel and Budget Committees of my desire to retire at the end of 2003, knowing that the Association's plans for '04 needed to take that into consideration. To say that the Association was gracious would be an understatement. My 18-year tenure as MBA's Director of Missions had been punctuated with many expressions of encouragement and affirmation. I do not remember a year when the Personnel Committee did not recommend and the Executive Board approve at least a modest salary increase. Both time and financial resources were made available for conferences and personal enrichment seminars. Vacation time was increased at regular intervals. At the association's annual meeting, on the occasion of my tenth anniversary, a surprise "This is Your Life" presentation was unveiled. Beth and Amy were unexpectedly ushered into the annual meeting. Alisa was not with them because she was in a Birmingham hospital that night giving birth to our first grandson, John Mark. Barbara, who had helped arrange the girls' surprise attendance, was now called up on stage. This time, both of us were surprised by the presentation of heavy hooded parkas, warm mittens, and a gift certificate for a cruise to Alaska, a delightful treat we enjoyed the following May.

On my fifteenth anniversary, I was given a cash award sufficient to cover expenses for a London, Scotland, and Ireland tour for two. It was on this tour I got to visit golf's historic "Old Course" at St. Andrews, Scotland. This was also the occasion of my first lesson in digital photography. While at the Cliffs of Moher a fellow tourist handed me his camera and asked me to take a picture of him and his companion with the cliffs in the background. He showed me which button to press, backed off, and posed. I "framed the photo" in the viewfinder and snapped the shutter. The gentleman thanked me, took the camera from my hand, turned it around 180 degrees, handed it back to me and said, "Now, how about taking a picture of us." Unknowingly, I had taken a picture of myself. Oh well, it wasn't the first time I embarrassed myself by thinking I knew more than I did.

The Association's Annual Meeting in October of 1985 had focused on joyfully welcoming their new Director of Missions. Eighteen years later in October of 2003, the Annual Meeting of the Montgomery Baptist Association was highlighted by an outpouring of appreciation for their retiring Director of Missions. A retirement dinner with all of my family in attendance was unforgettable. Alisa was present this time, along with 8-year-old John Mark, who celebrated by decorating his fingers with little green olives. State Convention and associational leaders from across the state were in attendance as were 200 plus Montgomery Baptists from nearly every church in the Association. Gene Hannah, Master of Ceremonies, kept the night light with humor, and Rick Marshall, on behalf of the Association, presented me with a spiffy new blue golf bag and a set of Callaway irons. Pictures and a recording of the event are forever treasured.

Epilogue

On February 1, 2004, for the first time in over 46 years, since November of 1957, I was not employed as the pastor of a Baptist church or the executive director of a Baptist association. During the next 4 months I was asked to preach at a few churches, but Barbara and I spent most of our time in search of our retirement home in Birmingham. The decision on Birmingham as our retirement destination was easily made. Barbara informed me shortly after we began talking seriously about retirement that I could live wherever I pleased, but she was living near the children and grandchildren. Since Beth and her 2 children lived in Homewood, a suburb of Birmingham; Amy lived in Northport, 60 miles west down I 59; and Alisa and her 3 children lived in Pell City (at the time), 30 miles east on I 20, no other location was even considered.

We engaged Wanda, a realtor, to help us find just the right house in our price range. Numerous trips to Birmingham ended in varying degrees of disappointment. In the meantime, I was getting our Montgomery house ready to sell. The front porch foundation had sunk just enough to create an unsightly mortar line on the house brick. I concluded the best solution to that problem was to cover the porch floor with terracotta tile, a task I tackled enthusiastically.

We also asked a Montgomery realtor friend to give us her suggestions for making the house a little more sellable. I don't remember her making any. A week or so after her initial visit, however, she called and asked if she could show the house. She had a client who was moving from Birmingham to Montgomery that she thought our house would just suit. The house was not ready to show. Bare 2X4s temporarily had replaced the white columns above the unfinished porch floor.

Long story short, our realtor friend was at our house at 8:00 the next morning with papers authorizing her to be our realtor. The young couple toured our house at 10:00 that morning and liked it. They brought the wife's father, who lived in Montgomery, by at 3:00 p.m. to look at the house and they made us an offer. We made them a counteroffer at 5:00 and by 7:00 that evening we had sold our house to the new Youth Minister of First Baptist Church, Montgomery. We were all happy, but Barbara and I did have some anxiety. We were now homeless with no place to go. The new owners graciously gave us 6 weeks to find a place, and even offered more time if we need it.

On Thursday, June 2, 2004, the moving van unloaded our belongings at our new home in Birmingham, Alabama, one day after I officially began a 15-month tenure as the Intentional Interim Pastor of First Baptist Church, Irondale. God's timing and blessings continue to be beyond amazing!

So, my pilgrimage of faith continues still down a path not fully known. Yet, I can walk it with confidence assurance my earthly future and my eternal destiny are in the hands of the loving Divine Shepherd. He who has faithfully guided me at critical junctures of my thus far will not abandon me now.

Amen!

Endnotes

Chapter 2

[1] In 1892 there were one-room schools at both Clover Bottom and Nonesuch but by the mid 40's I remember only a small 2 or 3 room school at Nonesuch across from Uncle George's garage.

[2] I use this spelling because that is on his tombstone in the Versailles cemetery.

Chapter 3

[1] A booklet entitled "The History of Southern Woodford County" self-published by author Cash Davis Bond contains the following entry, "Merritt and Sue McGohon…in 1909 and moved into a large brick house in Clover Bottom from whose porch Happy Chandler once made a speech to the local citizens when he was running for State Representative."

[2] Actually, the first job I remember being paid for was picking up rocks for half a day to clear a field on a farm where my uncle Robert lived, near Pinckard (in Woodford county between Keene and Versailles). On another occasion I made a couple of dollars picking strawberries for a nickel a quart at an orchard near Pinckard.)

Chapter 5

[1] William Henry Wishard, a doctor of the old school by Elizabeth Moreland originally published in 1920 has been republished by Andesite Press, 2017 and is available in paperback and hardback.

[2] The festival was organized by Henry County teacher Russell Bennett, a recent seminary graduate who would eventually become the outstanding Director of Missions for Long Run Baptist Association in Louisville and a professor at Southern Seminary.

Chapter 8

[1] Imagine my surprise to learn 30 years later that in 1939 the first Director of Missions for the Montgomery Baptist Association was John R. Wells. However, at that time his title was Superintendent of City Missions, and he was employed by the State Convention. His widow who lived in North Carolina stopped by my MBA office one day early in my ministry there looking for some old records. Unfortunately, I was away at the time but did talk with her later by phone for several minutes. I regret never getting to see her personally.

Chapter 9

[1] After Larry's wife, Susan, finished college they volunteered for SBC's Mission Service Corp serving two years in South America before coming back to attend Seminary in Texas. Following seminary, they were appointed as SBC Foreign Missionaries to Mexico where they served for many years. My relationship with Larry would lead to a 3-year partnership between the Montgomery Baptist Association and the Pueblo Convention in Mexico. Larry eventually became team coordinator for all of Central and Spanish speaking South America. Prior to his retirement from missionary service he was a leadership counselor and coach for missionary personnel in Asia.

[2] I am indebted to Dr. Blain Brownell head of UAB's Urban Studies department for this insight which came several years later in my learning curve.

[3] Fisher, Wallace E., <u>From Tradition to Mission: An Old Church Discovers the Secret of New Life</u>, Abingdon Press, 1965.

[4] The Doctor of Ministry degree required the candidate to be gainfully employed in the practice of ministry and it took approximately 3 years to complete. In each of the 3 years of study the candidate had to participate in a month-long, on campus, faculty guided seminar. Each seminar usually had a 5-10 book reading list for preparation. Students were assigned a faculty advisor who helped guide them through every phase of their work in pursuit of their degree. Each student would also secure an approved "field supervisor" with whom he would meet at least bimonthly during the regular semester to discuss a paper he had prepared on one of some 20 different aspects of his ministry. During the first two years all 20 papers would be discussed. Finally, the student was to select, plan and implement a project related to his ministry. In place of a dissertation he was to write about that project giving a rational for, description of and thorough evaluation of the project.

Chapter 10

[1] The description of a trip to Nigeria can be found in the chapter on Denominational Service.

[2] After 3 fruitful years on our staff Phil was called to First Baptist Chamblee GA. His talents would also take him to South Main Baptist in Houston and eventually to lead the national inter-denominational organization of church administrators.

[3] A bound copy of <u>Developing a Ministry to Apartment Residents in the South Avondale Community</u> can be found in the Library at Southern seminary and in my personal book collection

[4] These are mentioned as examples and are by no means intended as an inclusive list.

5 Charlotte's husband, Frank Stewart, an occasional golf buddie, was a professional bridge player who at the time sang in the Independent Presbyterian Church choir. They moved to Memphis, Tennessee and for years he has written a syndicated bridge column for the Memphis Appeal newspaper.

Chapter 11

1. A footnote on Baptist denominational life: 1) Each church is autonomous, thus totally self-governing. 2) Baptist churches cooperate with other Baptist churches in their local area, often their county, by joining and financially supporting a local Association. 3) They cooperate with other churches in their state by sending "messengers" to an annual State Convention meeting and financially supporting its work. 4) Churches cooperate nation-wide by sending "messengers" to an annual meeting of the Southern Baptist Convention and financially supporting its work. 5) "Messengers" express their personal opinions and vote their personal convictions. While elected by the church, they are not "delegates" authorized to act on behalf of the church. Thus, no local church is bound by any action of the denominational bodies with which it cooperates and to whose meetings it sends messengers. 6) Each church chooses the amount of financial support it will provide for the work of the various denominational bodies. 7) In like manner no denominational body is bound by the action of any other denominational body. This is the theory of "autonomy" but, since each body is dependent upon the voluntary support of its respective churches, actions by the various bodies though seldom unanimous usually have broad based support.

2 Each year messengers to the Alabama Baptist Convention's annual meeting elect an Executive Board to oversee the work of the convention and act on the convention's behalf when it is not in session. The Board is composed of 125 members, one from each of the 75 associations and the remaining 50 allotted to associations based on the total membership of the churches in the various associations. Persons are elected to the Board for a three-year term and are eligible for and usually reelection to a second term. The Board normally met four times a year for 2 to 3 hours and heard reports and recommendations from its Executive Secretary who managed a staff of approximately 100 members. The Board, at that time, also had an Administrative Committee of 15 members who met more frequently and served as the budget planning committee for the convention. The Board eventually changed its name to the State Board of Missions and the Administration Committee was renamed the Executive Committee.

3 The name given this position by most associations is Director of Missions or Associational Missionary.

Chapter 12

[1] The Montgomery Baptist Association was an association of 52 churches and 1 mission. Five of the churches were in Lowndes County, 2 were in Elmore County and the other 45 churches were in Montgomery county, 15 of which were rural or in very small communities, the other 30 were in the city limits of Montgomery or in very close proximity. They ranged in size from First Baptist Montgomery with over 2,100 resident members (though 7 more churches had over 1,000) to Lapine with 19. Three congregations were predominantly African American.

[2] The Executive Board was composed of the pastor and a lay member from each of the Association's 52 churches, plus the association's moderator, vice-moderator and recording secretary, elected at the annual meeting. It normally met quarterly to transact the business of the association between annual meetings.

[3] The origins of the Baptist Center Ministry are detailed in the book Farming the Inner City for Christ by Delores Cork, a Center volunteer.

[4] After retirement I met Debbie's brother, a good friend of Vestavia Hills pastor Gary Furr, one Wednesday night at the church. Dwight was professor and dean of the chapel at Georgetown College in Georgetown, Ky for a decade or more and for a time was interim pastor of Rosemont, my sister Ann's church.

[5] The early paid leaders of the Montgomery association had the title "Superintendent of Missions." In the late 1930's the Alabama Baptist State Convention employed 3 Superintendents of Missions to work in the state's 3 largest cities. Rev. John R Wells was employed to work in Montgomery. The next leader, and the first to be paid by the Montgomery Association, Rev. Blunt Davidson, had an office in a house adjacent to and owned by First Baptist Church. The church's construction of a new building required the demolition of the house. New office space for a new Superintendent of Missions, Rev. Frank Hixon, was provided by the Alabama Baptist State Board Missions in its newly constructed office building on South Boulevard. When the State Board of Mission needed that space for its own use, First Baptist Church, having received the property of Calvary Baptist Church when Calvary disbanded, gave that property to the association for "temporary" office space.

[6] By now the association had an Education Director, a part-time Baptist Center director, a receptionist/secretary and a financial/educational secretary.

Chapter 13

[1] When the IMB withdrew its support of the University, it also withdrew its support from the Hong Kong Baptist Seminary. Picking up full support for the seminary left the Hong Kong Baptist Convention strapped for funds to

continue its work of starting new churches. I spent a full day with convention leaders visiting the seminary and looking at various aspects of their work seeking ways we might be of help. We concluded supporting David was our best avenue of help.

2 Back in Montgomery Neal resigned his pastorate of the McGehee Road Baptist Church in order to begin a house church with several locations in the housing projects of Montgomery. By July, a pilot project was launched under Neal's leadership, sponsored by the MBA, and supported by volunteers from several MBA churches that would become Hope Community Church. The State Convention and the SBC's NAMB also became supporting partners. Neal eventually became a NAMB missionary with a focus on multi-family housing ministries and serves today as MBA's Director of Missions. Twenty years later Hope Church continues it ministry to the underserved of Montgomery.

Chapter 14

1 I was invited to consult with churches in Birmingham, Elba, Enterprise, Dothan and Wilmore, Ky. prior to retirement. Following retirement, the Memorial Baptist Church in Columbia, Missouri asked me to be their consultant in a strategy planning process. Also, during "retirement" I served as the Intentional Interim pastor for 4 churches which involved extensive consulting work (1st Baptist Irondale – 15 months; Leeds 1st Baptist – 21 months; Indian Springs – 30 months; 1st Baptist Center Point – 19 months). I also served both Irondale 1st and Leeds 1st a second time as interim pastor, but for a much shorter time, 6 months or so.

2 Not long after I retired, Jenkins left the office to become pastor of First Baptist Church, Athens. Since the Board was tightening its financial belt at this time, to my knowledge, he was not replaced. Following my retirement from the Montgomery Association, I was employed by the Birmingham Association on a part time basis as their Director of Leadership Development. When Ricky resigned, the Association asked me to be its interim Executive Director until Dr. Mike McLemore was called as its permanent director.

3 During my tenure, 3 new African American congregations were started and petitioned the association for membership. All 3 contributed financially to the work of the Association.

Past Recollections

October 1870, my sister Mrs. N. L. Unthank and I went to visit some relatives living near Mackville, Ky. where we remained until March, 1871. In January, my Aunt Mrs. Margaret McKittrick, myself, and others of our friends, determined to visit Harrodsburg, Mercer County; while there, we went out two miles east, near the road leading from that place to Lexington, to once more visit the place of our birth. I had for several years wished to make one more visit to the spot, the dearest to me on earth, and the most like home, where both of my Grandfathers lived for many years beside each other. But, Oh, how things had changed in appearance, those once dear happy homes. Nothing remained to make the place look home-like although, all looked changed and desolate, yet I felt as if standing on hallowed ground. On one of these farms my father was born and lived there, and died in the 25th year of his life. And on the other, my mother was born, and married to my father, John Stagg, on the last of December, 1807.

Not one of the families of either Grandparents are now living, all are gone, I only remain. By request of a relative I will relate what I have heard and know of our Grand-parents.

Mark McGohon and Elizabeth Dunn McGohon, my Grandfather was an Irish-man by birth. He came to America at the age of about 14 years. His father, Mark McGohon, Sr., came to America some time previous to try the New World, and if he liked the country and the prospects, he would return for this family and bring them over also. But while in this country the trouble began to brew between England and America, and he did not get to return as he had intended. He had previously written to his wife that he was intending to come soon, and wished her to dispose of all she could before his coming, so that there might be no delay, as he wished to return as soon as possible. He was at heart a warm Whig but dare not let it be known in his native country, Ireland, until he could get his family to America.

As he could not go for his family without great risk, he contracted with a ship Captain to bring his family over to New York on his return trip, taking for him also a letter of direction to his wife, while he would try to remain in New York until the return of the vessel and work at his trade, (ship-building).

The time was supposed to be about three months, as all vessels were sail vessels, and could not always be on time.

He worked and waited the appointed time, but the ship did not arrive in port, finally a year, and no tidings of ship or family. He came to the conclusion that the ship was lost, and greatly discouraged and almost heart-broken, he determined to enlist in the service of his adopted country until the close of the war, seven years. Yet he still grieved over the loss of his dear family.

Near the close of the war, several regiments or what remained of them, were ordered to meet at a certain point, I do not now remember the name of the place or the regiment to which he belonged, but Mark McGohon belonged to one so ordered.

-3-

During the balance of the day they wandered about hoping they might hear of their father, but could not. About the middle of the afternoon, Mark led his sister to a large pile of loose lumber, near which a great number of persons were passing continually, hoping that if their father should pass that way, he might notice them and be recognized by him. After hoping and waiting a long time, the sister began to cry from hunger and weariness.

A great many persons passed by them, looked at them and passed on manifesting no sympathy for them until late in the evening an old man came walking past them slowly, walked a short distance past, but turned about and came near them. He asked what was the matter with the little girl, awdn Mark told him that she was tired and hungry. He them said, why don't you go home? Mark said, "we have no home, our mother and little sister died on the sea, and was buried in the waters, and were brought here to New York this morning, and set down in this place." Have you no father? We had one a year ago, and he promised to wait for us here in New York but we have not found him yet. The man said, why this is not New York, this is Philadelphia, many miles from New York.

Mark said New York is the place we were to meet him. The old gentleman said, come go home with me, I will see what can be done for you. They went with him to his home and were very kindly treated by both the old gentleman and his wife. They had no family, except servants. They made every possible effort to find their father, but without avail or success. Three months these good people kept and cared for those destitute children. It was then thought best that Mark should learn a trade, so that he might in a little while be able to take care of himself, but his little sister was to remain where she was, as they had by this time become greatly attached to her, being sorry for her on account of her loneliness and possessing a lovable disposition. The old lady was not willing to part with her. Mark did not like his Master very much, he thought him cross and very exacting, indeed sometimes cruel, but he resolved to do the best he could and learn all that was possible, that he might be near his sister and try to comfort her.

He was sure his sister was kindly treated and for that reason he tried to bear his own misfortune as best he could.

It was not quite a year from the time of their landing in America, until his sister died, and Mark then felt as though he was indeed all alone in the world, with no one that cared for him, or that he really cared for. He at once determined on leaving his Master. A little while after the death of his sister, on a Saturday evening, he got permission of his Master to visit his old fried, but his main object was, to learn something in regard to the army and its division and of the nearest location of troops, so that if an opportunity offered soon, he would go, or try to get there if possible. Not many days after a regiment of soldiers passed on through Philadelphia tolerably late in the day, and Mark thought that was his chance to leave his unfeeling Master, therefore instead of going to sleep that evening, he got his little budget all ready and started after them.

Towards morning he came up to where the soldiers were encamped, he was taken before the officer, and was required to give an account of himself. He told a true story, with the exception of running away from his Master. Mark told the officer that he would like to go with them. At the age of 16 he was permitted to enlist as a soldier in the Continental army, which priveledge he was proud of as long as he lived.

After he had been in service about 3 years, the regiment to which he belonged, was
ordered to a certain point in Pennsylvania, and were encamped there for some little
time. Not far from their place of encampment was a well-to-do farmer, who kept
quite a good number of cows and had a large stone spring-house which kept the milk
nicely. To this farm the soldiers often went to get milk, two of the farmers
daughters, Mary and Elizabeth, or Betsey as she was called at home, always attended
to the milk, that was their part of the business in particular, when ever milk was
wanted, one of the girls always went to get it. Mark McGohon, although some-what
lame, was always very glad to go to Mr. Dunns spring-house for milk, as there was
really a greater attraction there for him than the milk, as the soldiers like it.
He had fallen in love with Betsey Dunn, and the errand of going for milk was a good
excuse he thought, for his frequent visits to the farm. Whenever Mark went for milk
Betsey would always go with him to the milk house, and give him of the very best, as
they had an abundance of it to spare.

Some of the soldiers were well pleased with the location of their encampment, but
after a time they received orders to march the next day. Mark went for milk that
afternoon, he told Elizabeth of his affection for her, that she was the only woman
he had ever really loved, except his own mother and his little sisters, and that
they were gone from him, and that he loved her only.

Tomorrow I must leave you, perhaps forever, but should my life be spared until the
close of the war, will you then become my wife? She told him she would, provided
he brought with him a good name and an honorable discharge. Mark went back to the
encampment, feeling that he had made, as he thought a very satisfactory days work.
When the war was over, and Mark McGohon had been honorably mustered out of service,
and felt that he was then a free man. He made hast to return to the only person
on earth that he really believed he loved, (at that time he had not seen or even heard
of his father) what must of been his disappointment when, after several days hard
traveling on foot, for there were no stage coaches or railroad cars to accomodate
travelers at that time, to discover that the family he had expected to find near their
old encampment had moved away and strangers occupied their place. He was informed
however, that Mr. Dunn had moved to the western part of the state (Pennsylvania)
near Brownsville, or where Brownsville now is. It was indeed a long and tiresome
journey, worn, weak and almost sick, he arrived at the place of his destination and
found the object of his search, Elizabeth Dunn, in good healthe, high hopes and still
true to her promise. Mark obtained employment in the neighborhood for some months.
In due time they were married and lived quite happily together, Elizabeth's great
and only trouble was, her husband would be out and after the Indians when ever they
came near the frontier. He had seen so much of their barbarity and meaness, that
he had determined to annihilate every one that came within reach of his rifle. He
had passed through many hard fought battles, and had sometimes been defeated, yet
he was still as brave and fearless as a lion. Fear was something he did not seem to
know. At that time little was known of the country west and southwest of Fort
Pitt, now Pittsburg. A few adventurous ones had passed over and down the Ohio River,
bringing glowing accounts of the country on bothe sides of the river.

Some thought the country on the south side was surely the garden spot of the world,
and that was out south of where Maysville now is. Others went to explore, and went
still farther south. The accounts that they brought on their return created in the
minds of some a great desire to visit that beautiful land. Mark McGohon was one of
that number. He and one or two of his neighbors set about building what was called
a deel-boat to float them down the Ohio River as far as they might wish to go.

171

By the next spring the new settlers began in earnest to make the land they had located on, ready for raising a crop for the next year or the coming season. The Indians had not troubled them much during the fall and winter previous, so that they were greatly encouraged, they had selected land as close together as was convenient for mutial safety and protection. They had planted their corn which was growing nicely.

But one morning near the last of June they got up in the morning to find five of the seven horses belonging to the fort gone.

They had tied them out in different places so that they might eat grass during the night. They knew well that the Indians had taken them as the trace could be seen very plainly through the grass, which was quite tall at the time. The trail was followed for some distance to find the course the Indians had taken. It was found to be towards the falls of the Ohio River, to which place they had a regular trace from the southern part of the state.

No time was to be lost, three men started on after the Indians. Taking the two remaining horses belonging to the fort with what arms and amunition they could carry to defend themselves as best they could in case of an attack by the Indians. After a hard and hurried march they at last came in sight of the Ohio River and the hills back from where New Albany stands today.

Some little distance below the falls there was a great sand-bar which extended out a considerable distance into the river on the north sid of the stream, as far as that bar reached it could be found by horses, leaving not a great distance for them to be obliged to swim. The trace ran directly this place. Just across the river on the north side was a beautiful plain or piece of level land, upon this land the persurers saw the Indians, also their own horses, five in number, one a beautiful whit mare which had been raised a pet, and had been given to Elizabeth by her father, Andrew Dunn, before she started from home.

The Indians expected to be pursued, and the men supposes that they had not stopped for anything as they appeared to be cooking something over a fire, and the horses were quietly grazing near them. The Indians made all manner of sport of the pursurers. Supposing they were then as far as they could or dare go,) which was quite true, one of the men proposes returning, as the horses they had with them were badly needed at home and it was very plain that the others were entirely out of reach. Mark McCohon said, wait a little, we need some rest and so do our horses.

In about two hours it was thought that the Indians were making preparations to go. Mark mounted the trunk of a large tree which has fallen near the bank and where he might be seen from the other shore as plainly as could be, at that distance. And calling out as loudly as he possibly could, Cope Nell, Cope Nell, she heard him and knew the call of her master, she broke for the water, the others followed and all landed safe on the Kentucky shore. The Indians tried hard to keep the horses back, but that was impossible when Nell started. Then Mark and his friends had their time for fun. But the Indians told them by their actions what they might expect soon, but for a good while they were not troubled at that fort as the other forts were, yet once in a while they would become alarmed and flee into their Stronghold, the Old Fort for safety. This matter went on until the ware of 1812, which settled the Indians, and the settlers had rest.

Mark was out in that campaign and returned unharmed.

Mark McGohon raised a family of ten children, seven daughters, and three sons. They had no deaths in their family until his wife died in the year 1822. His second son William also died in 1825, leaving three children, two daughters and one son. This grandson and one other are all of his descendants who at present bear the name of McGohon. Yet his descendants are scattered, some in their native state Kentucky, some others in Oregon, California, Iowa, Missouri, Wisconsin, Indiana and elsewhere.

Mark McGohon died in February, 1848. He was a man greatly respected by all who knew him. And was buried near Mackville, Washington County, Kentucky, with the honors of war. At the time of the old gentleman's death, he had but one child living, Mrs. Margaret McKittrick, of Washington County, Kentucky. She also has now passed away and blessed is the remembrance of them.

PERSONAL - Mark McGohon, the subject of this sketch, had two half-brothers, born to their father by second marriage, after the war was over, Peter and Daniel. Peter died, leaving no family. Daniel married and moved from Eastern Pennsylvania to Bracken County, Kentucky. He had a large family of daughters and I think but one son. He afterwards moved to the state of Ohio, near a town called Salem, where some of his descendants still live. The father, Mark Sr., never came west, but died in Cumberland County, Pennsylvania. Elizabeth Dunn McGohon was a daughter of Andrew Dunn and Lydia Mitchell Dunn. Lydia Mitchell's father, mother, and brother (14 years old) were all killed and scalped by the Indians on the same day, a few months after her marriage to Andrew Dunn. Lydia Mitchell's children were Andrew Dunn and William Dunn, Polly McGinnis, Elizabeth McGohon, Jenny Moreland, Lydia Presser and Rachel McCob. Jenny Moreland never came west. (John R. Moreland's mother and Betsey Hanley's mother).

Elizabeth McGuire
Age 81 years

October 24, 1889